The Philosophy of
Foucault

Continental European Philosophy

This series provides accessible and stimulating introductions to the ideas of continental thinkers who have shaped the fundamentals of European philosophical thought. Powerful and radical, the ideas of these philosophers have often been contested, but they remain key to understanding current philosophical thinking as well as the current direction of disciplines such as political science, literary theory, comparative literature, art history, and cultural studies. Each book seeks to combine clarity with depth, introducing fresh insights and wider perspectives while also providing a comprehensive survey of each thinker's philosophical ideas.

Published titles

The Philosophy of Foucault
Todd May

The Philosophy of Merleau-Ponty
Eric Matthews

The Philosophy of Gadamer
Jean Grondin

The Philosophy of Nietzsche
Rex Welshon

The Philosophy of Habermas
Andrew Edgar

The Philosophy of Schopenhauer
Dale Jacquette

The Philosophy of Kierkegaard
George Pattison

Forthcoming titles include

The Philosophy of Derrida
Mark Dooley and Liam Kavanagh

The Philosophy of Kant
Jim O'Shea

The Philosophy of Hegel
Allen Speight

The Philosophy of Rousseau
Patrick Riley, Sr and Patrick Riley, Jr

The Philosophy of Husserl
Burt Hopkins

The Philosophy of Sartre
Anthony Hatzimoysis

The Philosophy of Foucault

Todd May

ACUMEN

First published in 2006 by Acumen

Acumen Publishing Limited
15a Lewins Yard
East Street
Chesham
Bucks HP5 1HQ
www.acumenpublishing.co.uk

ISBN-10: 1-84465-056-1 (hardcover)
ISBN-13: 978-1-84465-056-9
ISBN-10: 1-84465-057-X (paperback)
ISBN-13: 978-1-84465-057-6

British Library Cataloguing-in-Publication Data
A catalogue record for this book is available from the British Library.

Typeset in Classical Garamond by Graphicraft Limited, Hong Kong.
Printed and bound by Cromwell Press, Trowbridge.

For Kathleen, David, Rachel and Joel

Contents

Abbreviations

AKDL *The Archaeology of Knowledge and The Discourse on Language* (1972).

ALCF *Abnormal: Lectures at the Collège de France, 1974–1975* (2003).

BC *The Birth of the Clinic* (1973).

CS *The Care of the Self* (1986).

CT/IH "Critical Theory/Intellectual History" (an interview with Gerard Raulet) (1988).

DP *Discipline and Punish: The Birth of the Prison* (1977).

EC "The Ethics of the Concern of the Self as a Practice of Freedom" (1997).

Gov. "Governmentality" (1991).

HFAC *Histoire de la folie à l'âge classique* (1972).

HS *The History of Sexuality, Volume I: An Introduction* (1978).

HSLCF *The Hermeneutics of the Subject: Lectures at the Collège de France 1981–1982* (2005).

IP "Intellectuals and Power" (1977).

MBPF "My Body, This Paper, This Fire" (1999).

MC *Madness and Civilization: A History of Insanity in the Age of Reason* (1965).

NB *Naissance de la biopolitique: Cours au Collège de France 1978–1979* (2004).

NGH "Nietzsche, Genealogy, History" (1977).

OGE "On the Genealogy of Ethics: An Overview of a Work in Progress" (1984).

OT *The Order of Things: An Archaeology of the Human Sciences* (1971).

PC "Practicing Criticism" (1988).

QM "Questions of Method" (1991).

SP   "The Subject and Power" (1982).
STP *Sécurité, territoire, population: Cours au Collège de France 1977–1978* (2004).
TP   "Truth and Power" (1980).
UP   *The Use of Pleasure: Volume 2 of The History of Sexuality* (1985).
WE   "What is Enlightenment?" (1997).

Acknowledgements

I would like to thank Acumen, and especially Steven Gerrard, Elizabeth Teague, Kate Williams, Sue Hadden and three anonymous reviewers for their generous help in improving the manuscript and seeing it through.

CHAPTER ONE

Introduction: who are we?

Why study a philosopher, a philosophically oriented historian, a thinker? Why grapple with a body of thought that is difficult, often elusive? Why forsake the pleasures of sport, the company of friends, a novel or a videogame for the slow, patient activity of coming to understand a set of texts that, far from inviting one in, seem often designed to keep one at bay?

These are not idle questions. One might be told, in response to them, that the rigours of thought are good for the mind, that grappling with difficult concepts is bracing, or strengthening, or a sign of good character. These are, it seems to me, bad answers. Not that a person should not have a good mind or a good character. But why study philosophy in order to achieve these? Would mathematics, or physics, or the law not do just as well? There is nothing less rigorous about these disciplines than there is about philosophy. They offer challenges to the mind, and in addition training in something that might come in handy down the road.

If one is to study a philosophical figure, if one is, to paraphrase James Joyce, to forge one's own soul in the smithy of their mind, there must be a better reason on offer than simply being told that conceptual difficulty is good for you. There must be something about the thinker's being *philosophical*, or, in the case of Michel Foucault, at least philosophically oriented, that is itself compelling. That reason need not be practical, in the traditional sense of the term. It need not lead to a job, or a social position, or recognition by a broader public. Ideology aside, there is no reason to believe that these are all that people seek. The reason one might study a philosopher can be less goal-oriented, or more subtle. But, given the alternative ways of spending one's time, the reason ought to be a good one.

The philosopher Gilles Deleuze tells us that:

> a philosophical theory is an elaborately developed question, and nothing else; by itself and in itself, it is not the resolution to a

problem, but the elaboration, *to the very end*, of the necessary implications of a formulated question. It shows us what things are, or what things should be, on the assumption that the question is good and rigorous.[1]

Deleuze suggests that a philosophical theory is not to be defined by the answer it gives but by the question it asks. The point of reading philosophy, to him, is not one of seeking solutions but of elaborating the implications of a question.

We must be clear here. Deleuze is not arguing that philosophy is about questions rather than about answers. Or at least he is not arguing it in any simple way. He is not saying only that it is the questions that matter rather than the answers. There is something empty, after all, in being told that if one asks the right question, then what comes after does not matter. What would the point of asking a question be, if the response did not somehow matter? When he talks about the elaboration of the necessary implications of a formulated question, he is talking not only about questions, but also about responses. Those responses, those elaborations, however, need not be as straightforward as answers to traditional questions. They need not be as narrow as answers to questions such as "Where do you live?" or "What is the GNP of Sierra Leone?" They can be difficult, or shifting, or open-ended. If they are to be worthwhile, however, they need to respond to a question that is *good and rigorous*. And that is where the riches of philosophy lie.

The point of reading philosophers is to follow their elaboration of the implications of a good and rigorous question. If the question is worthwhile, if it is a matter of what Deleuze elsewhere calls "the Interesting, Remarkable, or Important"[2], then there is a reason to engage in studying it. If we are to ask ourselves whether a philosophical work or a body of philosophical thought is worth pausing over, then we must, sooner or later, know the question that is being elaborated.

For Foucault there is, throughout the body of his work, a single question that receives elaboration. It is the question "Who are we?" This is not the only question he elaborates. Yet it is the one he asks most doggedly, the one that is never far from the surface of any of his works. In his hands, the question of who we are becomes a rigorous one, elaborated, if not to the very end, then very far along the way.

The question of who we are, or at least that of who each among us is, will be foreign to no one. Who has not, at least once or twice, asked this question? And, when asked seriously, rigorously, its answer – or its response – is not obvious. There are, of course, many institutions in our society that seem to provide easy answers. Our churches tell us: you are a child of God. Our politicians tell us: you are an American (or an Australian, or an Indian, or . . .). Our televisions tell us: you are a consumer. We are told who we are, and as a result we rarely ask. But if we do not ask often, we do ask sometimes, at moments when the obvious answers seem to fall away in the wake of a tragedy, or when boredom overcomes us and the easy answers lose their grip, or, more rarely, when a philosopher puts the question to us in a new way.

There are many ways to ask the question of who I am or of who we are. Foucault turns the question, reformulates it, asks it in a new way. To understand how he does so, to grasp the particular rigour he brings to the question, we must contrast it with other, more traditional ways of asking and elaborating.

We could do worse than to start with René Descartes. Although he is concerned more with the question of what we could know than of who we are, his legacy is perhaps greater in regard to the second question. The response he gives to the question of who we are is still with us; it still defines the framework within which most of us ask the question. The legacy of Descartes – one of the legacies Foucault will seek to undermine – remains our inheritance. How, then, does he answer the question of who we are?

For Descartes, the central question is one of what we could know. And the problem is that he wants to be able to give our knowledge a more solid foundation than merely a reliance on faith. He himself probably puts the issue best, at the beginning of his *Meditations*, in an ironic passage that at once challenges and denies that he is challenging the church authorities.

> It is absolutely true, both that we must believe that there is a God because it is so taught in the Holy Scriptures, and, on the other hand, that we must believe the Holy Scriptures because they come from God. . . . Nevertheless, we could hardly offer this argument to those without faith, for they might suppose that we were committing the fallacy that logicians call circular reasoning.[3]

Suppose, indeed. Descartes learns from the church's censure of Galileo to be circumspect in his deviations from church orthodoxy.

The foundation he offers is well known. It occurs in two steps: first, a proof of the existence of God and, secondly, a proof that God cannot be a deceiver. It is in the first step that he begins to answer the question of who we are. The first move in the first step is to doubt everything that he cannot be absolutely certain of. What remains after such doubt? Only the existence of a doubter, of a substance that thinks, perceives, imagines, etc. That, as it will turn out, is one of the two substances that comprise a human being. The other substance is physical matter. (There is a third substance in the universe as well, that of the divine.) But it is mental substance that is the key. That is what allows him to construct his proof of God and what seems most important about who we are. The other substance – physical matter – does not make its appearance until the sixth and last of his meditations. There the existence of physical matter in general, and Descartes's own body in particular, is a conclusion he arrives at on the basis of earlier proofs: namely, if God exists and is not a deceiver, then so much of what I experience as corporeal matter must be correlated with my actually having a body. "I also recognize in myself some other faculties, such as the power of changing location, of assuming various postures, and other similar ones; which cannot be conceived without some substance in which they inhere . . .".[4]

So who are we? We are beings made up of two substances, a mental substance and a physical substance. These substances are intimately related. Indeed, Descartes thinks they actually meet at a particular point, the pineal gland.[5] But the fact that they meet does not mean that they are the same kind of substance. He writes of the body's characteristics that:

> if it is true that they exist, [they] must inhere in some corporeal or extended substance, and not in an intelligent substance, since their clear and distinct concept does actually involve some sort of extension, but no sort of intelligence whatsoever.[6]

Of these two substances, it is the mind that is the most important in several respects. First, the body cannot be conceived without it. Second, it is the seat of our highest capacities, those of thinking, judging and free choice. Finally, it is the mind, the mental substance, that gives the body the particular animation it has. It is not that the body would not have any animation without the mind. Descartes argues that the body could, at least in principle, operate on its own. "[T]he human body", he tells us:

> may be considered as a machine, so built and composed of bones, nerves, muscles, veins, blood, and skin that even if there were no mind in it, it would not cease to move in all the ways that it does at present when it is not moved under the direction of the will, nor consequently with the aid of the mind, but only by the condition of its organs.[7]

But to do the particular things that a particular body does in the way that it does them requires a mind to be attached to it.

This way of thinking of ourselves remains with us. It has been passed down to us through our Judeo-Christian legacy, which in many ways both influenced and then followed Descartes. The main stream of this tradition holds the body to be a substance characterized by fault or sin or weakness and the mind to be a substance capable, if it so chooses, of departing from that corporeal inheritance. Think of such phrases as "mind over matter", or "you can do anything you put your mind to" or "it's all in your mind". These clichés, and so many like them, reveal a particular cultural inheritance committed to two ideas. First, there is an important separation between mind and body, a separation that Descartes characterizes by saying that they are different substances. Secondly, in this separation, the mental is privileged with respect to the physical.

Many current scientists would dispute Descartes's claim that there is a mental substance distinct from the physical one. They believe that what is called mental substance is nothing more than the working of the brain, or more broadly of the body. (Foucault's writings, by the way, are not contrary to such a viewpoint.) However, the weight of tradition lies heavily on most of us, and it remains difficult to think of ourselves otherwise than as beings that are defined as a particular combination of mind and body. Even when we seek to escape this inheritance, it finds it way back through our speech and into our conception of ourselves. Foucault is cognizant of this, and uses it, as we shall see in detail later, to invert our Judeo-Christian legacy when he declares in his book on the prisons that "the soul is the prison of the body" (*DP*: 30).

If we set Descartes aside for a moment to turn to a more nearly contemporary thinker, we shall see, beyond surface differences, important similarities that run through the philosophical tradition. At first it may be hard to imagine a thinker more different from Descartes than Sigmund Freud. Whereas Descartes privileges consciousness, Freud privileges the unconscious. Where Descartes sees a large measure of free will, Freud sees a long and often unsuccessful struggle to attain any freedom. Where Descartes allows reason to rid us of the burden of false conceptions, Freud sees us as being burdened by a history whose legacy one can never entirely escape.

So who are we, in Freud's view? This is a difficult question to answer, and not only because his writings can be elusive. Freud seems to present us with two distinct topographies of the mind: one that dominates his earlier writings and another that appears later on. The first one, in which the distinction between the conscious and the unconscious dominates, will be our focus. The second one, with its tripartite division into id, ego and superego, can be interpreted in light of the earlier one, and we shall leave it aside.

To think of human beings as having an unconscious, and furthermore to think of who they are as being largely a matter of what happens in that unconscious and how it expresses itself, is a revolutionary idea at the time of Freud's writings in the early twentieth century. He thinks of the idea as the third great blow to humanity's view of itself as a privileged being in the universe, after Copernicus's discovery that the earth revolves around the sun and Darwin's discovery of the evolution of species.

> [H]uman megalomania will have suffered its third and most wounding blow from the psychological research of the present time which seeks to prove to the ego that it is not even the master of its own house, but must content itself with scanty information of what is going on unconsciously in its mind.[8]

To say that we are largely a matter of our unconscious is to remove us from what the philosophical tradition has taught us to consider as our special relation to reason and self-awareness, a special relation that is central to Descartes, among others.

For Freud, who each of us is concerns how we live the historical conflicts that characterize our early life. Although the particular character of those conflicts is unique to each of us, there is a general pattern that all of them follow. First, those conflicts are centred around oral issues, then anal ones. Next, and most important, they concern the Oedipal complex (or, for girls, the Electra complex). Taking the boys' development as exemplary – which is Freud's approach – the boy falls in love with his mother. He would like to be rid of his father, who, after all, is the competition for his love. However, he fears the consequences of his father's wrath; as Freud has it, castration is the imagined consequence. Therefore the boy must suppress his feelings for his mother. This suppression creates an unconscious, which in turn swallows much of the boy's pre-Oedipal history and sets the stage for the resolution of later conflicts.

As Freud conceives the unconscious, it is not merely a container for conflicts or a safe haven for unacceptable feelings or thoughts. The unconscious does not merely receive; it also expresses. Just as it incorporates situations in later life, repressing the elements of those situations that remind us of earlier difficulties, so it emerges in indirect ways in our behaviour. For Freud, jokes, symptoms and slips of the tongue are ways the unconscious can express itself in our behaviour without those expressions being recognized for what they are.

One way to describe who we are, then, is as a certain type of engagement with the world, an engagement that operates largely on an unconscious economy of repression and expression. This economy is one that, with the help of a psychoanalyst, we can come to understand, at least to a certain extent. We need the aid of an analyst because the unconscious has no motivation to reveal itself; moreover, the project of self-understanding is, in Freud's view, a never-ending one. Therefore, each of us can, through a long and often painful process and with the assistance of another, come to some recognition of who we are, and perhaps can do something to overcome those aspects of ourselves that we would rather be rid of. But this ability is limited and is gained at a high price.

The other way to describe who we are is as a set of more or less successfully resolved conflicts. This way of describing us is not in conflict with the first. Rather, it focuses on a different aspect of Freud's view, on the history rather than the topography. If we are, on the one hand, largely an unconscious relation with the world, it is because we are, on the other, a determined set of conflicts that each of us faces. Those conflicts, again, are at once universal and individual. They are universal in that they unfold according to a pattern that holds for all human beings. They are individual in that that pattern is inflected in particular ways depending on a person's particular history.

The contrast between Freud's focus on the unconscious and Descartes's primacy of the conscious mind could not be sharper. Although the possibility of the unconscious does not occur to Descartes, it would be safe to say that, if it did, he would reject it. It runs against the entire grain of his philosophy, with its focus on conscious rationality. Moreover, one might well say that the idea of an unconscious violates the claim that God is not a deceiver, since the point of the unconscious is to engage in a systematic deception of consciousness. If, for instance, the little boy recognizes that he is suppressing his hatred and fear of his father, and later comes to understand that some of his actions express that hatred and that fear, the unconscious would not be performing its function.

Although these differences are crucial, there are important similarities between the approaches of Descartes and Freud. Two of them are fundamental for understanding Foucault's approach to the question of who we are: their individualized approach and, although it may seem to be the opposite, their universal character.

When Descartes and Freud ask who we are, they approach the question by asking who each of us is in his or her nature. The "we" of who we are is not a collective we. It is an individual I. For Descartes, the answer to the question of who we are is, in its most important elements, the same as the answer to the question of who each of us is. Each of us is a mind-substance and a body-substance engaged with each other, in which the mind – the conscious, rational mind – is the dominant aspect. That we could be who we are as a result of a collective experience is irrelevant for him. This is not to say that he denies that people have a collective experience. It is rather to say that, in undertaking to answer the question of who we are, he does not consider it. It is neglected rather than rejected.

With Freud the situation is more complicated. On the one hand, he does allow for collective experience. In fact, his book *Moses and Monotheism* speculates that one of the seeds of the Oedipal complex may be a result of the murder of Moses by the Jewish people. This would lend a historical and collective aspect to his developmental narrative. In addition, he allows that the particularity of a person's conflicts may be a result of his or her particular history. This seems to open the door to a collective determination of who someone is, an experience that one shares with others. On the other hand, he gives a fairly fine-grained interpretation of human development, one that privileges the unfolding of the individual within a developmental pattern that depends on what each individual undergoes. Who we are is a matter of who each of us is in the particular way each of us resolves a predetermined set of conflicts.

And here we can see the intersection of the individualized approach and the universal one. For Freud, as for Descartes, the universal and the individual go hand in hand. It is *because* they both have a universal approach to who each of us is that Freud and Descartes are focused on the individual rather than the collective. How can this be? To the extent that one believes that who we are has a universal character, that it is the same across times and places, one will also believe that the particularities of a person's or a society's history are irrelevant in determining who one is. It is to believe that what is essential about us is immune to the contingencies of a changing history. To put the point another way, it is to believe that what is essential about us is something that each of us contains, regardless of our or our culture's or society's particular experiences or histories. And thus what makes us who we are is something that is at once timelessly universal and radically individual.

Much of the history of philosophy will confirm this strange connivance between the universal and the individual in the approach to who we are. For a final example, one that might seem to fly in the face of what I have just said, we can look towards a more recent thinker: Jean-Paul Sartre. Sartre's career overlaps with Foucault's. In fact, he inhabits the intellectual generation that precedes Foucault's, the generation of the existentialists. For Sartre, especially in his earlier, more purely existential writings, the answer to the question of who we are can be summed up in a single word: freedom.

Sartre rejects any outside determination of who we are. We are simply what we choose to be. If thinkers like Freud and Descartes see us as having an essence it is our fate to live out, Sartre can be seen as diametrically opposed to them. "Atheist existentialism, which I represent . . . states that if God does not exist, there is at least one being in whom existence precedes essence, a being who exists before he can be defined by any concept, and that this being is man."[9] Rather than possessing an essential nature that is inescapably ours (Descartes) or a specific developmental scheme that will define us (Freud), we are instead nothing other than what we make of ourselves. We are the projects we choose to engage in. "What we mean is that a man is nothing else than a series of undertakings, that he is the sum, the organization, the ensemble of the relationships which make up these undertakings."[10]

Sartre's claim that one is nothing other than one's undertakings is inseparable from his claim that one is one's freedom. They are two sides of the same coin. For someone to be a free being, radically free in the sense Sartre would have it, is for them to be able to undertake any number of projects. It is for them to choose how to array the future that fans out in front of them. When Sartre defines human beings solely as the sum of their undertakings, what he is rejecting – and the earlier quote defining atheist existentialism hints at this – is the possibility that we are determined by something outside us, most likely God. It is the Judeo-Christian belief that a person's being is created in God's image that he takes aim at. For Sartre, we are not created in God's image. We are not created in any image. Whatever there is of image to be had in us is a product of our own creation.

Sartre's answer to the question of who we are seems to reject the approach embraced by both Descartes and Freud. For both of them, it is an essential nature that defines us. For Sartre, by contrast, it is precisely the lack of an essential nature that defines us. (One might argue here that Sartre is closer to Descartes than I am indicating here. After all, might Sartre's freedom and Descartes's ability to reason not be more intimately linked than I have indicated? Indeed they might. I will leave that issue aside here, since it does not affect the claim I am about to make.) The deep connection remains intact, however. Just as Descartes and Freud approach the question of who we are by means of the individual and the universal, so does Sartre. For Sartre, what is important about each of us – we can use the term *essential* here, if we do not confuse it with the essentialism that existentialism rejects – is our freedom. Each of us is defined by our freedom. And the reason for this is precisely that freedom is the crucial universal trait of human beings. It is what makes us what we are, or perhaps more appropriate, what we are not, since for Sartre, who was fond of paradoxes, "human reality must not be necessarily what it is but must be able to be what it is not".[11]

Someone familiar with the entire trajectory of Sartre's work might well object here that, in focusing on the writings from the 1940s and early 1950s, I have neglected his later, more Marxist-inspired work. It is in the later work where a collective determination is assimilated to the existentialism of Sartre's earlier career. I want to turn to Marx himself in a moment. This is an important issue, and deserves to be paused over more than I will here. I can only gesture at a response.

Sartre does not replace his existentialism with Marxism. To claim that he does would be, I believe, to deny the originality of his work. Instead, he grafts Marxism on to existentialism, showing how the individualism of his earlier work is actually compatible with the collective approach of Marx. In that way, he remains committed to the connivance between the individual and the universal that is characteristic of both Descartes and Freud. On the other side of things, however, there is a collectivist character to his later work that does bring him more nearly in alliance with Foucault. The two thinkers never converge, since Sartre always seeks universal categories, whether in his existentialist phase or in his later Marxist one. But, seen from the perspective of Sartre's later writings, they share more than they do if one focuses solely on Sartre's early career.

In looking at Descartes, Freud and Sartre (at least Sartre's existentialist period), we have seen that these thinkers – and, in as much as they are representative, the history of philosophy generally – approach the question of who we are by trying to isolate the important universal aspect or aspects of human being and claiming that each of us instantiates that aspect or those aspects. The approach is at once universal and individual. Is there anything wrong with this? There is. It is not that such views capture nothing of who we are. There is something to be said for rational self-consciousness as an important element of human being, even if one rejects the idea that humans comprise two different substances. There is an important truth captured in the idea that we are always engaged with the world in a conflicted way, even if one abandons the idea that that conflict can be traced to an Oedipal core. It seems right to say that freedom or something like it is a characteristic without which a full conception of human being would be lacking, even if the radical freedom Sartre posits goes beyond what one can accept.

But there is something missing as well. The accounts offered to us by Descartes, Freud, Sartre and others focus on purported general defining characteristics of human existence. But we are not generalities. We are not merely individual instances of a larger human character. We are specific human beings who have specific orientations and who deal with specific types of concerns in specific, if distinct, ways. With these more general accounts, it feels as though we were shown a particular aspect of the human body and told that that is who we are. It is as though Descartes showed us, say, the skeleton, and said, "That's you." To which Freud responds, "No; it's not the skeleton, it's the circulatory system." Sartre, in his turn, says, "In fact, it's the brain." These answers are unsatisfying, and not simply because each of them only captures an aspect of our corporeal structure.

The problem is not simply one of a limited perspective, as though if we added up all the aspects of these and other thinkers together we would then have a full account of who we are. All we would have then is an entire human body. But I am not simply my body. I am also the way it moves, the way it thinks and desires. I am its rhythms. I am the way it navigates through the world. In order to capture these aspects of who I am, I cannot simply talk about general aspects of human being. And, conversely, neither can I just talk about who I am as an individual. I have to talk about the world in which my navigating occurs, a world that has a specific character and that has unfolded its specific character in a specific way. As it will turn out, it is often the stamp of this world that, in important ways, makes me who I am, makes us who we are.

At first, we might say that we have to consider history. Why history? History, as Foucault thinks of it, is not just a matter of discrete events or movements that happened to precede us. Thinking of history in that way loses its connection with us, with the way it has helped make us who we are. Alternatively, we cannot think of history as that thing we need to understand to ensure that we are not condemned to repeat it. In some sense, that would be the opposite of Foucault's view of history. To think of history as something repeatable is to entertain the possibility that it has circular movements. Certain events that happened before us are capable, in some form, of returning. But that can't be right. Could it possibly be that, in the early twenty-first century, something that happened in the Renaissance could happen again? Or, if we tone down the idea, that something like what happened in the Renaissance could happen again? Surely, similar causes have similar effects. But in studying history, we are as much at a loss to isolate causes and effects as we are in anything else. What are the causes of the French Revolution, the New Deal, or globalization? The idea that we repeat history, even in kind, is at best an elusive one. In any case, there is another, perhaps better, way to approach our history.

Perhaps we should think of our history as the temporal movement that has deposited us on these particular shores. On this view, history is a part of us. It is not disconnected from us in the way the approach to history as a series of discrete events would have it. However, if history is a part of us, if it helps determine who we are, this is not simply in virtue of its structure. It is not because history is circular or because it takes some other shape that we are a product of it. It is because this particular history, with these particular events, led us to this place and not some other. The history that has brought us here could have been different. It did not have to take the paths it took. If it had, we ourselves would be different from who we are. But it took these paths, which means both that we are *this* rather than *that* and, in a lesson that will be equally important, we are *this* rather than *that* as a matter of contingency, not necessity. We did not have to be *this* rather than *that*, which means, among other things, that we do not have to continue to be *this*.

Already we can begin to appreciate the distance that separates Foucault from the tradition that includes Descartes, Freud and Sartre. For Foucault, who we are concerns not only what human beings are at their core. It is, more importantly, a matter of who we are now, of what we have been made to be by the history that has formed us. If we can recount that history, or, since history itself is complex, those histories, then we can address more adequately the question of who we are. We can start to think of ourselves as something more than generalities. We can situate ourselves and see who we are in terms of that situation.

Foucault is not the first to think of who we are as a matter of history. However, he thinks of it in a new way. In order to understand his view, we can approach it, again, by contrast. Here the contrast would be with Karl Marx. For thinkers of Foucault's generation, the generation of the 1960s and 1970s, Marx occupies a central place in all political and philosophical discussion. It is hard to imagine or to remember now, almost twenty years after the fall of the Berlin wall, how dominant Marxism was on the European political landscape. But dominant it was. In France, for instance, there was a Marxist party, the Parti Communiste Français (PCF), that ran candidates for office, that had a strong grip on the trade union movement, and that was the touchstone for progressive thought and action. Although in the uprisings in France in May and June of 1968, the PCF began to lose credibility by siding with the government in the suppression of the student and worker revolts, for many years before then the progressive who spoke outside the parameters defined by Marxist thought was very much an anomaly.

Marx thinks of who we are as a matter of history. This does not mean that he denies that there is a human essence. He does have, at least in his early writings, a commitment to the idea that humans are a *species-being*.

> Man is a species-being, not only because he practically and theoretically makes the species – both his own and those of other things – his object, but also – and this is simply another way of saying the same thing – because he looks upon himself as the present, living species, because he looks upon himself as a *universal* and therefore free being.[12]

For the early Marx, this species-being, this being who is in its essence free, productive and self-constituting, is alienated from itself under capitalism and requires a communist revolution to be achieved. But the fact that we have this species-being, even in an alienated form, does not mean that history is only secondary for Marx.

In Marx's view, who we are at a given moment is largely a matter of where we stand in the unfolding of our history. Human history can be seen as the unfolding of our productive relationship with nature and with one another. For Marx, human beings are part of nature, but a part of nature that, in surviving and reproducing itself, also refashions nature. It has been said that Marx reduces everything to economics. This may be true, but Marx's view of economics is far broader than our own. Economics, for him, is nothing less than the social interaction with the natural world through which we produce and reproduce ourselves. We make ourselves and one another through the production of our lives together, and this production occurs as a matter of our working and reworking the material world we find ourselves in, that is, nature.

As it happens, for most of human history this making and remaking occurs under conditions of scarcity. There is not enough for everyone to create for themselves an adequate life. People must compete for the scarce resources that are available. The result is that there are some who have more and others who have less. There are, as Marx puts it, classes. Those who have more can, and do, dominate those who have less; in turn, those who have less struggle against that domination. "The history of all hitherto existing society", he declares at the outset of *The Communist Manifesto*, "is the history of class struggles."[13]

This relationship of struggle is not constant. The character of classes, as well as those who make them up, changes. They change with changing economic conditions. The productive conditions of a particular society will change until the class relationships that comprise those conditions no longer fit them. When that happens there will be a revolution of some sort and a new set of class relationships will emerge. This will continue until scarcity has been overcome. For Marx, the possibility of overcoming scarcity is produced by capitalism because of its enormous productive capacity. However, the inequities of capitalism will allow scarcity to remain until the last revolution, the communist revolution, has ended all class relationships.

In this view of things, who we are at a particular moment is a matter of our place in history. More specifically, it is a matter of our place in a particular class in history. We do not have to see Marx committing himself to the idea that the entirety of who each of us is is reducible to our class position. We need not see Marx, although some of his interpreters do, as a determinist who argues that everything about a person is reducible to the class they occupy. Marx once argued that "Men make their own history, but they do not make it just as they please; they do not make it under circumstances chosen by themselves, but under circumstances directly encountered, given and transmitted from the past."[14] People may not be reducible to their histories, but they cannot escape those histories either.

If we are, in part at least, a product of our history, then is there anything in particular about how our history unfolds that makes us who we are? Or is our history contingent? Does it unfold without any necessary pattern or order? In Marx's eyes, there is a pattern, and it is a necessary one. Recall that, for him, class relations change when they can no longer be sustained as the economic conditions of a society evolve. For instance, late in the feudal world a nascent bourgeoisie arises, a class that is characterized not by ownership of the land but by ownership of small factories and large workshops. This rising bourgeoisie is excluded from positions of power and influence, which are retained by the landed aristocracy. The tension between these two classes is also, and for the same reasons, a tension between the structure of a society as it currently is (with the aristocracy in a dominant position), and the relationships between a group with an increasing share of economic resources (the emerging bourgeoisie) and a group that is, relative to this group, losing theirs (the old aristocracy). As Marx sometimes summarizes the point, there is a conflict between the mode of production and the relations of production. When this conflict becomes too much for a given mode of production to bear, then a revolution occurs that creates a new one. In this case, feudalism gives way to capitalism.

This is how history unfolds. The movement accords with what Marx's predecessor, Georg Hegel, calls the dialectic. In Hegel's view, history (and not just history: ideas, nature and much else) unfolds dialectically. There is a given situation. That situation is not a stable one. It is characterized by internal tensions. Eventually, those tensions overwhelm the situation and create another situation, one that is very different and perhaps even opposed at many points to the first situation. However, the second situation, like the first, is unstable; it has its own internal tensions. As the second situation unfolds, those tensions, as they did in the first situation, become sharper. Once again, they overwhelm the situation and a new situation is created. This movement, from internally unstable situation to rising tension to revolution to new situation, is how history progresses. For Hegel, as for Marx, history will eventually yield a stable situation where all the important internal tensions are resolved. That will be the end of history, at least as an evolving dialectic.

There are significant differences between Hegel's view of the dialectic of history and Marx's. First, for Hegel the dialectic is as much conceptual as, or even more so than, it is material. Marx, for his part, sees the dialectic arising on the basis of human beings' material productive relations with the natural world. Secondly, Hegel believes that the final stage of history arrives in the course of his lifetime, that he is witnessing the last stage of the dialectic. For Marx, the last stage of history needs another revolution, the communist revolution. He sees Hegel's thought stopping one stage short of completion. For both thinkers, however, there is a structure to the way history unfolds, the way it makes us who we are.

This is where Foucault parts company with Marx. In Foucault's view, to take history as unfolding in accordance with a necessary pattern or structure is not to take history seriously enough. It is to submit history to a principle outside the specific movement of its events, a principle that dictates the nature or the direction of that movement. History becomes subject to a transcendent principle outside it or an immanent principle that determines it. It is as though history does not exist on its own terms, but is rather an example or an expression of something ahistorical.

Such a view of history is essentialist, in the way that Sartre sees previous views of human being as essentialist. For Sartre, the Genesis story of creation, in which man is created in God's image, is essentialist. In this story man is simply an expression of an essence that he does not create. Man exemplifies a nature that precedes him. Sartre holds that human beings create their own natures. We do not express or exemplify pre-given ones. In much the same way a Marxist view of history is essentialist. It takes history as a matter of expressing the movement of the dialectic. History does not possess its own integrity; its existence is preceded by an essence.

We might say that, in this particular sense, history is existential in Foucault's eyes. This does not mean that history creates itself in the way that Sartre thinks human beings create themselves. That would anthropomorphize history. It is not that history creates itself; it is that it is not created by some transcendent, overarching or underlying principle. It does not necessarily progress or regress. It does not necessarily move in a circle. It does not necessarily repeat anything. It may progress, or regress, or circle, or repeat. But if it does, then this is because of particular local conditions that have arisen, not because it lies in the character of history itself to do so.

History exists on its own terms and must be studied on its own terms. That is what it means to say that Foucault takes history more seriously than others, like Marx, who have introduced history into their account of who we are.

Foucault addresses the question of who we are by appealing to history. He hopes to be able to give a richer, more robust answer to that question by abandoning both the universal/individual approach of Descartes, Freud and Sartre, and the ahistorically determined historical approach embraced by Marx. He jettisons the first because it neglects the role that our collective history plays in creating who we are. He rejects the second because it submits that collective history to a determining principle, and thus circles back to the universalism of the first approach. Instead, Foucault sees us largely as products of a contingent history. Our history has made who we are today, not because it had to, but just because it did, because at certain junctures it took one path as opposed to another. Perhaps it took that path because of the influence of local events, or perhaps because of some mistaken or overdetermined view of things that people had, or maybe because of chance. But for whatever reason, it did. And thus we find ourselves here as opposed to there.

15

We are not barred from ever getting there as opposed to here. Or better, if we are so barred, it is not because the nature of things prevents it but because local conditions cannot be turned in that direction. There is no deep reason that keeps us here instead of there. That, as I have said, will turn out to be a crucial point. We can already see that the world bequeathed to us by our history, and we ourselves, are much more malleable than previous thinkers have led us to believe.

We must ask what it means to say that we are a product, or largely a product, of a contingent history. This means more than it might seem on the surface. To embrace this view of ourselves is not simply to invoke either history or contingency. Nor is it only to declare an intersection between the two. In Foucault's hands, to say that we are a product of a contingent history is to commit to a view of ourselves that has a number of characteristics. Together, they add up to both a radically new approach to the question of who we are and an important opening on to the question of who we might be.

We can isolate five features of this view. First, who we are is largely a collective matter, or, to put it another way, the question of who each of us is individually is deeply bound to the question of who *we* are. Secondly, that collective determination of who we are is not something that we can simply shake off; in being historical, who we are is embedded in a historical legacy that is not simply a matter of choice. Thirdly, that determination is complex. It is not a single historical theme that makes us who we are at a given moment, but instead an interplay of themes that weave together, split apart, reform and transform. To see who we are, then, we must not look at ourselves with a bird's-eye view. We must look at our particular historically given practices. Fourthly, those practices are tied up not only with how we act but also with how we go about knowing things (or attempting to know them or thinking we know them) and especially how we go about knowing ourselves. Fifthly, although we have already seen this, this historically given complex of practices through which we know and, indeed, *are* is contingent and therefore changeable. We did not control how we became who we are, and who we are is not simply something we can walk away from; nevertheless, we do not have to be who we are. We can be otherwise. And to be otherwise, as it will turn out, is not simply something *I* can be. Usually, it is something that *we* can be: not all of us, to be sure, but certainly more than one.

Before turning to the specific histories in which Foucault traces the lineage of who we are, it would be worth lingering over these five characteristics. They frame the histories he gives. They keep alive the idea as we survey those histories that there is more going on than a mere recitation of facts. The first characteristic is that who we are is largely a collective matter. We

cannot think of ourselves simply as individuals, divorced from the historically given context in which we find ourselves. There are a number of theories that seem to want to consider us as atoms, as individuals separable from our specific context. For instance, the individualism of traditional liberal political theory seems to see us thus. Indeed, liberal political theory has been attacked by a movement called *communitarianism* for allegedly neglecting our embeddedness in specific contexts. Although Foucault is no communitarian – he tends to view those specific contexts with a more jaundiced eye than do communitarians – he ratifies the idea that who we are is not separable from them.

We need not turn to political theory, however, to see the individualism Foucault rejects. It is all around us. It lies in the notion, dear to many Americans, that one can be whoever one likes as long as one is willing to work at it. To be sure, this notion has its virtues. For instance, it offers optimism in the face of obstacles. However, it is, strictly speaking, mistaken on two counts. First, it assumes that each of us is an isolated individual, that our past and our future are not collective but individual matters. Secondly, and related, it assumes that the conditions in which each of us finds ourselves are not deeply a part of who we are, that each of us can shrug off our historically given social inheritance and assume another. This is certainly wrong. I, for instance, will always be someone who grew up in New York during the Vietnam War period. My peregrinations, no matter how far they lead me geographically or emotionally or chronologically from that time and place, will always be informed by the legacy of being raised in that city during that period. Who I am will always be, at least in part, a matter of that past. This is the second characteristic of Foucault's histories.

It is tied to the first one, that who I am is also inseparable from who other people are. After all, I was not the only person who grew up in New York at that time. There were others. Some of them I have remained in contact with, and others I have met later in life. The recognition is always immediate. There are things that we share, an outlook that we can, if not embrace, then certainly relate to, one that is foreign to many others I have met. Who I am, then, is a collective matter, not simply an individual one. And its tie to who I am runs deep.

For Foucault, this collective matter is common not only to a very specific time and place. It involves much wider themes, larger cultural orientations that, for him, operate across Europe, and sometimes the Western world, as well as across a number of practices. These themes are also of longer standing, often centuries in duration. The idea remains, however, that who each one of us is cannot be separated from a common history that has created the landscape we inhabit. Commonality, inseparability: two themes framing the histories of who we are that Foucault recounts.

17

But, someone will say, you are not solely a person who grew up in New York during the Vietnam War. You are more than that; your historical determination is more complicated. It comprises multiple sources that arise from vastly different arenas of experience. You spent years working in the field of psychology (at least until you started reading Foucault's histories of psychology); you are engaged in child rearing; you teach at a university; you are a serious runner; you have organized on behalf of various progressive causes. Surely the collective histories of these different practices are also determinative for who you are. You are not simply the result of being an adolescent in New York during the late 1960s and early 1970s.

This is true. It makes the histories of each of us complex. It also makes the histories of our particular contexts complex. There are norms of child rearing, of university teaching, of running, of progressive organizing. These norms, and the practices in which they are embedded, sometimes overlap and sometimes conflict. They are neither entirely isolated from one another nor reducible to a single theme that binds them. In order to study the emergence of each of them, we have to look close to the ground. A general history of our times will not do. Worse still, a history that focused on what the leaders of the time – those anointed by the media, the electoral political structure, or by themselves – would be entirely irrelevant. We must look where people live, at the practices that they engage in or that, one way or another, come to engage them. Over the course of his life Foucault says many things about his method, often from different angles, and often shifting, depending on his current interests. One of the most important and enduring, however, is this:

> In this piece of research [*Discipline and Punish*], as in my earlier work, the target of analysis wasn't "institutions", "theories," or "ideology," but *practices* . . . It is a question of analyzing a "regime of practices" – practices being understood here as places where what is said and what is done, rules imposed and reasons given, the planned and the taken for granted meet and interconnect.
>
> (QM: 75)

Practices are what people live. They determine who we are not by imposing a set of constraints from above, but through historically given norms through which we think and act. These historically given norms are, once again, neither divorceable from nor reducible to what people often consider their larger historical context. The insistence of psychology in so many business and educational practices, embedded in the larger concern with normality that is an ongoing theme of Foucault's research, cannot be separated from the emergence and domination of capitalism. But neither is

18

it reducible to capitalism in the way that many Marxists would have it, as a superstructure that is simply erected upon the economic base. It is a practice or a group of practices that interact with other practices, both economic and non-economic, and that share or borrow or cross-fertilize or reinforce important themes, all in complex ways.

The convergence, conflict and reinforcement of practices can create effects that are unintended by those who participate in them. For instance, as we will see in detail below, those who are members of monasteries in the early eighteenth century and before do not intend their rigid daily schedules to be part of the larger social development of what Foucault calls *discipline*, a term he uses to cover the minute observation and regimentation of daily life under the banner of normality. Monks of the time, in their isolation, do not foresee that their practices will intersect with those of the Prussian military or the prison reformers in order to foster the rise of normality as a crucial form of the operation of power in our world. However, since practices intersect with one another in various ways, even the relative isolation of monks cannot prevent the incorporation of their regimented life into other practices whose convergence gives way to disciplinary control. Foucault puts the point this way: "People know what they do; they frequently know why they do what they do; but what they don't know is what what they do does."[15]

If practices are engaged with one another in this way, then one can begin to understand the contingency of history, particularly in regard to its determination of who we are. The complexity of interacting practices does not lend itself to a single overarching theme. To see what is at play in our historical inheritance cannot be a matter of finding *the* key to unlock the mysteries of its workings; it must be a matter of looking at the unfolding, the evolution and the interaction of particular practices. In discovering who we are, there is no privileged place to look, as some Marxists would like to look at the economy. There is no privileged theme to discover, as some theorists would like to discover progress or dialectics or circular recurrence. There are only the particularities of what has come before, structured by the various practices in which we are all engaged.

This is not to deny that the contingency of history may give rise to important themes, themes that run across large swaths of a specific historical context. Foucault often seeks to understand such themes as discipline, normalization, bio-politics, or, in his earlier work, resemblance, classification, and death seen as a natural development of life. What it denies is that these themes structure the unfolding of history from above, within, or outside it. These themes emerge from the unfolding of practices. Once in place, they may, for a time, react back on those practices to give them further structure. But it is not because the themes have an independence from our practices that they do so; it is precisely because they are inseparable from them.

One of the aspects, and for Foucault one of the most important aspects, of this inseparability of themes from practices concerns knowledge. Although there are many shifts in Foucault's approach to history over the course of his career – changing from what has been called *archaeology* to *genealogy* to *ethics*, discovering the importance of power, turning from the external constitution of who we are to our own self-constitution – the pre-occupation with knowledge remains a constant with him. For Foucault, knowledge is something that always happens in our practices. One does not know something from a standpoint outside the practices that make one up. There is, as the philosopher Thomas Nagel puts it, no "view from nowhere". Our knowledge is situated in our practices. This situating has several implications.

First, our knowledge changes as our practices change. In the unfolding of our contingent history, we will know things in different ways depending on the state and structure of our practices at a particular time. To put the point another way, we will know differently at different periods. This does not mean that nothing we know is ever true, or that knowledge is merely a shifting opinion. If Foucault's perspective is right, then one cannot claim that nothing we ever know is true or that knowledge is merely a shifting opinion. Both of those views would presume that we can somehow exit our practices, and with them our knowledge, to obtain a view above or outside them: in short, a view from nowhere. But that is precisely what Foucault's perspective precludes.

A second implication of the embeddedness of our knowledge in our practices is that what goes on in those practices will affect how we go about the project of knowing. Our knowing is not only inseparable from our practices generally; it is inseparable from the norms and doings and sayings those practices consist in. This idea becomes important in Foucault's genealogical works, where the theme of power emerges as a central concern of his thought. If knowledge occurs within our practices, and power arises within those same practices, then there must be an intimate connection between knowledge and power. In contrast to those who would like to see knowledge as something that happens apart from the impurity of power relationships, knowledge and power are entwined. "Perhaps", Foucault writes:

> we should abandon a whole tradition that allows us to imagine that knowledge can exist only where power relations are suspended . . . These "power–knowledge" relations are to be analysed, therefore, not on the basis of a subject of knowledge who is or is not free in

relation to the power system, but, on the contrary, the subject who knows, the objects to be known and the modalities of knowledge must be regarded as so many effects of these fundamental implications of power–knowledge and their historical transformations.

(DP: 27–8)

Foucault's oft-cited concept "power–knowledge" does not reduce knowledge to power, as some have argued. Nor does it see our purported knowledge as simply masking relations of power. Instead, it takes power and knowledge to be embedded in practices whose history and effects Foucault takes it as his task to understand.

If who we are is a matter of our practices rather than of some human essence that determines us, then who we are is much more fluid and changeable than we are often taught. This is not to deny that the historical grip of our practices is a tight one. On the contrary, it is precisely the fact that our historical grip holds us so tightly that makes it seem to us that we cannot live otherwise than the way we do now, that we cannot be something other than what we are. However, if history is contingent, then its grip is not inescapable. How things are is not how they must be. By understanding our history we can intervene upon it. "My optimism", Foucault says:

consists . . . in saying that so many things can be changed, fragile as they are, bound up more with circumstances than with necessities, more arbitrary than self-evident, more a matter of complex, but temporary, historical circumstances than with inevitable anthropological constraints . . . You know, to say that we are much more recent than we think . . . [is] to place at the disposal of the work that we can do on ourselves the greatest possible share of what is presented to us as inaccessible. (PC: 156)

Circumstances rather than necessities; temporary constraints rather than anthropological ones; arbitrary rather than self-evident; fragile: that is the character of the historical trajectory that has brought us here. It has made us who we are not because it could not make us anything else. We can become otherwise. To do so, however, requires us to understand who we have been made to be, and, more important, to recognize the historically contingent character of that making. Otherwise, who we might be, as opposed to who we are, will seem to us to be "inaccessible".

It is only a small step to see that to be otherwise than who we are can only rarely be an individual task. One does not act, one does not create oneself, in a vacuum. If who *I* have been made to be is inseparable from who *we* have been made to be, and if who we are is bound to the practices we

21

engage in and that engage us, it is difficult to imagine how being otherwise can be accomplished without others. One does not create new practices on one's own. One does not alter the practices one participates in without it having effects on others. One does not understand one's own complex history without recourse to the work of those who have also attempted to understand theirs. If who we are is a collective project, then so is the project of being otherwise than who we are.

What is certain is that the project of being otherwise is not "inaccessible". We do not have to be who we are currently constituted to be. And in that sense, we might refine the question that frames Foucault's work. Rather than asking, "Who are we?", we might see Foucault asking the question, "Who are we *now*?" Although much of his historical work describes a trajectory that precedes us, he often ends his books by drawing lessons for the character of our current ways of being. It is not that the question of who we are is the wrong one; it is rather that the question of who we are, asked rightly, is the same as the question of who we are now. If we turn away from timeless or inescapable answers to the question of who we are, then, unless we take as our task a mere historical curiosity about who we once were, the point of our doing history, the goal of our research, is to understand who we are now.

In an essay on the philosopher Immanuel Kant, Foucault makes this clear. Responding to an essay of Kant's entitled "What is Enlightenment?", Foucault writes that what modernity offers us, and what much of the critical project of modernity has been, is a reflection on who we have been made to be and how we might escape the constraints of that making:

> The critical ontology of ourselves must be considered not, certainly, as a theory, a doctrine, nor even as a permanent body of knowledge that is accumulating; it must be conceived as an attitude, an ethos, a philosophical life in which the critique of what we are is at one and the same time the historical analysis of the limits imposed on us and an experiment with the possibility of going beyond them. (WE: 319)

Kant's text is a reflection on the Enlightenment written by someone who is living through it. It is an attempt to grasp, to understand the present as it is happening. That, in Foucault's view, is a striking feature of the modern era and a legacy of the Enlightenment: it promotes a critical relation to one's present. Foucault writes:

> [T]he thread which may connect us with the Enlightenment is not faithfulness to doctrinal elements but, rather, the permanent

reactivation of an attitude – that is, of a philosophical ethos that could be described as a permanent critique of our historical era.

(*Ibid.*: 312)

Foucault takes himself, like Kant, to be inscribed in that ethos. Foucault is not anti-modern: nor is he postmodern. He is, at least in his own eyes, precisely modern. He seeks to understand the present and who we have been made to be in that present, not to satisfy a passing curiosity but to open up the possibility for new ways of being.

Foucault never does tell us, aside from offering a few suggestive phrases, what these new ways of being should consist in. That is our task, the task of each of us alone and many of us together. His task consists in asking about our present, asking who we have come to be in the present. But the task is not an idle one. Rather, "this task requires work on our limits, that is, a patient labor giving form to our impatience for liberty" (*ibid.*: 319). It is directed at once towards our present and towards our future. It is at once a historical analysis and an invitation to change. It is at once the project of a single individual, alone in a dusty archive, immersed in faded documents, and of those who engage in conversation with the works that emerge from that immersion, and, yet again, of those who, having read him or heard of his work or anticipated his words with their own lives, would converge on a project of self-understanding and self-transformation that can use the material of who we are in order to create new possibilities for who we might be.

Near the end of his life, Foucault puts the point this way:

As for what motivated me, it is quite simple; I would hope that in the eyes of some it might be sufficient in itself. It was curiosity – the only kind of curiosity, in any case, that is worth acting upon with a degree of obstinacy: not the curiosity that seeks to assimilate what it is proper for one to know, but that which enables one to get free of oneself.

(*UP*: 8)

With Foucault, we must ask who we are, who we are now. We must follow the thread of this question in his texts and the responses, always partial, that he gives. But this path will, in the end, prove useless unless there is the passion for who we might be. Foucault does not provide that. He can reveal the contingency of who we have been told that we are, but he cannot inflame the desire to be otherwise. That must come, if indeed it does come, from those whose own lives are at stake.

CHAPTER TWO

Archaeological histories of who we are

How might we embark on a historical approach, or a set of historical approaches, to address the question of who we are? Because of the complexity of our historical inheritance there are many avenues of entry. No single one among of them is preferred or exhaustive. There is no Archimedean point. Foucault himself, at different times in his life, offers different interpretations of his own approach. Usually, those interpretations depend on what is motivating him at the time; he tends to see his previous writings in light of current interests. There is, however, a traditional classification of his published writings into three periods: archaeology, genealogy and ethics. The first period encompasses the time from his first major publication, *Histoire de la folie à l'âge classique* (partially translated into English as *Madness and Civilization*) through his last methodological work on archaeology, *The Archaeology of Knowledge*. The other major works of that period are *The Birth of the Clinic* and *The Order of Things*. The second period is characterized by two major works, *Discipline and Punish* and the first volume of *The History of Sexuality*. The final period encompasses his last two published volumes of the history of sexuality, *The Use of Pleasure* and *The Care of the Self*. If we are to give dates to these periods, we might say that the archaeological period runs from 1961 until 1968 or 1969, the genealogical period until 1978 or so, and the ethical period until his death in 1984.

How useful is this periodization? Although it is the standard one, many have argued that the divisions in Foucault's approach are far less decisive than it would seem to suggest. If Foucault sees continuity in his own work, even if that continuity differs in character depending on the different stages of his career, should we not also see his writings as forming a more or less continuous whole? Or, if we take Foucault seriously in those moments where he seems to say that each of his texts is a singular experiment, should we not jettison periodization from the other end? Should we not argue against periodization precisely because there is nothing like a continuous whole characterizing his works, nor even an important continuity between any one and its successor?

There are reasons to embrace any of these readings of his corpus. We will, at least roughly, follow periodization here, although along the way I will point out reasons to be leery of it. There will be reasons to see the continuity, and reasons to see the singularity, of each work. We cannot treat all of his works here without betraying the riches that each brings; we will focus on those most often discussed. And even so, betrayal will be inevitable.

Throughout our readings, however, there will be a single theme that returns, one that characterizes the entire trajectory of Foucault's publications. What all these periods have in common is that they are framed by a historical concern with the emergence of who we are.

The history of madness

The history of madness (in *Histoire de la folie*) is his first major work. It is the first work where he speaks in his own voice, the voice that will be recognized over the course of the rest of his career. Before the book on madness, and in keeping with the intellectual tenor of the time in Europe, Foucault writes under the convergent influences of phenomenology and Marxism. In an interview he speaks of this early period:

> we should not forget that throughout the period from 1945 to 1955 in France, the entire French university – the young French university, as opposed to what had been the traditional university – was very much preoccupied with the task of building something which was not Freudian–Marxist but Husserlian–Marxist: the phenomenology–Marxism relation. That is what was at stake in the debates and efforts of a whole series of people. [Maurice] Merleau-Ponty and Sartre, in moving from phenomenology to Marxism, were definitely operating on that axis.   (CT/IH: 21)

Histoire de la folie breaks decisively with the early project. Phenomenology takes a person's subjective experience to be the crucial object of investigation. It seeks to understand the structure of a person's experience, to unfold that which, although experienced, needs to be reflected upon in a rigorously descriptive way if it is to become accessible to the understanding. Foucault's book on madness rejects phenomenology. It shifts the ground from the project of unpacking and detailing an experience that has not yet been fully clarified to a historical investigation of the different structures for treating madness. It is those structures that frame the subjective experience.

Rather than asking, as the phenomenologists did, "What is it like to experience such-and-such?", Foucault asks instead, "What are the shifting historical frameworks within which such-and-such – in this case madness – is experienced?" The investigation no longer concerns what the individual undergoes; it concerns the historical conditions of their undergoing it. If we use terms loosely, we might say that the axis of investigation has shifted from inside the individual to outside.

In order to grasp these shifting historical frameworks, we cannot take madness as an objective given. It is not that there is this disease or this structure or this way of being called madness that has been experienced differently in different historical periods. Why should we assume that beneath the frameworks within which madness is treated, there is some constant that informs them all? This would assume too much. Alternatively, we need not assume the opposite, that there is nothing that any of these frameworks is looking at, that they are all preoccupied with an illusion. Rather, we should make no assumptions about the object of study and treatment called "madness". We should look at the historical frameworks for what they are, and, more important, for what they reveal to us about ourselves, rather than for what they may or may not reveal about the object of their investigation.

In order to do this, Foucault suggests that we return to the point at which madness becomes distinguished from reason. "We must try to return, in history, to that zero point in the course of madness at which madness is an undifferentiated experience, a not yet divided experience of division itself" (MC: ix).[1] The experience of madness emerges from a historical context in which madness first appears as such, as an experience distinct from reason. Foucault begins his investigation just before that context in order to trace its development.

In the Middle Ages, he writes, madness does not have a distinct character, or at least it does not have the character we have come to ascribe to it, as the Other of reason. Instances of what we would call madness are woven more seamlessly into the fabric of medieval experience. As the Middle Ages come to a close, however, the figure of madness begins to appear. Soon the mad will take the place, both figuratively and literally, of the medieval leper. The houses of leprosy will be cleared. They will, at least in part, be replaced by the madhouses. As lepers were once the object of practices and rituals of exclusion, hidden at the edges of medieval life in lazar houses, now the mad will occupy their place. It will be the same gesture, in any case: exclusion and confinement.

In what guise do the mad begin to make their appearance – that is, their appearance as mad? Foucault answers this question by appeal to the arresting image of the Ship of Fools. Ships of Fools were said to be ships that towns filled with their mad, sending them off on uncertain journeys, but at least ridding the towns of their presence. Why, however, would their presence constitute a threat? In the late medieval and early Renaissance period, madness comes to be associated with mysterious nether regions. It is associated with animality, with darkness, and ultimately with death.

> The dawn of madness on the horizon of the Renaissance is first perceptible in the decay of Gothic symbolism; as if that world, whose network of spiritual meanings was so close-knit, had begun to unravel, showing faces whose meaning was no longer clear except in the forms of madness. (MC: 18)

In the disintegration of the medieval perspective, madness appears as the indecipherable symbol of hidden truths. It is the dark underside of existence that can neither be escaped nor understood. As such, it is an object of both fascination and repulsion.

In Foucault's eyes, it is no accident that two of the major authors of the time, Cervantes and Shakespeare, often give madness pride of place in their works. For Cervantes, the figure of Don Quixote constitutes a madness that is at once foolish and wise, but in any case possessed of an unsettling power. In Shakespeare's plays, one need only refer to the madness of Hamlet or the twisted truths of King Lear's fool to recognize the importance he accorded the mad experience.

The Ship of Fools encapsulates this combination of fascination of repulsion. On the one hand, the ships are objects of painting, of discussion, and of public policy. On the other, their purpose is to depart, to leave, and to let human kind alone. Do these ships actually exist? Foucault says they did. Other historians are sceptical. Later, after recounting Foucault's own history of madness, we will need to return to the question of the historical status of his account. Is his account accurate, and what effect might particular inaccuracies have upon it? For the moment these questions can be placed to the side.

What is clear is that the ambiguous status enjoyed by madness during the late medieval and early Renaissance period declines, and by the seventeenth century madness is no longer the figure of darkness or of death. There is a historical break. Madness becomes more pedestrian. It is not a stalking animal within each of us, nor is it a sign of impending disintegration; it becomes mere folly. (During the Renaissance, madness was, at times, also conceived as folly, but not as *mere* folly.)

> Madness is here, at the heart of things and of men, an ironic sign that misplaces the true guideposts between the real and the

chimerical, barely retaining the memory of the great tragic threats
– a life more disturbed than disturbing, an absurd agitation in society, the mobility of reason.   (MC: 37)

One can glimpse this change in the treatment of madness in Descartes's
Meditations. Recall the movement of doubt that is Descartes's method of
philosophical reflection. In order to arrive at what must necessarily be true,
what cannot be suspect, and what therefore can serve as the foundation
of the rest of our knowledge, one must doubt everything that cannot be
held certain. The senses are doubted. Mathematical knowledge is doubted.
Descartes even raises the possibility of an Evil Genius that systematically
deceives him and clouds his thought. What is not entertained, what cannot
reasonably be entertained, is the possibility that one is mad.

When doubting the senses, Descartes raises the possibility that one is
mad, only to dismiss it and then approach the issue from another direction:
that one is asleep. As for madness, he writes:

> how could I deny that these hands and this body are mine, unless
> I am to compare myself with certain lunatics whose brain is so
> troubled and befogged by the black vapors of the bile that they
> continually affirm that they are kings while they are paupers . . . or
> that their body is glass? But this is ridiculous; such men are fools,
> and I would be no less insane than they if I followed their example.[2]

The problem that madness raises may be a true problem. One can reasonably doubt the evidence of the senses, including the evidence one has of the
character of one's own body. After all, in dreams we experience at times the
disintegration of our body's character and capacities.

If the problem of doubt can be sustained by sleep, however, it cannot by
way of madness. Madness is outside the pale, because it is outside the prov-
ince of truth. As Foucault writes:

> In the economy of doubt, there is a fundamental disequilibrium
> between madness [*folie*] on the one hand and dream or error on
> the other. Their situation is different in their relationship to truth
> and to what is being sought; dreams or illusions are surmounted in
> the structure itself of truth; but madness is excluded by the subject
> who doubts.   (HFAC: 57)

Dreams and illusions can place our beliefs in doubt because they still inhabit
the realm of the true and the false. We can think about them, consider
them, hold them before the light of truth and the shadow of falsity. In a

word, they are subject to reason. Madness is not. It is beyond, or perhaps beneath, "the structure of truth". "If *man* can always be fooled, *thought*, as exercise of the sovereignty of a subject that is obliged to perceive the truth, cannot be insane" (*HFAC*: 58).

Whence this change in attitude towards madness? How did madness lose its fascination? How did it fall from its initial status as symbol of our darker regions to a subject unworthy of the project of thought? Foucault does not say. During this period of his thought, he focuses, more emphatically than he does later, on the discontinuities between historical periods. As he explains later in his methodological study *The Archaeology of Knowledge*:

> the great problem presented by such historical analyses is not how continuities are established . . . the problem is no longer one of tradition, of tracing a line, but one of division, of limits; it is no longer one of lasting foundations, but one of transformations that serve as new foundations, the rebuilding of foundations. (*AKDL*: 5)

We shall return to this idea later, but it is worth recognizing one of the motivations for his emphasis on discontinuity. It is to prevent us from thinking that we can hold our history, and indeed ourselves, clearly before us. If thought has ruptures, if it has breaks, then it is not on a continuous path of progress toward the Truth. We can no longer think that one day we will know ourselves, that nothing will escape our intellectual gaze. The progressive view of history, that view of history that tells us we are on a path that leads inevitably closer to the truth of things, is a temptation that must be fought. Introducing discontinuities into history is one way to do it, because it stymies the attempt to see each historical period as a further development or refinement of the previous one.

There is, for Foucault, always an Other or Others to our thought. Or, to put the point another way, thought can always be otherwise than it is. There is always more to think than our current categories would lead us to believe. This should not be surprising for a writer whose first major work approaches madness as the Other of reason.

Returning then to Descartes's dismissal of madness, Foucault sees in it not a singular event, and not, as we just saw, a cause of a new way of treating madness. Descartes is not the initiator of a new approach to madness. His dismissal of madness is itself a reflection of a larger shift in the relation between reason and madness. It is emblematic rather than initiating. There is at this time, however, another, greater emblem of the change in reason's relation to madness. Foucault marks the date of this change as 1656, fifteen years after the publication of Descartes's *Meditations*. That year sees the decree that establishes in Paris the Hôpital Général. The Hôpital Général is hardly the only large institution of confinement in France. It certainly is not the first. In addition to older established hospitals, there are the abandoned lazar houses that will soon be housing the mad. What makes this particular institution unique is something else: "the Hôpital Général is not a medical establishment. It is rather a sort of semijudicial structure, an administrative entity which, along with the already constituted powers, and outside of the courts, decides, judges and executes" (*MC*: 40). Within a few months of the establishment of this semijudicial structure, Foucault says, nearly one per cent of the population of Paris finds itself confined to one hospital or another.

Is one per cent of the population mad? Does the decree of 1656 allow the police authorities to diagnose Descartes's fools on every street corner in Paris and elsewhere (since, as Foucault makes clear, the Great Confinement is not limited to Paris, or even to France)? No. It is not a question simply of rounding up the mad. Rather, there is a more general sensibility in which madness finds itself caught up.

> Between labor and idleness in the classical world ran a line of demarcation that replaced the exclusion of leprosy. The asylum was substituted for the lazar house, in the geography of haunted places as in the landscape of the moral universe. The old rites of excommunication were revived, but in the world of production and commerce. (*Ibid.*: 57)

It is work as an economic and moral matter that structures the rise of the Great Confinement. Those who can work are morally worthy; those who cannot are to be excluded.

We must be careful here not to see a false historical continuity that Foucault seems to be suggesting. It may appear that there is a historical constant, a role of exclusion or "excommunication" that must be played by somebody. Earlier, it is leprosy that plays that role; later, it is madness and the refusal or inability to work. This seems to me to be a misreading of Foucault's intent. The rhetoric is indeed suggestive, but I take it as little more than that. There is an earlier exclusion and a later one. They share similar rituals and even some overlapping sites. But that is all. There is no universal or absolute need for exclusion that is played out now upon one part of the population and later upon another. Rather, there are various inclusions and exclusions that occur in given social and historical contexts. Foucault is following a particular one, recognizing at the same time that it is not the only one.

In any case, reason's view of madness during the period of the Great Confinement occurs through the lens of work: "madness was perceived through a condemnation of idleness and in a social immanence guaranteed by the community of labor" (*ibid.*: 58). Madness is part of a larger phenomenon that Foucault labels *unreason*. The person of reason is engaged in work. He (more likely than "she" in this historical period) is part of the community of labouring beings that takes his sense of himself from that engagement. To labour is not simply an economic matter. It is also, and more deeply, a moral one. As Foucault notes, the cheap labour provided by the houses of confinement does not yield much economic value. In fact, by competing with work outside those houses, it may do more economic damage than good. But prosperity is not the issue here. One works not in order to contribute a certain amount to the greater social wealth; one works because it is the right thing to do. People of reason labour. To refuse to labour is to be a creature of unreason. And to be a creature of unreason is to invite exclusion from the community, at once moral and geographical, of those who recognize and engage in the work that is a person's calling.

Madness, then, is swept up in the larger phenomenon of unreason. It does, however, occupy a distinctive place: that of animality. The mad person is one who has descended or regressed into an animal state. That is why, Foucault says, although in most cases unreason, the refusal to work, is hidden during this period, madness is allowed to be displayed. Madness is an object lesson. It shows how far human beings can descend into unreason from the state of madness. If reason is distinct both from unreason and from animality, then the madman exhibits the link between the latter two clearly, and in doing so shows, by contrast, what it is to be fully human.

The view of madness as animality is in keeping with Descartes's own theoretical exclusion of madness. If, for Descartes, madness is the inability to engage in reason, for the entirety of what Foucault terms "the classical period" (roughly, the middle-to-late seventeenth to the end of the eighteenth century), madness is treated as a particular form of general unreason, a descent into bestiality that cannot share in what makes us who we are. We are far removed here from the madness of the early Renaissance. There is nothing mystical or threatening about the mad, nothing to give one pause over the fragility of one's existence or the powers that threaten it. "The animal in man no longer has any value as the sign of a Beyond; it has become his madness, without relation to anything but itself: his madness in the state of nature" (*ibid.*: 74).

We must be careful here not to interpret the fall into the state of nature in terms of a framework closer to our own. We are used to seeing in the animal the absence of free will. To descend into nature is to be caught up in determinism. We are, the story goes, animals ourselves, but animals that, however one accounts for it, possess a free will that allows us to recognize and to extricate ourselves from the immediacy of our circumstances. We are not like a wasp or a squirrel that is bound to its instincts, reduced to its "hard-wiring". When we think of the descent into animality, that is how we are tempted to think of it.

This would be a mistake. "It is not on this horizon of *nature* that the seventeenth and eighteenth centuries recognized madness, but against a background of *Unreason*; madness did not disclose a mechanism, but revealed a liberty raging in the monstrous forms of animality" (*ibid.*: 83). Madness, in the classical period, does not harbour a determinism; instead it harbours a licentious freedom, a freedom that cannot be harnessed to the requirements of reason. It is this reason, in turn, that is the recognition of the constraining requirements of a civilized society, and above all the requirement of work.

Treatments of madness, then, although they may seem to our eyes to be crude forms of medical intervention, should not be interpreted in this way. Madness is not yet mental illness; it is not yet to be submitted to the medical model. "[A]t this extreme point, madness was less than ever linked to the domain of correction. Unchained animality could be mastered only by *discipline* and *brutalizing*" (*ibid.*: 75). Madness is, ultimately, a moral matter and must be treated as such. Madness will be treated, and Foucault details a number of the treatments that madness receives, from immersion in water to the administration of bitters and to travel. However, that treatment remains caught in the ethical web that the classical period weaves around its view of the mad. "Being both error and sin, madness is simultaneously impurity and solitude; it is withdrawn from the world, and from truth; but it is by that very fact imprisoned in evil" (*ibid.*: 175).

In the second half of the eighteenth century, things change again. A new orientation toward madness arises, one that sets the stage for our more contemporary view. We are not yet at the inauguration of the contemporary view; that will have to await the interventions of Samuel Tuke and Philippe Pinel. However, a couple of the themes that will soon receive their full articulation in the work of these two emerge before their appearance on the stage of madness. In the second half of the eighteenth century, the unity of unreason begins to unravel. Poverty comes to be distinguished from madness not only in the latter's character as pure libertine animality, but in the association of madness now with indolence rather than impoverishment. During the latter half of the eighteenth century, it is the rich rather than the poor who are at risk of madness.

How does the link between poverty and unreason come undone? Here Foucault offers a causal explanation rather than, as usual, simply demarcating a break. In the economic change from mercantilism to industrialism there arises a need for unskilled labour. Mercantilism relies on trade and small-scale production. Industrialism requires a large labour pool.

32

Therefore, confining those who are able to perform unskilled labour in the name of unreason begins to run counter to the emerging economic imperatives. "In the mercantile economy, the Pauper, being neither producer nor consumer, had no place: idle, vagabond, unemployed, he belonged only to confinement . . . With the nascent industry which needs manpower, he once again plays a part in the body of the nation" (*ibid.*: 230).

We must be careful in approaching this shift of concern about madness from poor to rich, since it remains a shift on more or less the same ground. Madness is still tied to the absence of work. But the absence of work is no longer tied to impoverishment; it finds new moorings among the idle rich. The release from work brings with it an unbound leisure, one that can loosen a person's ties to the world of reason and work. For Foucault, this new view of madness can be located particularly in three themes: the association of madness with excess wealth, the bond posited between madness and an immodest religious fervour, and a concern that arises around too much reading and speculation. These are preoccupations of the rich. It is those who do not have to labour that have an excess of wealth; it is they who are ready to embrace new religious fads; and it is they who have the time for reading and speculation. All of these occur at the expense of a labour that keeps one's feet on the ground: that prevents one from drifting off into the ethereal realm where madness lies ready to weave its spell.

This shift is accompanied by a general withdrawal from the project of confinement. The poor, being creatures of unreason, could be confined in large numbers without harm to society. Now they must be reintegrated. They are not to be replaced by the rich, even though they have become objects of the fear of madness. As we noted before, Foucault does not believe that there must always be an exiled or confined group. Confinement is not a historical constant that is foisted upon different groups at different times. With the rise of the industrial economy, the fracturing of the unity of unreason, and, in France at least, the humanist pretensions of the French Revolution, confinement itself begins to lose its grip as a cure for social ills.

It is in the wake of this loss of confinement's grip that Tuke and Pinel's project at the end of the eighteenth century of the "liberation" of the mad is able to take place. Before turning to their work, it is worth pausing a moment over their historical reputation. Tuke and Pinel are canonized in the history of psychology and psychiatry for breaking the chains – often literal ones – of confinement that, until their time, are the lot of the those deemed mad. It is they who recognize the brutality of confinement and heroically step in to end it and to create newer, more humane methods of treating madness. Modern psychotherapy often traces its lineage back to these figures who, it is claimed, are the first to intervene on behalf of those who are mentally ill rather than against them. The establishment of Tuke's Quaker Retreat in England and Pinel's order to remove the chains of those confined at the hospital at Bicêtre together form the moment at which modern psychiatry is born. They mark the moment of the birth of the hospital as asylum, as a space of cure, in contrast to the previous age of hospitals as places marked solely by their role as institutions of confinement.

There are three questions one might pose to this account. First, does the work of these two figures, by their own efforts, destroy the idea that confinement is the proper way to treat madness? As we have seen, it does not. Confinement comes into disrepute before the end of the eighteenth century. Their work, although contributing to its demise, does not by itself create it. The historical break has already taken place before Pinel arrives at the door of Bicêtre in 1793.

Secondly, what are we to make of the brutality exhibited toward the mad? From our perspective, the confinement of the mad is undoubtedly barbarous. We should bear in mind, however, that this barbarity is not intended to be so. It is not anger or a desire for vengeance or mere cruelty that motivates the confinement of the mad in the seventeenth and eighteenth centuries. It is the entire organization of the relation between reason and madness. Given the view of madness as a type of unreason rooted in a libertine animality, confinement makes a certain kind of sense. The fact that it does so does not exonerate it. It is not that confinement is or has ever been a good thing just because people once felt they had reason to confine, any more than US slavery would be justified by the fact that Europeans believed Africans to be inferior. The point rather is the historical one that what Tuke and Pinel intervene upon is not an intended brutality but the remnants of a way of looking at madness.

If the brutality of the classical period toward the mad is unrecognized as such, this can lead one to ask whether there is an unrecognized brutality in the treatment of the mad in our age. This is the third question, the most important and most unsettling one. We look upon the treatment of madness in the classical period and see an unremitting cruelty in their confinement. That we do so is, as we just saw, half right. But why do we miss the other half? Because we believe ourselves to be enlightened – both morally and scientifically – about madness in ways that our predecessors are not. However, do not those in the classical period see themselves as enlightened? Their thought is not incoherent, and, given the framework that Foucault depicts, their theories about and actions towards what they take to be madness are neither arbitrary nor baseless. Is it possible that we, because we see history as progressive, and in particular as progressing towards where we now stand, are blind to our own barbarities towards what was once called madness and is now called mental illness?

It is this disturbing possibility that Foucault pursues in his chapter on Tuke and Pinel. What he discovers is something other than the story that has been handed down to us about the heroism of their actions. Tuke and Pinel do not liberate madness from its chains; rather, they change the composition of those chains. From then on, it is not iron that would bind those declared mad. Their bonds will be less obvious but more pervasive. Instead of the physical bonds of confinement, henceforth there will be the moral bonds of shame and guilt.

Consider this passage, quoted in *Madness and Civilization*, regarding one of the first of the mad whose chains Pinel removes. Pinel orders that, in regard to this man, who believed he was Christ:

> everyone . . . not address a word to this poor madman. This pro-
> hibition, which was rigorously observed, produced upon this self-
> intoxicated creature an effect much more perceptible than irons
> and the dungeon; he felt humiliated in an abandon and an isolation
> so new to him amid his freedom. Finally, after long hesitations, they
> saw him come of his own accord to join the society of the other
> patients; henceforth, he returned to more sensible and true ideas.
>
> (Cited in MC: 260)

The effect of silence, of complete social isolation, is "more perceptible than irons and the dungeon". This is Pinel's liberation of the mad. Not the freedom from bondage, but instead the submission to a more secure bondage. Foucault describes the shift characterized by Tuke and Pinel's methods, one that focuses on moral rather than physical constraint. In addition to silence, these methods include infantilization, religious inculcation, verbal confrontation, and an endless judgement on the madman's behaviour. Finally, in a move that remains with us intact after two hundred years, there is the elevation of the status of the doctor, what Foucault calls "the apotheosis of the *medical personage*" (*ibid.*: 269). This elevation at once creates a nearly unshakeable trust in the doctor and, in the same gesture, lends an aura of the sacred to the doctor/patient relationship.

I can recall the power of this apotheosis from my own experience. When I was younger I worked in a mental hospital. Although the nursing staff spent many more hours talking with and listening to the patients, when doctors came to interview a patient, they never asked any of the staff for their impressions, and the interview itself, even if only a few minutes, was considered the final word in patient assessment. It was never questioned publicly, and rarely even earned much grumbling among the nursing staff. Even today, there are few people who visit psychiatrists who do not feel that they are in the hands of someone with almost shamanistic power.

The new approach to madness that the work of Tuke and Pinel embodies does not heal the rift that arises in the late Renaissance between the mad and the sane. There is no more commerce between those who are isolated as mad and those who sit in judgement on them than there is when unreason is segregated and confined. "The science of mental disease, as it would develop in the asylum, would always be only of the order of observation and classification. It would not be a dialogue" (*ibid.*: 250). This is not to claim that physical bondage is better than the moral treatments that remain in force today. (Although here one might ask what the role of the recent dominance of pharmacological approaches to madness might play: does this represent another historical break in the perspective on and treatment of madness?) It is, rather, to stake out three positions. First, it is a misnomer to speak of the liberation of the mad. A shift in constraints is misdescribed by the term *liberation*. Secondly, this shift does not heal the rift between what is called madness and what is called sanity. The rift in the conversation between madness and reason that Foucault describes emerging through the sixteenth and seventeenth centuries is a legacy that we have not yet escaped. As Foucault says, "The language of psychiatry, which is a monologue of reason *about* madness, has been established only on the basis of such a silence" (*ibid.*: x–xi).

Finally, all this can be understood only if we abandon the view of history as a movement of progress. History is not of its nature progressive; it does not necessarily move from the more primitive to the more enlightened, from the barbaric to the civilized. History has neither telos – a goal – nor a structured movement. We can see this clearly if we abandon our commitment to historical continuity and allow ourselves to see breaks instead, moments in which one way of looking is replaced by another, not as an improvement on or a refinement of the earlier way, but simply as a new framework or perspective.

What do we make of Foucault's history of madness? It is an early work, one about which Foucault periodically expresses reservations. However, one can ask about the character of its larger project. What does this history seek to do? What is its point? For the philosopher Jacques Derrida, *Histoire de la folie* is a grand attempt that is, by the nature of its project, a necessary failure. In Derrida's view, "Foucault has attempted – and this is the greatest merit, but also the unfeasibility of the book – to write a history of madness *itself*."[3] Foucault tries in this book to heal the rift that the classical age has created. He seeks to put madness back in dialogue with reason, to restore the voice of madness that reason's monologue has suppressed.

This, Derrida argues, is a project that cannot succeed. One cannot speak in the name of madness without speaking as the mad do. Otherwise, one speaks for them in the language of reason. One continues the monologue rather than establishing a dialogue.

> [I]s not an archaeology, even of silence, a logic, that is, an organized language, a project, an order, a sentence, a syntax, a work? ... *Nothing* within this language, and *no one* among those who speak it, can escape the historical guilt – if there is one, and if it is historical in a classical sense – which Foucault apparently wants to put on trial. But such a trial may be impossible, for by the simple fact of their articulation the proceedings and the verdict unceasingly reiterate the crime.[4]

The charge levelled against Foucault here is one that has come to be called a performative contradiction. Foucault betrays in act what he claims to want in theory. In Derrida's eyes, this is the inescapable fate of Foucault's project. One cannot construct an archaeology that seeks to restore the voice of madness. An archaeology must be articulated in a systematic fashion. It must be a project of reason. Therefore, it cannot bring us any nearer to the mystical but irrational sense of mad speech that madness has in the early Renaissance, and even less so to the time in which madness is not differentiated as a particular experience.

Is this in fact what Foucault is after in his discussion of madness? Derrida relies on a quote from the preface to the book, one that follows the citation above that "the language of psychiatry, which is a monologue of reason *about* madness, has been established only on the basis of such a silence". The text continues, "I have not tried to write the history of that language, but rather the archaeology of that silence" (*MC*: xi). This seems to Derrida to imply that what is at issue is a discussion, not from the standpoint of reason, but from that of those who have been named mad by reason and then silenced.

However, we need not interpret the passage this way. As Derrida points out, the project such an interpretation calls for would be an impossible one. Moreover, it does not seem to be in keeping with the rest of the book, which is indeed a history of how the mad have been categorized as such, discussed, and treated. Perhaps it would be better to turn things around. Rather than interpreting the book in light of this suggestive but not entirely clear passage, it would be best to interpret this passage on the basis of the book that follows it. In order to do that, we should pause over the passage's term "archaeology".

Foucault's methodological reflection *The Archaeology of Knowledge* appears in 1969, eight years after the first edition of *Histoire de la folie*. As

Foucault notes in the latter book, the methodology he attempts to construct there is not meant to be a faithful reflection of what goes on in the earlier books. The books he refers to are *Histoire de la Folie*, the book on medicine *The Birth of the Clinic*, and the book we shall discuss shortly, *The Order of Things*. (In French, title of the last book is *Les Mots et les choses*, which in English means *Words and Things*.) *The Archaeology of Knowledge* does not simply reconstruct a common methodology employed in the earlier works. This, in any case, would be fruitless, since their approaches, although broadly similar, differ somewhat from book to book. Instead, Foucault seeks to articulate a methodology that those books are, to a greater or lesser extent, attempts to achieve. Nevertheless, much of the broad framework he offers there does capture what is going on in the earlier works.

In the conclusion to *The Archaeology of Knowledge*, Foucault sums up his earlier projects this way:

> The positivities I have tried to establish must not be understood as a set of determinations imposed from the outside on the thought of individuals, or inhabiting them from the inside, in advance as it were; they constitute rather the set of conditions in accordance with which a practice is exercised, in accordance with which that practice gives rise to partially or totally new statements, and in accordance with which it can be modified. (*AKDL*: 208–9)

What Foucault has in mind here is a very precise approach to history, one that resists the idea of continuities and the idea that the historical structure of knowledge in a given practice or group of practices during a given period can be changed by the conscious efforts of individuals to change it (for example, Tuke and Pinel).

For Foucault, there are certain regularities that govern what can and cannot legitimately be said in particular practices at particular times. It is not that it is impossible to say certain things. The limitation is not a physical or a legal one. It is, rather, epistemic; that is, it has to do with knowledge. If certain unacceptable things are said, or if things are said that might be acceptable if uttered by the right authorities but not by this particular person, they will simply not be recognized. It would be like a spectator's getting up in a courtroom to declare an accused person either innocent or guilty. Such a gesture would not be recognized. (In fact, the person would probably be thought mad.)

These regularities function as rules of a sort. But they are not conscious rules dictating what can be said. They are not recognized as limitations by the speakers who are bound by them. In addition, these regularities do not channel speech into particular claims; they allow for the possibility of debate and contradiction. Instead they are unconscious structurings of discourse, setting the character and boundaries of how debate and discussion can happen. A couple of years later, in the English preface to *The Order of Things*, Foucault famously refers to these structurings as "the positive unconscious of knowledge" (*OT*: xi). These structurings are not principles dictated by the outside, transcending the practice itself and then imposed on it. But neither are they a set of boundaries and conditions agreed upon by the participants. They are the framework, the perspective, by means of which (1) the participants in discussion recognize one another in their proper role as participants and (2) the statements of those participants are recognized as contributions to a particular discussion, or as establishing certain points, or as making certain claims, or as performing certain acts.

Foucault introduces the term *archive*, and says that "the *archive* defines a particular level: that of a practice that causes a multiplicity of statements to emerge as so many regular events, as so many things to be dealt with and manipulated" (*AKDL*: 130).[5] On that basis he defines an archaeology. "Archaeology describes discourses as practices specified in the element of the archive" (*ibid.*: 131). Here we can see the elusive idea Foucault is trying to capture. In contrast to a view of history as continuous or progressive, archaeology takes history to involve particular structurings of what can and cannot legitimately be said, as well as how and by whom they can legitimately be said during certain periods (or at least in certain groups of practices during those periods, a point to which we shall return).

Those structurings can and do change. When they change, this is not because of an improvement in knowledge or through the efforts of an individual, although those things can contribute to a change. Foucault, as we saw earlier, does not say much about why they change. But, because knowledge is structured in this way, however the change happens, it constitutes a break or a rift with the previous structuring.

If we interpret Foucault's archaeology of silence in this way, then *Histoire de la folie* does not appear to be what Derrida says it seeks to be. There is no such thing as an archaeology of silence, if by that we mean a historical account of what is suppressed, of what is not allowed to express itself. The book on madness is not a book *about* madness. It is a book about reason, about reason's monologue on madness. What *Histoire de la folie* seeks is not to give voice to those who have been labelled mad; as Derrida points out, no archaeology can do that. Rather, it articulates the various ways in which, once madness is established as such, the discourse on madness is structured. The account of these structurings happens in three successive stages: the Renaissance, the classical period, and the early modern period. The focus, however, is on the classical period.

If we see things this way, the history we have summarized makes more sense and is more coherent. The book is an archaeology of the historical structurings, the archives, of reason in its monologue upon madness.

What, then, do we make of the phrase "the archaeology of that silence"? It is not an archaeology of a silence itself, but rather an archaeology of a *silencing*: of the forms it has taken, the successive structures of the discussions it has elicited, the practices of experimentation and treatment to which it has given rise. To put the point another way, it is not an archaeology of the mad; it is an archaeology of *us*, the ones who are caught up in reason.

Histoire de la folie is a discussion of who we are. It focuses on one of the most important aspects of our being, our reason. It discusses the way in which reason has established then maintained the establishment of its Other – that which lies outside it, that against which it defines and defends itself. Moreover, it suggests that reason is to be thought of as something other than a timeless human quality. Far from being the essential core of who we are, as philosophers from at least Descartes up to the present day have thought, reason is a mutating historical project. It takes different forms at different times. In much of the classical period, for instance, reason is aligned with a certain morality, a morality that was itself allied with labour. Reason, Foucault suggests, is bound to several conditions from which it has always distanced itself: history, everyday practices and its Other. Reason is neither timeless nor ethereal. It is, instead, temporal and grounded in our world. One might say of it what Foucault later says about truth during an interview:

> Truth is a thing of this world: it is produced only by virtue of multiple forms of constraint . . . Each society has its "general politics" of truth: that is, the types of discourse which it accepts and makes function as true; the mechanisms and instances which enable one to distinguish true and false statements, the means by which each is sanctioned. . . .　　　　　　　　　　　　　　　　(TP: 131)

The lesson of *Histoire de la folie* does not concern those who have been called mad, at least not directly. It concerns those of us who have not fallen under that label. It is, contrary to Derrida's reading, a coherent discussion of who we have been and of who we have become, and it is addressed to those who are capable of both understanding that discussion and recognizing themselves in it. The book leaves us at the threshold of our particular structuring of reason. It offers witness to its historical birth, and allows us to see the origin from which it came.

But is it accurate? Are the facts that Foucault brings forward in the book actual facts? Do the facts point in the direction Foucault suggests? There has been some historical assessment of Foucault's works, although those who read Foucault philosophically and those who read him historically are, unfortunately, rarely in dialogue with each other. My own orientation is philosophical, so I can offer little in the way of historical judgement of his work. However, this is an area that should not be ignored. Some historians have found his work compelling.[6] Others have criticized it from a viewpoint that seems foreign to his projects, offering claims of fact that seem to oppose his perspective but do not, or claims that are irrelevant to his perspective. Still others have quibbled with some of his claims but found his overall perspective intriguing.

In order at least to get a sense of the historical debate about Foucault's work, we can focus on an article that is particularly critical of Foucault's history. It illustrates both what kinds of critique might be relevant and what might be less so. An article by the historian H. C. Midelfort[7] takes issue with a number of historical claims Foucault offers. Among his historical criticisms we can isolate four of them for discussion.

First, Midelfort claims that, contrary to Foucault's assumption, there is no record of such a thing as a Ship of Fools. "There are references to deportation and exile of mad persons to be sure . . . Occasionally the mad were indeed sent away on boats. But nowhere can one find reference to real boats loaded with mad pilgrims searching for their lost reason."[8] Secondly, "the grand renfermement [Great Confinement] was aimed not at madness or even at deviance, but at poverty".[9] Moreover, this confinement is motivated not by a new structure of reason but by an ecclesiastical tradition of long standing that banished the poor. Thirdly, for the mad at least, the period of confinement does not end with the emergence of a new view of the relation of reason to madness. In fact, it is only recently that the use of large institutions for the insane has come under criticism. "With regard to madness, therefore, we are witnessing the end of the age of confinement only now, as drug therapy and community mental health centers increase in popularity at the expense of in-patient hospitals."[10] Finally, Foucault's history is insensitive to differences across Europe. He privileges the French experience at the expense of other countries that have treated the mad very differently from France. Related to this, Foucault neglects the internal history of France. There is too much diversity in any given period to reduce it all to a particular structuring, especially one of reason.

The first criticism is an example of an irrelevant fact. Foucault does indeed claim that there were Ships of Fools, sent away by towns in search of their reason. However, nothing hangs on the fact that there were not. There were works of art depicting Ships of Fools, and those considered mad were indeed sent away, as Midelfort says, and often on boats. What Foucault is interested in is the rise of a certain fascination with madness. The existence of beliefs and art about Ships of Fools, regardless of the real existence of such ships, has no bearing on the emergence of this fascination.

The second criticism, that it is poverty rather than madness that motivates the Great Confinement, is one that Foucault largely *agrees* with. He points out, as we saw, the link between reason, morality and work. Moreover, he traces the decline in confinement to a different view of poverty. Midelfort might insist here that, be that as it may, it is ecclesiastical tradition rather than a change in the character of reason that motivates the confinement. But that raises the question of why it happens at this particular moment rather than earlier. If there is no change in the way people see things, why do the authorities suddenly start confining large numbers of their fellow citizens? Although Foucault does not offer a causal history of events that led to the Great Confinement, he does offer a view of how people saw things such that confinement begins to make sense at that time when it would not have earlier. Ascribing confinement to a long-standing ecclesiastical tradition does not explain this.

The third criticism is an important, although perhaps not critical, one. It raises the question of the relation of physical confinement to the moral constraints exemplified in the work of Tuke and Pinel. Foucault differentiates, we have seen, between confinement as a general matter and the rise of the asylum. However, it may well be that there is a more complex relationship between physical and moral confinement than Foucault admits. This would not detract from his general claims about reason and madness, but would require a more nuanced view of the relation of physical and mental bonds than the one he has offered.

The most urgent issue is the final one. First, Foucault often privileges France in his histories. This raises the question of how far one can generalize his conclusions beyond the French archive. Midelfort refers to the work of psychiatrist and historian Klaus Doerner entitled (in the English translation) *Madmen and the Bourgeoisie: A Social History of Insanity and Psychiatry* as a positive alternative to Foucault's history of madness. In that work, Doerner divides his history into three parts, dealing with England, France and then Germany. He finds both similarities and differences among these countries, but discusses each on the basis of its own experience. Oddly, although Midelfort sees Doerner's work as an alternative to Foucault's, Doerner himself does not see it that way. He takes issue with some of Foucault's interpretations (largely because, as he acknowledges, his approach is more straightforwardly dialectical than Foucault's), but he accepts many of Foucault's claims without reservation. Moreover, he refers to Foucault's book as "the first important approach to a scientific sociology of psychiatry".[11]

Doerner's praise notwithstanding, the question of the relevance of Foucault's privileging of France for the experience of other countries is an important one. It is a question that concerns more than historical accuracy. If, as Foucault believes, we are largely products of a contingent history, then we can look nowhere else than at the particularities of that history in order to understand who we have become. Foucault knows this. And to understand ourselves aright, we must understand how far a historical portrait drawn from a particular place can be generalized. We cannot appeal to some universal essence that lies within ourselves or our history in order to give an account of who we are in general, and especially of who we are now. There is nowhere else to turn but to what has happened. (Of course, *how* we understand what has happened, our mode of approach to ourselves and our history, is also crucial.) Although this book is philosophical in orientation, the question of generalizability, as well as that of historical accuracy, should always be with us. We shall return to both in the discussion of the book on the prisons.

In addition to the question of how far Foucault's histories can be generalized across Europe, there is also the question of internal diversity. Foucault's early histories, those grouped in what is called his archaeological period, have been read as positing themes that characterize an entire period. In contrast to the later genealogical works, which focus more self-consciously on particular areas of experience, his archaeologies are often understood as claiming that the themes he discusses, the structurings he cites, apply not only to the specific areas under study but across an entire culture as well as across an entire continent. Not all of his interpreters embrace this view,[12] but it is a common one, and Foucault admits later that it is a view that could easily be ascribed to his work.

It is not difficult to see how such a view could arise in regard to the book on madness. There he discusses reason as though it were a monolithic thing, covering a large swath of who we are. When reason changes, we change. Foucault does not say this. He does not say that who we are is a matter of reason. Nor does he say that reason is always the same across a particular culture at a particular time. However, in the way that he focuses on reason, in the way he situates his discussion relative to thinkers like Descartes, in the way he creates a division between reason and its Other – madness – he creates the impression that what holds for reason in the particulars in which he discusses it holds for other aspects of who we were and are.

Words and things

If *Histoire de la folie* leaves this impression, *The Order of Things* reinforces it. In that book, Foucault introduces the concept of the *episteme*, a concept that founds the book's approach. He defines his project this way:

> what I am attempting to bring to light is the epistemological field, the *episteme* in which knowledge, envisaged apart from all criteria having reference to its rational value or to its objective forms, grounds its positivity and thereby manifests a history which is not that of its growing perfection, but rather that of its conditions of possibility; in this account, what should appear are those configurations within the *space* of knowledge which have given rise to the diverse forms of empirical science . . . on the archaeological level, we see that the system of positivities was transformed in a wholesale fashion at the end of the eighteenth and beginning of the nineteenth century.   (*OT*: xxii)

This view of an *episteme* is, we see at once, in keeping with the general methodological approach Foucault describes in *The Archaeology of Knowledge*, published three years later. Although the latter book does not use the term *episteme*, the term *archive* plays a similar role. In any case, at issue is looking at the "positivities" of our knowledge not by means of an account of the progress of knowledge, but rather by means of the structurings that, in a given historical period, form its "conditions of possibility". The issue is not so much what is said, or better the truth of or evidence for what is said, but rather how what is said arises from what can be said, or at least legitimately said, at a particular time and place.

Foucault sees this project as related to the book on madness, but also different in important ways:

> The history of madness would be the history of the Other – of that which, for a given culture, is at once interior and foreign, therefore to be excluded (so as to exorcize the interior danger) but by being shut away (in order to reduce its otherness); whereas the history of the order imposed on things would be the history of the Same – of that which, for a given culture, is both dispersed and related, therefore to be distinguished by kinds and to be collected together into identities.   (*OT*: xxiv)

There are at least three things worth drawing attention to in this passage. First, the history of the Other he speaks of, the archaeology of a silence, is referred to, contrary to Derrida's interpretation, from the side of reason. It is how reason sees its Other, not how the Other is in itself, that the book on madness addresses. Secondly, and this is the main point of the passage, whereas the book on madness defines reason by means of the foil it creates for itself, the current book seeks to define something not by what it opposes but by what it is or by how it works. That is why Foucault uses, in this book and the methodological one, the term "positivity". The structurings he discusses are not limits. They do not stop knowledge or claims of knowledge from occurring. They are positive structurings; they create the space in which knowledge happens.

Thirdly, the passage speaks in a very general way about culture. By invoking the concept of the *episteme*, Foucault seems to indicate – and this passage reinforces it – that he is addressing an epistemological structuring that operates across all forms of knowledge in a culture, or at least all empirical sciences. In *The Archaeology of Knowledge*, he admits that this would be a reasonable interpretation of the text, writing that "in *The Order of Things*, the absence of methodological signposts may have given the impression that my analyses were being conducted in terms of cultural totality" (*AKDL*: 16). It is an interpretation that, when the English translation appears in 1970, Foucault is at pains to distance himself from. He writes in the preface to the English translation that the book "was to be not an analysis of Classicism in general, nor a search for a *Weltanschauung* [world-view], but a strictly 'regional' study" (*OT*: x).

On the one hand, in the original text it is difficult to see the various *epistemes* he discusses as something other than archival layers that stretch across the map of knowledge during particular periods. On the other, however, aside from his general methodological claims he focuses his discussion on three specific areas of knowledge: those that have more recently come to be called *economics*, *biology* and *linguistics*. He finds similar structurings of knowledge running across these fields, and, moreover, similar changes in structurings during different time periods.

As with the book on madness, the discussion unfolds in three stages. Foucault begins a little later, with Renaissance thought, then spends the central part of the book on the classical period, and finally turns towards more recent developments. His treatment of the Renaissance does not distinguish the three fields that are to become his concern, with the exception of an account of language that he appends to the end of the discussion of the general *episteme*. (This also can contribute to the idea that the structurings he discusses later are relevant for other fields of knowledge aside from the three he focuses on.) Renaissance knowledge, he finds, can be summed up in the idea of *resemblance*. There are relations of resemblance among different elements and aspects of the universe. The project of knowledge is to discover those relations. This project cannot be carried out through the use of empirical methods of discovery, since resemblances are an invisible aspect of the cosmos that is woven into it rather than something one can discover through observation or experimentation. To discover resemblances, one needs to interpret the cosmos rather than to perceive it.

To get a grasp of how resemblance structures knowledge, one can appeal to the example of the microcosm and macrocosm. The idea of microcosmic and macrocosmic resemblances stretches at least as far back as Plato. In the *Republic*, Plato offers what is one of the most lasting examples of their relation in the history of philosophy. Socrates is seeking to discover what justice in the soul is. The challenge he confronts is that it might be difficult to see justice at the level of the soul; it might be elusive or undetectable. He offers his interlocutors the possibility of looking at something larger than the soul, in order to be able to see justice more clearly.

> [S]ince we aren't clever people, we should adopt the method of investigation that we'd use if, lacking keen eyesight, we were told to read small letters from a distance and then noticed that the same letters existed elsewhere in a larger size and on a larger surface.[13]

The larger object Socrates suggests is that of a city, and so they design a just city in order to allow justice to appear more perspicuously.

The just city, as it turns out, is a harmony of three elements: the merchants, who work to make money; the guardians, who protect the city; and the rulers, drawn from among the guardians, who rule the city. This harmony is reflected in the soul. The merchants are like the soul's desires, seeking satisfaction. They form the appetitive part of the soul. The rulers are like the soul's reason, guiding the soul along its proper paths. That is the soul's rational part. And the guardians are the soul's spirit. The spirit is that which, if it is not corrupted by the appetites, aligns itself with the soul's reason in order to keep one noble or honourable.

In this example there are several salient aspects. First, the discovery of justice as a harmony of parts of the soul does not arise through empirical research but rather through an exercise of analogy. It is not observed; it is instead recognized through a reflective enquiry. Secondly, the analogy works from the larger to the smaller and back again, as though the cosmos is constructed so that cities and souls reflect each other. There are invisible bonds of resemblance that suffuse the cosmos; the project of knowledge is to understand them. Finally, although the brief summary here does not show this, the work of interpretation that this analogy requires does not rely on anything obvious that either the city or soul presents to Socrates or his fellow knowledge seekers. That it was the three classes of the city that were the relevant factor in discovering justice is a matter of patient theoretical construction and subtle reasoning. It does not present itself as immediate or obvious. Further, finding their analogy in the soul requires more reflection and interpretation. The project of drawing out resemblances, then, is not a simple matter of seeing them. It requires patient intellectual work.

The patience of this work becomes particularly evident when one realizes that resemblances can occur in a variety of ways. Foucault isolates four of them: *convenientia, aemulatio, analogy* and *sympathy. Convenientia* occurs through proximity: the soul is proximate to the body, and so each is built to resemble the other. *Aemulatio,* Foucault says, is *convenietia* but without spatial proximity; it is resemblance at a distance. *Analogy* allows for resemblances that occur by thematic likenesses between more disparate objects. *Sympathy* is a free-floating resemblance that suffuses the cosmos. These forms of resemblance form the framework within which the Renaissance's epistemic project takes place.

In this framework, language functions as a participant rather than as an external element. The operation of language, like other things, is woven into the fabric of resemblances that constitute the universe. It is a natural part of the cosmos. "The relation of languages to the world is one of analogy rather than signification; or rather, their value as signs and their duplicating function are superimposed; they speak the heaven and the earth of which they are the image" (*OT*: 37). The language that articulates the world is also of the order of the world; they are inseparable in the Renaissance *episteme*.

And when they do become separated, when the working of language is no longer of a piece with the cosmos, the Renaissance *episteme* has given way to the classical one. If Renaissance knowledge can be summed up in the idea of resemblance, then the classical period receives its summation in the word *order*. Order is a matter, not of analogy, but of representation. If we are to understand classical order, we must approach it by way of language as a representing medium.

Representation begins when the relation between the sign and what it signifies is no longer a natural one. "In the seventeenth and eighteenth centuries, the peculiar existence and ancient solidity of language as a thing inscribed in the fabric of the world were dissolved in the functioning of representation; all language had value only as discourse" (*ibid.*: 43). There are objects on the one side and the signs that represent them on the other. Their internal bond is sundered. In saying this, however, one must be careful. It is not that language has withdrawn from its place in the universe to become something else, something other. Rather, it is that the relation between signs and their signification has lost its status as a natural one. For instance,

Foucault says, a sign can become an object for another sign; a linguistic sign can become the object of a representation. The issue, then, is between signs and what they signify, not between language and the rest of the world. We might say that the change is a matter of linguistic operation rather than ontological status.

What is the relation between signifier and what it signifies in the classical period? The sign effaces itself before the object it signifies, and in turn the object reveals itself without remainder in the sign:

> [T]he signifying element has no content, no function, and no deter-
> mination other than what it represents: it is entirely ordered upon
> and transparent to it. But this content is indicated only in a repre-
> sentation that posits itself as such, and that which it signifies resides,
> without residuum and without opacity, within the representation
> of the sign. *(Ibid.*: 64)

The relation between signifier and signified is exhausted in the relation of representation. There is no longer, as there was in the Renaissance, a silent web of resemblance that would constitute the aether in which signs and their objects are immersed. And there is not yet, as there will be later, a human consciousness that must be taken into account because of its effect on the operation of language. There is no third thing: the relation is a binary one.

It might seem here that representation does not break the relationship between words and things. There seems to be an internal bond. After all, if signs efface themselves before their objects, is that not because of some deep tie between sign and object? Does not representation without remainder imply that there is a bond between signifier and signified?

Foucault is not arguing that there is no relation between a sign and its object. We are not yet in more recent views of language that see language as a social phenomenon imposed on nature from without. What no longer exists in the classical period is a web of resemblances in which language fits. The internal bond that is lost is the aether of resemblance, the cosmic play of *convenientia*, *aemulatio*, *analogy* and *sympathy* that binds all of existence together. It is that bond that is broken with the emergence of classical representation.

If the primitive source of knowledge is that of representations, then the project of knowledge becomes that of ordering those representations. We should think of the term *order* not as an overarching Order in which everything has its place, but rather as a project of ordering that is at the heart of classical knowledge. Our signs are no longer texts with hidden meanings to be deciphered; they are now representations that must be put in a proper order so that understanding can occur. One starts with the simple ones, and then builds more and more complex systems of representations. Thus the idea of the table, the table that gives the proper order to things, becomes central to the classical *episteme*:

> The sciences carry within themselves the project, however remote it may be, of an exhaustive ordering of the world; they are always directed, too, toward the discovery of simple elements and their progressive combination; and at their center they form a table on which knowledge is displayed in a system contemporary with itself.
>
> (*Ibid.*: 74)

We must be clear here. What Foucault is describing is not the position taken by various sciences – especially those concerning livings beings, money and value, and grammar. Order is not what these sciences claim. Nor is he characterizing what they see themselves as engaged in. Order is not the project itself; it is the framework, the structuring of the project. Within this structuring, many debates take place. The structure of order allows for opposition and contradiction. What it does not allow for are claims and positions that cannot be fitted within the context of order. It requires an ordering of representations into their proper tables.

To see the project of order at work, consider the emergence of natural history. Foucault points out that natural history is not the same thing as biology. The latter is concerned with the concept of life, the former with the concept of living beings. Living beings need not be brought under the sway of a single concept unless there is already a commitment to that concept underlying the epistemic project. Natural history does not have that concept. What it has is a project of ordering.

Ordering, in contrast to the *episteme* of the Renaissance, starts with observation. We observe a plenitude of living beings in the world. There is no necessary hierarchy of order, no Order that is presented to us. The project of ordering lies in utilizing observation so as to achieve order. Language will be the lynchpin, since representation allows objects to be given to us as they are:

> [N]atural history has as a condition of its possibility the common affinity of things and language with representation; but it exists as a task only in so far as things and language happen to be separate. It must therefore reduce this distance between them so as to bring language as close as possible to the observing gaze, and the things observed as close as possible to words. Natural history is nothing more than nomination of the visible. (*Ibid.*: 132)

For natural history, the visible is the privileged means of access to the observable. It is the visible that can reduce the distance between things and their terms, more than the other senses. However, this reduction is only the first step. Nomination, if it stays at the level of simple naming, is not enough. There is representation, but not yet order. The nomination of natural history must create order among the diversity of nature and the names that represent it. Nomination must create a structure. It does so by means of:

> four variables only: the form of the elements, the quantity of those elements, the manner in which they are distributed in space in relation to each other, and the relative magnitude of each element... For example, when one studies the reproductive organs of a plant, it is sufficient, but indispensable, to enumerate the stamens and pistil (or to record their absence, according to the case), to define the form they assume, according to what geometrical figure they are distributed in the flower (circle, hexagon, triangle), and what their size is in relation to other organs.
>
> (*Ibid.*: 134)

First, then, one starts with simple representations, in this case the elements; then one observes and records how those elements are combined in terms of quantity, spatial relation and relative magnitude. And out of these combinations one builds tables. Those tables show the place of each living being relative to its neighbours. One creates a taxonomy. In this sense, one *botanizes* living beings. As Foucault tells us, "The book becomes the herbarium of living structures" (*ibid.*: 135).

How are these tables created? This is the subject of much debate within natural history during the classical period. One approach would be to select what seem to be the central elements, and arrange the taxonomy around them. This, of course, can be accomplished in numerous ways, depending on the elements one selects at the outset. Another approach would be to start with an exhaustive description of a particular living being, and then move to the next one, listing only the differences between it and the first one, and so on. Here one does not begin with a relatively arbitrary choice of privileged elements, but with an arbitrarily chosen living being. These approaches are exclusive: one cannot use both at the same time. However, they are both projects framed by the ordering characteristic of the classical *episteme*.

In the course of building a taxonomy, language itself undergoes reflection. As things are brought into a systematic relation with one another, so are the terms that represent them. And because of this, there is a close relationship between natural history and language, perhaps closer in a sense than between natural history and its successor field, biology:

> We must therefore not connect natural history, as it was mani-
> fested during the Classical period, with a philosophy of life, albeit
> an obscure and still faltering one. In reality, it is interwoven with a
> theory of words . . . it decomposes the language of everyday life,
> but in order to recompose it and discover what has made it
> possible . . . it criticizes it, but in order to reveal its foundation.
>
> (*Ibid.*: 161)

Near the beginning of the nineteenth century, the classical *episteme* undergoes an upheaval. It is one that will induce epistemic changes, changes in the structure of the archive that frames the investigations of natural history, the theories of money and value, and general grammar, and perhaps the entirety of Western knowledge (depending on how generally one reads the claims Foucault advances). Natural history will become biology, the theories of money and value will become economics, and general grammar will become linguistics. The change that occurs might be characterized as the addition of a new depth or dimension to the world of knowledge.

To see this new dimension, we can turn to the emergence of biology. Biology, unlike natural history, is concerned with life. It is not an investigation simply of living beings that are to be ordered, but of the organic nature that underlies them. This new investigation "was to be based on a principle alien to the domain of the visible – an internal principle not reducible to the reciprocal interaction of representations. This principle (which corresponds to labor in the economic sphere) is *organic structure*" (*ibid.*: 227). Life in biology, labour in economics, hidden grammatical structure in linguistics: these are the new concepts around which the project of knowledge is to be undertaken.

It is not simply that new concepts, however important, have been added to the lexicon of the classical *episteme*. These concepts do more than just broaden an epistemic structure that is already in place. Instead, they form the pivot around which the entire structure changes. Once the depth of an underlying reality is brought into the framework of knowledge, the goal of ordering and the assumption of representation are lost. Ordering is lost because it is in thrall to the visible. One orders the visible, one brings what can be seen and what can be said of what is seen closer together. However, the depth introduced by the nineteenth century is not of the order of the visible, but rather that of an underlying structure or nature. To investigate *that* is not merely to add a dimension to ordering; rather, it is to abandon it.

Representation is lost because of the assumption that words and things (recall the French title of the book, *Les Mots et les choses*) no longer match up as cleanly as the classical age thought they did. Now there are elusive depths and dimensions that undergird the visible and its representation. One can no longer count on the effacing of the sign before the object or the ability of the sign to render the object without remainder. In fact, it is precisely the remainder that is of interest.

This slackening of the bonds of representation corresponds to two spaces of depth, one on the side of the sign or the observer, the other on the side of the object. For both human beings and the world they confront, there is more to be understood than presented itself in the classical period. This "more" is not that of the Renaissance, with its resemblances folded into the cosmos. It is instead the more of an elusive depth that always lies beyond one's ability to grasp it conceptually.

Those who have studied Kant will recognize this dual depth Foucault characterizes. It is the depth of the noumenon, both on the side of the object to be known and the subject who acts. In fact, Foucault comments that the empirical studies of biology, economics and linguistics are the other side of the same epistemic framework that harbours transcendental philosophy. For the former:

> the conditions of possibility of experience are being sought in the conditions of possibility of the object and its existence, whereas in transcendental reflection the conditions of the possibility of the objects of experience are identified with the conditions of possibility of experience itself. The new positivity of the sciences of life, language, and economics is in correspondence with the founding of a transcendental philosophy.   (*Ibid.*: 244)

Although, as Foucault notes, the character of transcendental philosophy will change radically in the new *episteme* from that of Kantian philosophy, the introduction of depth can be glimpsed in the example of his philosophy.

This new *episteme*, which Foucault thinks we are near the end of (at least at the time of publication, 1966), is characterized by a particular instability. The instability can be grasped in the preceding quote. There is an oscillation in this *episteme* between the empirical and the transcendental, each forming, although insufficiently, the epistemic ground of the other. Because of the hidden depth on both sides of the equation, neither the empirical sciences nor transcendental philosophy can complete their tasks of grounding their knowledge. The empirical sciences cannot do this because the depth they seek is not reducible to empirical methods; they must appeal to transcendental philosophy. Alternatively, transcendental philosophy is a self-reflection on a self that always, ultimately, eludes the reflection. There is more depth than can be grasped by reflectors themselves; thus there is a constant appeal outside transcendental philosophy to the empirical sciences.

This oscillation appears in four guises. The first Foucault calls "the analytic of finitude". The person engaged in reflection or investigation is finite in character and in knowledge. As such, finitude becomes both the object of investigation in the arising human sciences of biology, economics and linguistics, and the limitation on knowledge of the investigation itself, since it is a human being who is doing the investigating. The second guise is the "empirico-transcendental doublet", in which human being, *man* as Foucault calls it, is at once the ground and object of investigation. The third guise is "the *cogito* and the unthought", in which thinkers keep seeking the unthought grounding of their own thought, which in turns recedes further toward the horizon as they pursue it. Finally, there is "the retreat and return of origin". It is an endless search for an origin that must be there because it is founding, but cannot be grasped precisely because it is founding: it founds the search that is seeking it.[14]

The underlying commonality among these four guises is a kind of depth that performs three roles at once. First, it is constitutive of our approach to the question of who we are. Secondly, it is the object of investigation. Since representation can no longer be taken for granted, one must delve into the depths of man in order to discover the origins or seek the ground of knowledge. Finally, it is that which always escapes the attempt to grasp it. It is a depth that in the same gesture both constitutes who we are and eludes our understanding it.

What centres this *episteme*, then, is the idea Foucault calls *man*. Man is not the human biological entity. Nor is he the creature with reason, nor even Aristotle's featherless biped. Man is the privileged moment of the current *episteme*. Man is at once the source and object of investigation, the being in depth that creates the paradoxes inherent in the modern framework of knowledge. Man is what seeks to know himself, but in order to do so must treat himself as at once the knower and the known, and must constantly oscillate between the two. Man is at once the subject and the object of knowledge. This is, of course, an impossible task, an endless one that can never be completed. For as close as one gets to being known, one must always recognize that it is oneself – as knower – that is engaged in the knowing, and therefore that there is still something left over to be known: the part that is doing the knowing. It is like trying to see one's own eyes.

Kant refers to Hume as the philosopher who awakens him from his dogmatic slumber. Foucault borrows that image, saying that, in the modern *episteme*, we are in the midst of an "anthropological sleep", a type of dogmatic slumber that dreams only of man, or better, that dreams itself as man dreaming of man. That sleep is characterized by the emergence of the human sciences, the sciences of man and by man.

For Foucault, then, "man is a recent invention" (*OT*: 386). This does not mean, as some have misunderstood it, that human beings are a recent invention, or that we have only recently come to recognize human beings as something special within nature, or that we shall soon give way to another type of creature. What is recent is man as the privileged source and object of investigation:

> Man had been a figure occurring between two modes of language; or rather, he was constituted only when language, having been situated within representation and, as it were, dissolved in it, freed itself from that situation at the cost of its own fragmentation: man composed his own figure in the interstices of that fragmented language.   (*Ibid.*)

Man, the being of depth that arises when representation no longer captures the relation of words and things, is a historical entity. And, like all historical entities, man will pass and something new will arise. Not human beings: *man*, in the very particular sense that it has arisen in the current *episteme*.

Foucault concludes *The Order of Things* with the oracular but ultimately historical claim that if the current *episteme* begins to lose its grip on us, then "man would be erased, like a face drawn in sand at the edge of the sea" (*ibid.*: 397). We should not take this pronouncement as a prediction of some kind of ontological fall of human beings, or their dissolution into some other world. Rather, we should take it as offering the possibility that, just as knowledge was once arranged in such a way that man as the privileged figure of depth does not occur, so it can be arranged that way again. In the three *epistemes* Foucault investigates, the position of man as at once subject and object of knowledge arises in only one. There is no reason not to believe that this *episteme*, like previous ones, will pass, and with its passing will also pass man.

The Order of Things, like *Histoire de la folie*, is a book about who we are, about who we take ourselves to be. And in that sense it is at the same time a book about who we are not. What the book accomplishes is to take a view of who we are, the view given through the recently arising human sciences (and specifically biology, linguistics and economics) and to show that that view is historically situated. The human sciences do not tell us who we are; or better, they do not tell us who we are in a way that is absolute and unsurpassable. Rather, they are investigations into who we are that are situated within a certain way of approaching us, a certain *episteme*, and its specific orientation. This does not mean that we are *not* what the human sciences tell us we are. To claim that would require a bird's-eye view of who we are. But if Foucault is right about the existence of *epistemes*, there is no bird's-eye view from which to pass such a judgement. Rather, his claim is that we do not have to take ourselves as being what the human sciences tell us we are. There are other ways for us to see ourselves; indeed, there have already been other ways. *The Order of Things*, then, is a book about who we are in a very specific sense. It is a book about the historical character of who we take ourselves to be.

Although, like *Histoire de la folie*, this book concerns the question of who we are, it approaches its subject matter differently from the earlier book. As Foucault notes, rather than seeing us from the viewpoint of our exclusion of the Other, it seeks to articulate the structure of the Same. It tries to describe the historically situated frameworks in which we have appeared to ourselves as living, speaking, exchanging beings. There is another difference as well. Although the book on madness is concerned not only with the discourse on madness, but also with the knowledge of madness, *The Order of Things* focuses exclusively on knowledge. *Histoire de la folie* spends much of its time on theories of madness and of particular types of madness. But it also discusses the treatment of the mad: the practices through which the mad were engaged, manipulated, confined and observed. *The Order of Things* is solely concerned with knowledge in its theoretical aspect. Nevertheless, both are concerned with the question of who we are, and especially with that question as it arises in our historically situated knowledge of ourselves.

Earlier, we isolated five elements that are characteristic of Foucault's approach to the question of who we are. Foucault sees our determination as collective, as one that we cannot just shake off, as complex, as involving both acting and knowing, and as historically contingent. We can see three of these elements clearly in play in both of the books we have recounted. That *Histoire de la folie* and *The Order of Things* see our determination as collective, historically contingent, and one we cannot just shake off is straightforward. The collective character of our determination arises from Foucault's account being historical rather than individual. He focuses on the way *we* see things – or have seen them – and the way *we* act. In contrast, for instance, to Sartre's early work, he does not account for who we are by looking at the individual, but rather at the framework of our collective viewpoints.

The archaeological method displays the historical contingency of our being who we are. Foucault's refusal to account for how *epistemes* change reflects, as we saw, a leeriness about progressive views of history. By allowing historical breaks or discontinuities into his narratives, he rejects the idea that each *episteme* is a necessary improvement on the previous one. But in such a rejection, there is also a commitment to historical contingency. Since later frameworks do not necessarily stem from earlier ones, the order of historical frameworks is not pre-given. There is no particular reason why representation had to follow resemblance, or why the mad had to be liberated from physical bondage in order to suffer moral bondage in the late-eighteenth century. Foucault does not deny that earlier events can cause later ones. However, he does not seek to account for that causality, which implies that he does not see a pattern that governs historical change. Historical change, is, then, contingent.

That we cannot just shake off the historical frameworks in which we find ourselves is not something Foucault argues for explicitly. Rather, it follows from his approach. He is at pains, for instance, to show that Tuke and Pinel do not initiate a new epoch in the treatment of the mad, but instead reflect larger changes that both precede and accompany their work. Foucault does not argue that nothing can be done to change historical frameworks; in fact, they do change. But he does not see those changes as being wrought simply by individual initiative. One might want to argue here that, since he does not account for historical breaks, he must think that nobody has any ability to contribute to historical change. We are all simply prisoners of our own *epistemes*.

That would be taking Foucault's reticence to account for change too far. Foucault is agnostic about our relation to historical change, not atheistic. To say that we cannot simply shake off our historical heritage is not to say that we can have no effect on it. Can we, as individuals or in a collective manner, create historical change? Foucault does not tell us his views on this. His reluctance to discuss how people affect the historical trajectories he recounts has led many people to think that he is a fatalist. This charge has followed not only his archaeological works, but his later genealogical ones as well. In the latter case, the accusation is more stinging because, as we shall see, the genealogical works are more politically charged. Their stakes concern who we are as a product of relations of power, and specifically relations of power and knowledge. When power is at stake, the claim that we can do nothing about it seems more despairing, or even cynical.

However, there seems to be no reason not to take Foucault's histories to be anything other than what he often says they are: tools to be used to understand our situation. He does not give us ontological accounts of who we are, and he is not seeking to answer questions about free will and determinism. The freedom he accords us comes not from within the deep structure of human beings, but from within the fragile and contingent nature of our history. Therefore, he does not see himself as owing us a general account of the ways people can or cannot affect their historical situation, but instead an account of the situation itself.

There are two qualities we have not discussed yet: the fact that who we are is a matter of both acting and knowing, and the complexity of who we are. As to the first, it appears most clearly in the book on madness. *The Order of Things* is a more theoretically focused work. Foucault does not discuss there the use of the human sciences in non-theoretical situations, although he recognizes that there is an interaction between theory and practice. In the *Archaeology of Knowledge*, for instance, he writes that:

> the determination of the theoretical choices that were actually made is also dependent on another authority. This authority is characterized first by the *function* that the discourse under study must carry out in a *field of non-discursive practices*. Thus, General Grammar played a role in pedagogic practice. . . . (*AKDL*: 67–8)

Even in that work, however, he privileges the discursive level, as evidenced by the terms "archive", "discursive formation" and "statement" that govern the methodological structure he erects.

When he moves to his later genealogical works, Foucault will articulate a deeper interaction between the discourse of the human sciences and their practice and application. At this stage of his investigation, Foucault is more interested at the discursive level than at the level of practice, although practice does appear in the book on madness with regard to the treatment of the mad, and it appears as well in *The Birth of the Clinic*, which describes the rise of clinical medicine and the views of life and death that arise in its wake.

The issue of complexity is itself a complex one. It depends, in part, on one's view of the status of archaeology. We have seen that Foucault is unclear at this stage in his writings about the range of application of his analyses. Is the relation of reason to madness in *Histoire de la folie* a matter all of reason? Does the reason that takes particular forms in relation to its Other characterize the entire structure of reason in a given period? If there is no such thing as an ahistorical Reason, is there such a thing as a historically situated Reason? We might ask the same questions about *epistemes*, about the extent of their reach in particular historical periods. Sometimes Foucault characterizes them as structures that lie beneath entire cultural formations. At other times he denies this. In *The Archaeology of Knowledge*, for instance, he writes that: "The relations I have described are valid in order to define a particular configuration: they are not signs to describe the face of a culture in its totality" (*ibid.*: 159). When we turn to Foucault's genealogical works, we shall see a more clearly demarcated set of limitations on his analyses. At the archaeological stage, it is unclear whether the archaeological layers he uncovers are meant to characterize a smaller or larger part of the terrain he is investigating.

In viewing the last two characteristics of Foucault's work, we have seen two sets of questions arise. The first concerns the relations between the discursive and the non-discursive. Although Foucault claims at times to be investigating both, the archaeological works place their accent on what is said at the expense of what is done. Is there a separable relation between the two, or is it rather that in order to understand one requires at the same time an investigation of the other? To understand what is said or what can be said does there not have to be an investigation of the doings in which those sayings are caught up, which frame them and confer their legitimacy or illegitimacy? Alternatively, does the relation between the two not also flow in the other direction, where certain sayings create or prevent or transmute the doings they come into contact with? Perhaps it would be best to drop the distinction between the two altogether and to investigate the practices in which both arise simultaneously.

The other set of questions concerns the status of the archives Foucault describes, their specificity and their generality. Archaeology, which works across a particular chronological stratum, seems to imply a commonality among discourses in a given historical period, both within a culture and across cultures. Is Foucault committed to this? Should we follow the lead of the works themselves, which seem more expansive in this regard? Or should we instead ratify some of the comments he makes about the works, often afterwards, which point to a more limited scope? Foucault himself seems to struggle with this problem.

There is a third set of questions as well, one that relates to the status of the works themselves. In *The Archaeology of Knowledge*, Foucault tells us, consistent with the approach of his writings, that "it is not possible for us to describe our own archive, since it is from within these rules that we speak, since it is that which gives us what we can say" (*AKDL*: 130). This statement raises two questions, one having to do with the statement itself, and the other with its implication for his histories. As far as the statement itself goes, there is a problem of what is known philosophically as reflexivity. If it is not possible for us to describe our own archive, how does he know that we speak within its rules? To know that would seem to imply that we can step outside our own archive, at least far enough to recognize that it *has* a particular set of rules. But that is precisely what Foucault says cannot be done. To say that one cannot describe one's own archive is a bit like saying "I always lie." There is something self-defeating about it, since it assumes a standpoint that the statement itself denies. It seems that the best Foucault can do in this area is plead ignorance about the archival nature of his own discourse. His attempt to situate us historically within an archive is self-refuting.

The implication for his histories is this. If we are speaking from within our own archive, and if its rules and norms are as ungrounded and as changeable as, say, that of the classical or the modern *episteme*, what does that mean for the status of his historical narratives? Should we take them as accurate depictions of the frameworks of knowledge that operate in the periods he describes? Or should we instead, and perhaps more consistently, see them simply as descriptions that come from a particular archive, no worse and no better than competing descriptions that could be offered from the perspective of different archives?

Foucault concludes *The Archaeology of Knowledge* with a written self-interview. It is an honest piece of self-reflection during which he asks himself, "What then is the title of your discourse? Where does it come from and from where does it derive its right to speak? How could it be legitimated?" He responds thus: "I admit that this question embarrasses me more than your earlier objections . . . my discourse, far from determining the locus in which it speaks, is avoiding the ground on which it could find support" (*ibid.*: 205). The question of the status of Foucault's archaeological writings is one that he never resolves.[15] It remains, alongside the issue of the relation of the discursive and the non-discursive and the question of the general scope of the archaeologies, among the challenges facing Foucault's archaeological project. He does not adequately answer them, because he moves on to another project, or at least modifies the project enough to give it another name. Genealogy replaces archaeology.

Should we reproach him for this? Does he owe us an account of the success or failure of archaeology to address these questions? He does not think so. When he confronts himself, at the outset of *The Archaeology of Knowledge*, with the charge that he keeps changing the character of what he is doing, he responds to himself by saying, "Do not ask who I am and do not ask me to remain the same: leave it to our bureaucrats and our police to see that our papers are in order" (*ibid.*: 17). This is, I believe, the right response. Not because one should never answer for anything one writes. But because one need not answer for *everything* one writes, every aspect of one's perspective. Sometimes it is enough just to move on.

Many philosophers spend the early part of their careers staking out a small piece of philosophical territory, and the rest of their professional lives patrolling that territory rather than investigating what else might be out there. It is, for all but very few philosophers – those who can mine a particular problem more deeply with each investigation, always finding a hidden seam with new riches – a sad and futile exercise. Foucault does not do this. He moves on. His archaeologies are a type of investigation, his genealogies another. If Foucault does not offer us the model of philosophical consistency, if he changes direction several times over the course of his career, and if he loses (or gains) readers in the process, perhaps we should not fault him for this. Perhaps we should see his works as he sees them: investigations, enquiries into who we are and how we got to be that way. And if we find a particular enquiry to be unhelpful – because it is unenlightening, mistaken, unclear, or for some other reason – we too can just move on, find something more helpful, more exciting, more challenging. The stakes, after all, concern who we are and who we might be. To mistake these stakes for something less would be to lose the thread, not only of Foucault's larger enterprise, but of our own.

CHAPTER THREE

Genealogical histories of who we are

In May and June of 1968, events in Paris and elsewhere – events that have both discursive and non-discursive aspects – alter the character of French life. They also alter the character of French thought. To recount these events in anything like the complexity they deserve is beyond the scope of this book. Moreover, any approach to the "events of May" or "May '68" invites controversy. No period in French history since the Second World War has generated as much discussion as these two months in the late 1960s. Are the events revolutionary, or are they just the indulgence of middle-class students? Have they had a long-lasting impact on French culture or politics, or are their effects localized to a time and place? Do they contribute to the rise of an independent French approach to the world, or simply stall its economic development? Are the events primarily a cultural phenomenon, or do they rise (or descend) to the level of politics? One cannot interpret the events without becoming, implicitly or explicitly, committed on these and other questions.[1]

Let us be brief. In May 1968 students at the university at Nanterre go on strike to protest their administration's temporary closing of the university in the wake of demands for "anti-imperialist" study. These strikes are soon followed by workers' strikes, and intersection of these strikes brings together, at least temporarily, two sections of the French population that are traditionally separate from each other. In Paris, barricades are built in the streets, and it looks for a brief period as though President de Gaulle's government might fall. It would be the first revolution in modern Western Europe, succeeding where the revolts of 1848 and 1871 fail. The French Communist Party takes a stand against the students and workers, largely because it is caught unawares by the events and does not find itself in the vanguard, where it considers its rightful place to be. By mid- to late June, civic order is restored. The character of many French citizens' sense of themselves, however, is transformed, as is the landscape of French intellectual life.

Up until the events of May, the French political scene could be neatly divided into the communists on the left and the liberals on the right. There are, of course, gradations in between, but the primary battleground concerns these two ideologies. One is either with Sartre the communist or Raymond Aron the liberal. The events do not change the liberal side. If anything, they reinforce the liberal view of the irresponsibility of radicalism. On the left, however, everything changes. The political bankruptcy of the French Communist Party, which had aligned itself with the rightist de Gaulle, is there for all to see. No longer would communism in France be the hope of the left. Or, more accurately, no longer would the communism of the French Communist Party, or any other party claiming to speak for the masses, be the left's hope. The Party betrays the workers. It does not lead them in the moment of transformation. It does not even follow; it resists from the right, in the name of its own leadership. The left will have to look elsewhere for its models.

This change does not involve a shift from one set of allegiances to another. There is, at this time, no other systematic competing set of ideas to embrace. Party communism does not have an alternative. And yet this, as it turns out, is the good news. The intellectual culture in France in the decade or so after May '68, particularly in its political thought, is among the most fruitful in recent history. There is an explosion of political, or politically relevant, thought from a number of angles that comes to occupy the place vacated by the French Communist Party. Not only Foucault, but also Gilles Deleuze, Jean-François Lyotard, Luce Irigaray, Jacques Derrida, Julia Kristeva, Alain Badiou, Jacques Rancière and others provide political reflection (or politically charged philosophical reflection) that points in new directions and offers new ways to conceive our relations to the world and to one another. Times of crisis, when the old order comes unglued and the new one has not yet coalesced, can act as a spur to creativity. Think of the Renaissance, for instance. The post-May period in French intellectual culture is one of those times.

Foucault is not in Paris during the events of May. He is teaching instead at the University of Tunis in Tunisia. However, soon after the events of May he returns to France to head the philosophy department at Vincennes, a gathering (some would call it a ghetto) of the French intellectual left. After the publication of *The Archaeology of Knowledge*, he does not publish a book for seven years. His shorter writings and activity, though, take on an increasingly political tinge. This tinge is in evidence in the inaugural address of his appointment to France's most prestigious institution of higher learning, the Collège de France. There he discusses the "will to truth" as a power imposed to limit discourse and prevent creative thought, and he announces his future research programme. It comprises two aspects.

The first is a critical one that isolates "the forms of exclusion, limitation and appropriation" of discourse (*AKDL*: 231). The second is a genealogical one that shows "how series of discourse are formed, through, in spite of, or with the aid of these systems of constraint: what were the specific norms for each, and what were their conditions of appearance, growth, and variation" (*ibid.*: 232).

The second project is the one that Foucault eventually embraces. And in embracing it, he shifts his focus from the more purely discursive to incorporate the non-discursive as well. He describes the rise and the effects, especially political effects, of various practices and their intersection. And, as he mentions in his inaugural address, he gives this historical description the name *genealogy*.

What is genealogy? Most of us are probably most familiar with the term in its application to familial lineage. To trace a family genealogy is to trace one's ancestors, to follow backwards (or forwards) the marriage and kinship lines that yield oneself, one's siblings, one's children. There is something of this going on in Foucault's genealogies. The idea of asking who one is by way of tracing how one has arrived at this point is certainly in accordance with his method. In addition, as we shall see, just as the roots of a family genealogy become more dispersed the further back (or the further forward) one goes, Foucault's genealogies do not found themselves at a particular privileged starting point. There is no pristine moment of origin, no point of creation. Everything begins dispersed, without centre or unity.

However, there are important differences as well. First, instead of tracing the evolution of marriages Foucault traces the evolution of practices. Secondly, and following directly from this, the question of who one is becomes, as it is in the archaeological works, a collective question rather than an individual one. The product of a Foucauldian genealogy is not an *I*; it is a *we*. Thirdly, in as much as familial genealogies seek to give a single answer to the question of who one is (and, of course, they need not do so), Foucault breaks with that approach. Unlike a family genealogy, of which there can only be one, genealogies of practices are many and various. We are involved in many different practices, and although particular ones may be more importantly determinative for who we are, no single one or no single group has a privileged position, one that guides the others or to which the others can be reduced. Fourthly, Foucault's genealogies are tied to the politics of truth. It is not simply practices that Foucault is interested in: it is the politics and epistemology of those practices, and especially the bond between their politics and their epistemology.

The term genealogy is one that Foucault borrows from Nietzsche. Nietzsche uses it to describe the emergence of what he thinks of as force relations in regard to particular institutions or practices. These forces are, broadly speaking, active and reactive ones. Active forces are at once creative and destructive; if they are destructive, though, it is as a by-product of their creativity. Active forces seek to express themselves, whether by artistic or martial or athletic or other means. Reactive forces, by contrast, do not seek to express themselves. They are, as their name implies, forces that react to active ones. Essentially, reactive forces are those that are unable to express themselves, as active forces do, so their form of expression is parasitical upon that of active ones. That form of expression is largely negative; they seek to undermine the expression of active forces. For Nietzsche, then, reactive forces are in a close alignment with resentment, with a hatred for the expression characteristic of active forces.

The question for Nietzsche is, given a particular institution or practice, what is currently dominating it, active or reactive forces? This is where genealogy comes in. Genealogy is the tracing of the history of an institution or a practice by asking which forces have taken hold of it, active or reactive ones. One cannot project back from one's current position the meaning or origin of an institution or practice. History is, in Nietzsche's eyes, the struggle for dominance among and between active and reactive forces. He points out, in *On the Genealogy of Morals*:

> that everything which happens in the organic world is part of a process of *overpowering*, *mastering*, and that, in turn, all overpowering and mastering is a reinterpretation, a manipulation, in the course of which the previous "meaning" and "aim" must necessarily be obscured or completely effaced.[2]

This approach has several elements that find their way into Foucault's own genealogies. First, genealogy does not search for an origin, a wellspring from which the practices one is investigating can be understood in their essence. For some who seek to understand particular practices, the key is to dig beneath all the historical transformations in order to discover the original character of the practice. Martin Heidegger, for instance, holds that in order to understand the question of Being we need to go back to its original asking, before it was buried under the weight of the metaphysical tradition. Genealogy rejects this approach. Of course, all practices begin somehow. However, their beginning does not give us any privileged insight into their essential character.

The reason for this, and this is the second element Foucault adopts, is that there is no essential character that practices contain. For Nietzsche, as for Foucault, what counts is not essence but historical legacy. To discover the character of a practice is to trace the roles it plays, the intersections with other practices it maintains, the meanings ascribed to it and that emerge from it, over the course of its evolution. Foucault departs from Nietzsche in Nietzsche's attempt to interpret this evolution in terms of active and reactive forces. For Foucault there are no forces that form a framework for interpretation. However, the difference here amounts to less than it might seem.

In Foucault's genealogical writings, as in Nietzsche's, there is a strong normative flavour. Foucault at times characterizes his works as description rather than recommendation, but this is a bit disingenuous. As we shall see, Foucault is clearly critical of the penal project of rehabilitation, as he is of the interpretative projects that have come to surround our sexuality. Nietzsche uses value-laden terms – active and reactive – in his genealogical studies. They form the normative framework of his approach. If Foucault does not have an overt normative framework, he certainly knows what he doesn't like, what he finds, in the term he sometimes uses, *intolerable*.[3] This is the third element he borrows from Nietzsche.

Those familiar with Nietzsche's and Foucault's writings might wish to object here that, although their genealogies are both normatively laden, there is a very different set of norms to which each is attached. After all, Nietzsche's view is aristocratic. He has no use, as he repeatedly insists, for anything democratic. For him, it is the strong and the creative that are worthy; he is not concerned with the oppressed. Foucault, on the other hand, never ceases to speak alongside (although never in the name of) the oppressed. Whether it is the mad, prisoners, homosexuals, or outcasts, he embraces those who find themselves in positions of weakness rather than strength.

There is something to this objection. Nietzsche, indeed, is no democrat. However, it would be easy to make too much of this difference, for two reasons. First, Nietzsche's active forces are themselves in danger of becoming outcasts. The mass of humanity – for which, to be sure, he displays no sympathy – always seek to destroy or at least to marginalize active forces. This is why he says "the strongest and most fortunate are weak when opposed by organized herd instincts, by the timidity of the weak, by the vast majority . . . Strange though it may sound, one always has to defend the strong against the weak."[4] Secondly, there is an important similarity between the objects of Nietzsche's and of Foucault's criticism. They both target the mindless conformism that characterizes contemporary society. For Nietzsche, that conformism is a product of the dominance of reactive forces; for Foucault, it has more to do with historically grounded realities such as the emergence of capitalism and the evolution of church doctrine. However, both share a revulsion against conformity that characterizes the world each of them lives in.

The debt that Foucault owes to Nietzsche in adopting the genealogical approach becomes clear in an essay he publishes in 1971, a year after his inaugural lecture at the Collège de France and four years before the appearance of his first full-length genealogy, *Discipline and Punish*. The essay, entitled "Nietzsche, Genealogy, History", is at once a rendering of Nietzsche's genealogical method and an announcement of his own. It begins with the lines, "Genealogy is gray, meticulous, and patiently documentary. It operates on a field of entangled and confused parchments, on documents that have been scratched over and recopied many times" (NGH: 139). These words are perhaps a better characterization of Foucault's more detailed approach than Nietzsche's method of painting with broad brush strokes, but it does emphasize the historical character of both projects. The similarity deepens as the essay unfolds.

After a critique of histories that rely on the concept of origins and grand beginnings, Foucault notes that Nietzsche's genealogical method is engaged in a twofold task: *Herkunft* and *Entstehung*, or in the English translation *descent* and *emergence*. Together they constitute a historical approach that abandons the ideas of history as having particular aims or goals, as being a unified goal with a decipherable meaning, and as having an essential origin that has made us who we are or, alternatively, from which we have strayed. Descent approaches history by means of seeking the separate, dispersed events that have come together in a contingent way to form a particular practice. Rather than looking for the golden threads that bind history together, descent seeks the coming-to-be of a practice in events that are often small, ignored, close to the ground, and disparate from one another. Emergence, on the other hand, describes the "hazardous play of dominations" (*ibid.*: 148) that forms the history of a given practice or group of practices. Emergence, in Nietzsche's view, is a matter of the domination of active and reactive forces. Rather than seeking the meaning of a practice in the goals it sets itself or the role it sees itself as fulfilling, Nietzsche asks whether a practice is oriented towards creation and expression or instead toward resentment and small-mindedness. But emergence can be seen, and Foucault will see it this way, as a matter of what effects, deleterious or helpful, the uses to which practices are put give rise at different times and places.

Together, descent and emergence offer a view of history that traces the emergence and dissolution of practices and of the unities those practices temporarily form with other practices. It is a history without origin, goal, or meaning. It is a history in which disparate practices come together and then disperse in unpredictable ways; and it is a history in which this coming together and dispersing produce a number of unforeseen effects that can result in a variety of dominations. This does not imply, however, that recounting this history is pointless. After all, human beings are without origin, goal, or meaning. Genealogy, then, is a project of telling us about who we are. It tells us without reference to the framing assumptions of much of the history of philosophy.

And in doing so, it tells us two other things as well. It allows us to see how aspects of ourselves that we thought were natural or inescapable turn out instead to be historical, and in fact historically contingent. We did not have to become who we are, and in turn we can become something other than what we are. It also allows us to see some of the effects of being who we are now, effects that perhaps we would rather not be party to.

There is no single story of who we are that Foucault has to tell. His genealogies do not seek to cover the broad sweep of our historical legacy. More clearly and more consciously than in his archaeological works, Foucault takes his genealogies to trace *aspects* of who we have come to be, of who we are now. If our history is a matter of the unfolding of temporary unities from dispersed origins, then who we are is a matter not of any particular unity but of a variety of overlapping and intersecting unities of practices. Although at times Foucault uses images that suggest he is describing an entire cultural formation, a close reading of his genealogical works shows that those images are rhetorical more than substantive. In each case, Foucault describes an important part of who we are and how we came to be that way. In no case does he take himself as accounting for all of it. The writer John Berger observes, "Never again will a single story be told as though it were the only one."[5] It is an observation that Foucault's writings embody.

There are two major works of Foucault's that fall clearly under the category of genealogy: the book on the punishment entitled *Discipline and Punish* and the first volume of *The History of Sexuality*. Of these, only the first is a full-fledged historical study. The latter is both methodological and programmatic. It offers a clear delineation of the method that was used in the prison book and is to be used in a larger study of sexuality, and it offers a brief historical framework for the genealogical study of sexuality. The latter project, for reasons we shall discuss more fully below, is never completed. Instead, Foucault turns from his proposed study of sexuality to the larger project of self-making, and at the same time widens the historical scope of his study. He starts with the Greeks rather than, as is his wont, the Renaissance or early post-Renaissance.

A history of the prisons

Discipline and Punish displays an important similarity to Foucault's book on madness. In both, as will also be the case with the book on sexuality, he performs what we might call an *inversion* of a received view. In *Histoire de la folie* the inversion takes place with regard to the work of Tuke and Pinel. On the received view, both are thought to be liberators of the mad, unchaining them and releasing them from their barbarous conditions. Foucault argues that, although this may be true, there is an opposite movement as well, a rechaining of the mad. Released from their physical bonds, the mad will now be bound by moral bonds that are as sure as, if not more sure than, the physical bondage to which they were previously subject.

We must be careful here not to misunderstand the inversion Foucault performs. He does *not* argue, although the view has been ascribed to him, that things were better in earlier periods and have now become worse. Nietzsche's work often suggests this type of historical decline or regression. It is not Foucault's position. The inversion he performs is not a simple one, in which we are told that things have become better when in fact they have become worse. To deny the assumption of a progressive history does not require that one embrace the assumption of a regressive history. The inversion Foucault's studies perform seeks to show that what has been called a progressive history moment is accompanied by a movement that is also deleterious. This does not *reverse* the assumption of historical progress; it *complicates* it.

What is the story of historical progress that Foucault reverses in his book on punishment and the prisons? It is a story we are all familiar with, even if we have no background in penal study. It is a story of penal progress from vengeance to rehabilitation.

In the early history of punishment, punishment takes the form of retribution. The offender is treated as something beneath or beyond human concern. Having committed a crime, the offender is subject to any form of punishment the social body deems appropriate to mete out. Torture, physical and psychological abuse, public humiliation: these are all among the range of punishments available to a society that wants only to get back at criminals for the wrongs they have committed. It is probably worth noting that this sentiment, which was once thought obsolete, can be seen on full display in the United States before the implementation of a death penalty. It is inscribed on the placards and etched in the faces of those who stand outside the prisons anticipating the execution. There are fewer reminders of how little distance we have travelled from the time of public torture more powerful than those gatherings.

In any case, so the story goes, we have (death penalty celebrations notwithstanding) become more civilized. Rehabilitation has replaced torture and public punishment as the preferred response to crime. Rather than simply punishing criminals for what they have done, we now seek to change them, make them into something that can navigate society in a different way. Crime, on this view, is not simply an act that requires vengeance; it is a behaviour that requires intervention. The criminal is not simply to be punished for committing an act. Once the criminal is in the custody of the state, the proper approach is to work on the criminal so as to promote a different style of engaging with the world, a different "behavioural repertoire". Whether by instilling proper work habits, or offering insight into the causes of the aberrant behaviour, or breaking individuals down boot-camp style and rebuilding them, or reinforcing good habits while seeking to extinguish bad ones, or by some combination of these, criminals are not simply to be harmed. They are to be improved.

In this way, the treatment of criminals has become more humane. It is no longer a ceremony of degradation or abuse. Rather, it is a policy of improvement. Criminals no longer fall outside the realm of human concern. While punishment of some form is in order, the criminal is at the same time to be treated as someone who was once and will again be a member of society. Penal intervention must be constructed with that recognition in mind. This is the progressive story of penal history.

The first few pages of *Discipline and Punish* do little to undermine that story. Foucault recounts the public torture of an attempted regicide named Damiens that takes place in 1757. The spectacle is gruesome. It involves burning and peeling skin from the offender, drawing and quartering, slicing limbs, all in an order that would seek to cause the maximum amount of pain. This account is immediately followed by one that could not provide a greater contrast. It is a prison schedule from eighty years later. It describes in a detached fashion the mundane routine to be followed by the inmates of a prison for youthful offenders, offering a rigorous, minutely detailed account of what is to be expected of them at each hour of the day.

It is easy to see here the received view of penal history at work: the contrast between the public torture and humiliation (during the procedure Damiens often called out for God's pity) of the procedure applied to the regicide and the regimentation of the penal practice that follows it. The first is an exercise in vengeance, the second an exercise in rehabilitation. Foucault's placing of these two approaches side by side shows that he recognizes that there is something to the received view. But it is also misleading. That is where the genealogical history begins.

Foucault's history does not, as his recitation of the case of Damiens exemplifies, take issue with the early part of the received view. Criminals are tortured and degraded before the reforms of the late-eighteenth and early-nineteenth centuries. In fact, torture occurs at two points in the criminal procedure, one secretly and the other publicly. The first point is during interrogation. In order to obtain confessions, pain is inflicted on the suspect's body. This may ring false to modern ears, where a person is presumed innocent until proved guilty. (Recall, though, that former President Ronald Reagan's Attorney General, Edwin Meese, once defended the denial of rights to suspects by saying that if they weren't guilty, they wouldn't be suspects.) However, during the classical period, guilt occurs by degrees. "Thus a semi-proof did not leave the suspect innocent until such time as it was completed; it made him semi-guilty; slight evidence of a serious crime marked someone as slightly criminal" (*DP*: 42). A suspect, then, is always deserving of torture.

It is during punishment that the criminal's body is subject to pain, and becomes public. In France the procedure is called *supplice*, which translates into English as *torture*. However, we should not think of *supplice* as a simple barbarity performed upon the body of the criminal. *Supplice* is not chaotic or arbitrary. It is a measured and calculated response to criminality, one that has three elements: the infliction of a measured amount of pain; the regulation of that pain; and the ritualistic character of the application of techniques producing pain. *Supplice* is a tightly choreographed public ritual of agony, and it finds its seat in the nature of criminality itself.

Criminality is often thought of, among other ways, as an offence against the social body. This is as true of earlier periods as it is now. However, the character of the social body in, for instance, pre-Revolution France is different. It is not the people but the sovereign, the king, who is considered the bearer of the elements of the social body. Whereas in democratic regimes, at least in principle, the people are thought to be the constituents of the social body, in earlier monarchies the king plays that role. It is not as though there are no people, but rather the character of the people is thought to be distilled in the body of the sovereign. The French – *c'est moi*. Thus an attack on the social body is an attack on the king, and in a very literal way. Criminality is an attack on the social *body*, on the body of the king. It is a personal attack: an injury attempted against the regal body.

In order to re-establish the sovereignty of the regal body, the social body, that has been attacked, one must restore the balance of power. (Here we shall use the term *power* in a traditional sense. It is a term, as we shall see, that Foucault complicates later in this work.) Or better, one must restore the proper imbalance of power. If the criminal can get away with an attack, this proves the weakness, the vulnerability of the social body. The punishment of a crime, then, must involve an assertion of the power of the sovereign. Criminals must be made to feel that power at the same site at which they sought to attack it in the sovereign. They must be made to feel it in their body. Hence the elaborate tortures whose goal is to maximize pain and to assert the unassailable power of the sovereign in a way that is unmistakable both to criminals and to the people alike. As the criminal is taught a lesson in power, the people are both restored to the security their sovereign can offer them and warned against violating that sovereignty themselves. "The public execution", Foucault says, "has a juridico-political function. It is a ceremonial by which a momentarily injured sovereign is reconstituted. It restores that sovereignty by manifesting it at its most spectacular" (DP: 48).

One can see then why punishment cannot be a blind rage. However agonizing it may be for the criminal, it remains an expression of the sovereign, and thus must bear the stamp of both his power and his bearing. In order to do so it must be controlled. To strike without control is a display of weakness, not strength.

There are at least two potential difficulties with this particular exercise of the power to punish. The first is that the grand display of this asymmetry of power can backfire. Alongside the public awe at the power of the king, and alongside the fear that that power invokes, it can also happen – and it did happen – that the public comes to identify with the object of punishment, and thus becomes resentful of the sovereign. This is particularly true when the criminal displays dignity under torture or when the punishment seems to go too far into the realm of the spectacular or when the criminal derides the authorities for their own abuses. In cases like these, the public comes at times to identify with the criminal, and this leads to resistance against these exercises of sovereignty. In addition, all criminality represents a rebellion against the current social order, a rebellion that would find sympathy in a large portion of a public who suffers under great disparities in wealth and comfort that are part of the structure of that order. The cure for all this, it would seem, would be to soften punishment, to make it less an expression of power and more an expression of justice.

And indeed there is a reform movement that seeks to soften punishment. But not only soften it. A number of changes are taking place during the second half of the eighteenth century:

> [T]he shift from a criminality of blood to a criminality of fraud forms part of a whole complex mechanism, embracing the development of production, the increase of wealth, a higher juridical and moral value placed on property relations, stricter methods of surveillance, a tighter partitioning of the population, more efficient techniques of locating and obtaining information.   (DP: 77)

Because of these changes, and in particular because of the change of property relations to which many of these relate, another concern comes to the surface as well.

Up to this point punishment is as sporadic as it is gruesome. To be sure, the consequences of getting caught are dire. However, many people do not get caught; and this is the second difficulty with *supplice*. The arrangement works tolerably well as long as the institution of private property is in its infancy. But as it matures, with it grows the necessity of a more universal form of punishment. All property must be protected, and since property is dispersed among many individuals, protection from criminality must be afforded to all of them:

> The true objective of the reform movement, even it its most general formulations, was not so much to establish a new right to punish based on more equitable principles, as to set up a new 'economy' of the power to punish . . . so that it should be distributed in homogeneous circuits capable of operating everywhere, in a continuous way, down to the finest grain of the social body. (*Ibid.*: 80)

The question becomes, how is this to happen? How can one construct a penal structure that will protect against all the petty crimes that had once been tacitly tolerated, while at the same time generating universal respect so that it does not suffer the same problems as *supplice*?

To this, the penal reformers have an answer. One must design punishments that are calibrated to crimes so as to ensure deterrence. If the loss to be incurred outweighs the gain of the crime, and if one is certain that by committing that crime one will also incur that loss, the crime is less likely to be committed.[6] "To find the suitable punishment for a crime is to find the disadvantage whose idea is such that it robs for ever the idea of a crime of any attraction" (*ibid.*: 104). In addition, the populace is less likely to become upset with the authorities. Since the response is not to perform an outrage upon the body but to deter crime, then there is no spectacle to which the public is called to react. A sober system of measured punishments is what is needed to eliminate crime – particularly crime against property – to ensure public order, and to be capable of universal application.

Why is it then that, rather than adopting this system of punishments, each designed to deter the crime it responds to, only one type of punishment emerges for everyone during the early nineteenth century? Why is it that there emerges a single answer for all crimes, an answer that remains with us today? Why imprisonment?

The subtitle of *Discipline and Punish* is *La Naissance de la prison*: the birth of the prison. It is at this point that Foucault's genealogical method begins to emerge. Up to this point, it is easy to think that the story Foucault is telling is a linear one, that it traces a singular thread through its chronological weave. This would not be genealogy as Foucault describes it in his essay on Nietzsche. It would involve a unity of origin rather than a dispersion that comes together into a temporary unity. And because of this it would invite a reading that sees history as either progressive or regressive. Either punishment is better and more humane than it used to be or it is worse.

This is not how Foucault approaches the birth of the prison. To be sure, there is a certain continuity between earlier and later forms of punishment. They are both, after all, ways of dealing with criminality. And, moreover, both involve the application of particular techniques to the body. However, the later form of punishment, which Foucault calls *discipline*, is not merely a development from an insular history of punishment. If it were, then one would expect that the advice of the reformers of the late eighteenth century would have been taken. It is not. In fact, the emergence of the prison is in direct contradiction to the ideas of the reformers. Rather than matching punishment to crime, it affords a single punishment for all crimes.

To account for this emergence Foucault looks beyond the prison to other, more far-flung practices:

> The "invention" of this new political anatomy must not be seen as a sudden discovery. It is rather a multiplicity of often minor processes, of different origin and scattered location, which overlap, repeat, or imitate one another, support one another, distinguish themselves from one another according to their domain of application, converge and gradually produce the blueprint of a general method. (*Ibid.*: 138)

Among these minor processes are the regimented time schedules characteristic of the monastery and the precisely calibrated movements that are taught to the soldiers of the Prussian army. These and other practices gradually converge on the issue of punishment, and over the course of the late eighteenth and early nineteenth centuries yield the "blueprint of a general method" of discipline.

Discipline, as Foucault uses the term, is more specific than simply the control of the behaviour of others. It may be defined as the project for the body's optimization, for turning the body into a well regulated machine by means of breaking down its movements into their smallest elements and then building them back into a maximally efficient whole. This project does not simply concern individuals, however. It also concerns their relations. Discipline must ensure that space is properly partitioned so that individuals can relate to one another in maximally efficient ways. It must ensure the proper time coordination among activities as well as within them. It is a process that is applied both to bodies and to the interaction between them.

The ability to accomplish this requires an enclosed area in which the movements of individuals and the partitioned space of their relations can be monitored and intervened upon. That is what a prison is.

If discipline sounds like training for factory work, it should. It is also, however, how schools are run: break down what is to be learned into manageable segments, and then have students master each segment before moving on. It is how businesses are run, how hospitals are run, often how athletics is taught, and how we run our lives. As Foucault asks, "Is it surprising that prisons resemble factories, schools, barracks, hospitals, which all resemble prisons?" (*DP*: 228).

Foucault isolates three central aspects of disciplinary training: hierarchical observation, normalizing judgement, and examination. Hierarchical observation involves a certain "economy of the gaze". There are observers and observed. The observer is to monitor the observed from a hierarchical distance so that the observer sees but is not seen and the observed is seen but does not see (or at least does not see the observer). In this way, the observer can see what the observed is doing, what they are not doing, and how well or poorly they are doing it. For their part, the observed, since they are continuously monitored, become subject to the gaze of the observer. They must always be "on". They can never let up. They must be as efficient as possible.

Normalizing judgement is a binary operation that works by means of both conformity and individualization. Conformity is to the norm itself, the standard that each must strive to meet; individuality is the requirement of a set of interventions on particular individuals in order to get them to achieve the norm. These interventions are trained upon minute elements of a person's behaviour. They come to bear at very specific points in the behavioural unfolding of an activity, seeking to maximize it through rewards, punishments, or other types of motivation. Think of a child who cannot use her fork in the proper manner. "Here", the parent says, "first hold it like this. Good, very good. Now bring it down to your food. No, not like that, that's wrong; like this. Yes, better . . .".

The emergence of normalization is a revolution not only in penal reform but also in the conception and character of who we are. Foucault describes normalizing judgement as directly opposed to earlier approaches to punishment, which operate "not by hierarchizing, but quite simply by bringing into play the binary opposition of the permitted and the forbidden; not by homogenizing, but by operating the division, acquired once and for all, of condemnation" (*ibid.*: 183). In earlier forms of punishment, one does not worry about where one stands in relation to the norm or the normal. The reason for this is that there is no norm or normal. There are acts that are forbidden, and others – the rest – that are permitted. For the former there are dire consequences, if one is caught. For the latter there is no need for intervention. There may be traditions governing behaviour, but there are no norms of the kind discipline develops.

Contrast that with our more normalized society. Who among us does not wonder whether their behaviour is normal? Who among us is not constrained by the concern that they may be weird, or off, or not like everyone else? Who is not driven in part by the motivation to avoid the need for counselling or therapy or some other intervention whose goal is to put one back on the right track? Who does not feel the shadow of normality over their shoulder? In older forms of punishment, the binary division between the permitted and the forbidden leaves one side of that division alone. In a society in thrall to normalization, no behaviour is immune to scrutiny. As my therapist friends say, everyone is a little sick, so everyone can benefit from some therapy. When they say it, they mean it as an advertisement for their profession; but it reveals a deeper truth, one Foucault finds in the emergence of discipline:

> The power of the Norm appears throughout the disciplines. Is this the new law of modern society? Let us say rather that, since the eighteenth century, it has joined other powers – the Law, the Word (*Parole*) and the Text, Tradition – imposing new delimitations upon them. (*Ibid.*: 184)

We might recall here the analysis, in *Histoire de la folie*, of the emergence of the moral character of therapy in the practices of Tuke and Pinel. The bonds placed by these figures are no longer physical ones; they are moral and psychological. Concurrent with the rise of normalization, there is also the rise of psychology as both a science of the normal and a practice of turning the abnormal into the normal. Psychology, as a study of and intervention into human behaviour, has its roots and its orientation provided by the twin poles of conformity and individualization characteristic of the normalizing judgement of discipline.

Here we see at work one of the concepts for which Foucault has become famous and, at times, notorious: power–knowledge. It is probably the most often misunderstood concept in his corpus. The concept of power–knowledge denies that one can hold knowledge to be divorced from power, that one can partition off all the relations of power in which people are involved in order to achieve a knowledge purged of political impurities, a neutral ground, so to speak. "Perhaps", he says, "we should abandon a whole tradition that allows us to imagine that knowledge can exist only where the power relations are suspended and that knowledge can develop only outside its injunctions, its demands, and its interests" (*ibid.*: 27).

This does not mean, however, that all knowledge is reducible to power relations or that knowledge is simply a mask for power. That would not be power–knowledge: it would just be power. Instead, we should think of knowledge as something that is embedded in, inseparable from, power relations, but still a form of knowledge. In fact, as we shall see in detail when we discuss power in the context of the first volume of Foucault's history of sexuality, the emergence of knowledge and its object can occur at the same time. Psychological knowledge, for example, is part of a larger whole – discipline – that does not simply understand but at the same time creates who we are.

To put the point another way, power does not only stop things from happening. It is not merely a negative or repressive operation. It also creates things. If this is the case, then psychological knowledge is not simply a mask for power. It actually is knowledge, but it is knowledge of something it has also participated in creating:

> These "power–knowledge relations" are to be analysed, therefore, not on the basis of a subject of knowledge who is or is not free in relation to the power system, but, on the contrary, the subject who knows, the objects to be known and the modalities of knowledge must be regarded as so many effects of these fundamental implications of power–knowledge and their historical transformations.
>
> (*Ibid.*: 27–8)

In addition to hierarchical observation and normalizing judgement, discipline involves a third element: examination. We have all been subject to it, whether in school, during job training, or in a hospital. The examination forms an element of the feedback loop of discipline. It marks out where each of us stands relative to the standard, the Norm, to which we are being compared. If hierarchical observation seeks to maximize efficiency by overseeing activity, the examination provides the feedback necessary to recognize the degree to which that efficiency has been internalized, the degree to which it has become part of us, or, in the terms we have been using, has become a part of who we are now.

Foucault sums up the elements of discipline and their operation in the arresting image of Jeremy Bentham's Panopticon. Bentham, the founder of modern utilitarian moral theory, offers in 1791 a design for a prison (one that is never built) that he calls the Panopticon. Essentially, the Panopticon is constructed like a ring around a central core. The ring holds the prisoners, the central core the guards. The prison is constructed so that the guards can look out and see inside all the prison cells. The prisoners, however, cannot see into the central core. Therefore, although one cannot watch all the prisoners at once, no prisoner can see who is being observed and who is not. One must act as though one is always being observed, since at any particular moment one might be.

But there is more. In the Panopticon, since one cannot see the guards, and since one must assume that one is being watched all the time, there do not actually have to be any guards in the central core. The prisoners, in essence, guard themselves. They act as though they are under surveillance even if there is nobody there to observe them. And that, Foucault concludes, is our condition. Given the suffusion of discipline across broad swaths of our society, we are in a condition of what he calls "panopticism". Even if there is no one watching us, even if we are not being monitored, we act as though we are. We wonder why we are normal, as we mentioned a moment ago, because we are our own prison guards. In a society filled with psycho-services, from therapists to social workers to personnel counsellors, there is no need for everyone to be watched. As these services proliferate, most of us will begin to watch ourselves.

We saw above that there are some continuities between penal discipline and earlier forms of punishment, in particular that both had to do with penality and that both are focused on the body. We can see now that the later forms of each are, although continuous in one sense, in another sense far removed from their earlier versions. Penality is no longer a project of punishment. It is not even, strictly speaking, a project of deterrence. It is a project of normalization, of what penal theorists call rehabilitation. Rather than vengeance there is care. Rather than torture there is discipline. Those who currently impugn the prisons for being too soft on prisoners are right in a sense. The project of imprisonment is no longer one of extracting a price for an injury against the social body. However, those critics miss the larger disciplinary whole into which this "softer" treatment fits.

The role of the body has changed as well. It has changed from being a site of pain to being a site of normalization. It is the place where our psychological state, our normalization, is created. When Foucault calls his study of the prisons "an element in a genealogy of the modern 'soul'" (*DP*: 29), we can see why. The modern soul is the psychological soul, one whose moral components are embedded in a logic of the normal and the abnormal. We are held in thrall to this modern soul, not simply because it is imposed on us but because, at this particular time in our history, it is who we are. Or better, since there is nothing that solely is who we are, it is, as Foucault says, "an element" of who we are: a centrally important one. And because we are held in thrall to it, and because it is one of the crucial sources of our conformity, it is no surprise when Foucault, inverting the old Christian formula, declares that "the soul is the prison of the body" (*ibid.*: 30).

Of course, as many will point out, the prison as a project of rehabilitation is a failure. Recidivism rates are high, many prisoners consider the therapeutic aspects of prison a joke, and, as we have come to understand, many projects of psychological therapy have at best uneven success in changing attitudes or behaviour. The prison as a site of discipline has not created the kind of environment in which discipline can take hold. And yet the prison remains the major response to criminality. How does Foucault explain this?

He does not deny the failure of the prison. What he seeks to understand instead is its continuance in the face of its failure. There must, he believes, be some function that prisons continue to serve if demonstrated failure is not enough to dismantle them. In fact there are two, one having to do with prisoners themselves and the other with the society at large. Regarding prisoners, the prison becomes part of an entire system where certain criminals who cannot be rehabilitated can at least be monitored. Prisons, parole officers, police, informants: all these become relays in a larger system of surveillance where criminality can be overseen, at times even utilized, when it cannot be eliminated. The dream of the early prison reformers, or later of the practitioners of discipline, is indeed a dream. There will always be criminality, particularly in societies where goods are as unevenly distributed as they are in Western societies. Therefore, where one can impose discipline successfully, one does. Where one cannot, one uses the same resources to construct a system of surveillance that can at least monitor what it cannot change.

The effects of the prison on the society at large are perhaps more important. It is not simply the prison itself, but the larger "carceral archipelago" (*DP*: 298), composed of social workers, psychologists, psychiatrists, personnel counsellors, judges, the legal system, family doctors, and others of which it is a necessary part. The carceral archipelago generates important effects on the texture of our society. Near the end of *Discipline and Punish*, Foucault isolates six of those effects. The carceral archipelago blurs the line between the legal and the illegal, allowing for continuous disciplinary intervention. It can recruit the delinquents it creates in order to monitor crime. It makes the idea of punishment itself seem natural or inevitable, particularly since it is done without violence but instead by means of softer disciplinary procedures. It permits a new form of law, one that is no longer beholden to the binary opposition of the permitted and the forbidden. It allows the proliferation of procedures of examination and normalization throughout society. Finally, it reinforces the importance of the prison itself, regardless of its failure, as the ultimate and often most threatening site of disciplinary intervention. In short, the carceral archipelago, of which the prison is a central element, sustains the disciplinary character of society even when it cannot accomplish the disciplinary project of rehabilitating criminals.

Discipline and Punish is Foucault's most sustained genealogical discussion of who we are now. We can see in it all the elements of a genealogy: the dispersed character of origins, the effects of what Nietzsche would undoubtedly call reactivity, the historical contingency of the unfolding of practices, the lowly character of the practices themselves that wind up converging to create (part of) who we are. We shall shortly turn to the view of power that underlies this work, a view that receives substantial elaboration in Foucault's next book, the first volume of his history of sexuality. Before that, however, it would be worth pausing again to ask after the accuracy of Foucault's history of discipline. It is a question that Foucault himself recognizes as legitimate, since, in that next volume, he raises it himself. Discussing his view of power as creative rather than simply prohibitive, he asks, "Beyond these few phosphorescences [the suggestive historical changes he has just discussed in regard to sexuality], are we not sure to find once more the somber law that always says no? The answer will have to come out of a historical inquiry" (*HS*: 72).

Perhaps the most sustained alternative to Foucault's history of the prisons is Pieter Spierenberg's *The Spectacle of Suffering*.[7] Spierenberg sees his own work as a contrast to *Discipline and Punish*, and writes that his project is one that "attempts to construct a 'counter-paradigm' to Foucault's".[8] Along the way, Spierenberg makes a number of criticisms of Foucault's work, many of which seem to be based on a misreading of Foucault's book. For instance, he writes that "Foucault speaks of the 'political danger' immanent in executions, which he considers the real cause of their eventual disappearance".[9] Spierenberg concedes that there is resistance to executions at times, but notes that there is no evidence that this alone leads to the end of public executions. As we have seen, however, Foucault's genealogical method resists the very idea of a "real cause". Causality is complex and dispersed, and Foucault indicates that the decline of public executions has as much to do with economic and political changes as it does with any resistance to the practice itself.

Spierenberg's main thesis, however, is that Foucault is mistaken to think that there is a sudden historical break in the late-eighteenth and early-nineteenth centuries that leads to the demise of torture and the emergence of discipline. Using archival research not only from France, but also from other places in Europe,[10] particularly England and the Netherlands, Spierenberg seeks to show that the emergence of the prison is a slower process occurring over a longer period of time than Foucault ascribes to it, and that older practices continue to exist alongside the newer disciplinary practices of the prison. "The fact that the completion of the privatization of repression took about two-thirds of the nineteenth century in most Western European countries adds up to a critique of Foucault's views."[11] Does it?

First, one must concede that Foucault's research is often centered on France. Spierenberg's work, like Klaus Doerner's on madness, draws from a wider range of countries. Secondly, in as much as Foucault ascribes a radical break, Spierenberg's work would serve as a corrective. It is not clear, however, that the ascribed break is as radical as Spierenberg makes it out to be. In his archaeological period, Foucault talks in terms of decisive historical discontinuities. The situation is more complicated in the genealogical works. Those involve emergences that appear more nuanced. That there is, sooner or later, a new historical situation is certainly one of Foucault's claims. Spierenberg does not deny this. However, when Spierenberg calls Foucault a "structuralist", as he does in the text, he seems to be thinking more of the approach of some of Foucault's archaeological works than his genealogical ones.

For instance, when Spierenberg writes that "From his structuralist perspective he is describing a system and it is irrelevant to him which particular point in time one picks to investigate that system",[12] that irrelevance would apply more to an archaeological view of archives than it would to a genealogical view of the interweaving of historically extended and modified practices. In an archaeological view there is, within a given archive, a stability of discursive rules that remains until a historical break. In a genealogical view, however, the practices that converge and diverge do not necessarily do so in accordance with any larger cultural (or subcultural) themes. Who we are is not *this* at one time and *that* at another. The themes that comprise us are fluid and historically staggered.

In that sense, Spierenberg, by according as much historical weight to what happens outside of France as within it, helps reinforce the fluid character of history in a way that Foucault does not emphasize in *Discipline and Punish*. That would make it a contribution to a genealogical history rather than an undermining of it. The extent to which Spierenberg's analysis is historically better than Foucault's is beyond my expertise to say. However, as I mentioned earlier, Foucault's work, both genealogical and archaeological, lies at the intersection of both philosophy and history. We should see his works, then, as engaging and open to both disciplines.

From the philosophical perspective, there are several novel contributions of *Discipline and Punish*. It questions a progressive view of history without embracing a regressive one. It inverts the traditional Christian-inspired view that the body is the prison of the soul. It subjects aspects of ourselves that we might have thought to be immutable to a contingent history. It places knowledge in the context of politics. These changes are not isolated from one another. For instance, if there are aspects of who we are that are matters of historical change rather than being immutable, and if that historical change is contingent, then our history cannot be one of necessary progress or regress. Or again, if knowledge is a matter of politics, then the Christian heritage of the privileging of the soul over the body can come into question, not only epistemologically but also politically.

Underlying all of these contributions is another one. Utilized in the book on the prisons, and explained in the first volume of his history of sexuality, is a new view of the operation of power. It is not that all of these other changes are reducible to this new view of power. Rather, it is that they all appeal to it; moreover, it gives each of them a force they would lack without it. At a first go, we might say that for Foucault, power acts as much as or more through what it *creates* than through what it *represses*.

There is a traditional view of power that informs almost all political thought. It can be seen particularly in the liberal tradition of political philosophy. The view is that power works primarily if not solely by stopping certain things from happening. Here is a rough sketch. In the social contract, individuals give up certain of their freedoms to the state. In this way, the state becomes extraordinarily powerful. It can intervene in people's lives in order to prevent them from doing all sorts of things. There must, then, be checks placed upon the state. Those checks prevent the state from overstepping its legitimate bounds. The checks can be internal to the state, for instance a separation of powers of the kind the US Constitution provides; they can also be external, for instance in limiting the powers of the state to dominate public discussion, as in freedom of the press; finally, they can be a combination of the two. However these checks work, they must allow individuals to be able to conduct their lives with the protection and support of, but not the undue interference by, the state.

This brief, admittedly inadequate, sketch of liberal political philosophy is meant to illuminate two related themes that characterize that philosophy: the centrality of the state and the negative view of power, that is, the view of power as repressive. These themes lean upon each other. If we look at power from the standpoint of the state, we are likely to see something large, imposing, and repressive. Power is what states have that can interfere with the ability of individuals to carry out their lives. Think of the military, the police, prisons. From the other side, if we look at the state from the standpoint of a repressive or negative power, we are likely to see something monolithic that needs to be curbed so that it does not become tyrannical.

But suppose we approach power in a different fashion. Suppose we turn away from the state and look closer to the ground at our everyday practices. Suppose we take a genealogical turn and ask, "Where and how does a particular form of power arise?" instead of the liberal question of "Who has power?" In that case, power can appear very differently from the way it does in liberal theory. This is not to say that Foucault denies that there is such a thing as repressive power or that the state possesses it. This is a common misreading of his work. Rather, it is to say that often the more effective forms of power come from below rather than above, from our practices rather than from the state. It is also to say that this often more effective power operates by creating objects rather than by repressing them.

It should be emphasized here that the emergence of this form of power is itself a historical matter. It relies on more advanced technologies of communication, more dominant population centres such as cities, the rise of medical and related health sciences, and greater economic integration:

> [I]f it is true that the juridical system [the binary system of the permitted and the forbidden with its repressive view of power] was useful for representing, albeit in a nonexhaustive way, a power that was centered primarily around deduction [*prélèvement*] and death, it is utterly incongruous with the new methods of power whose operation is not ensured by right but by technique, not by law but by normalization, not by punishment but by control, methods that are employed on all levels and in forms that go beyond the state and its apparatus. (*HS*: 89)[13]

If creative forms of power are at one time marginal, they are now central in the practices in which we engage and through which we become who we are, who we are now.

If we are to deepen our understanding, we must ask two questions: what does Foucault mean by power, and how does it work? The first question is one that Foucault mostly avoids. He does not, he tells us, want to give us a theory of power, but rather to describe its operation in particular historical situations. Nevertheless, using the term as centrally as he does, he must have something in mind. And in an essay entitled "The Subject and Power", he does offer a tentative definition of power:

> In effect, what defines a relationship of power is that it is a mode of action which does not act directly and immediately on others. Instead it acts upon their actions: an action upon an action, on existing actions or on those which may arise in the present or the future. (*SP*: 220)

Foucault contrasts power and violence. Violence forces a body to do something; it compels without the possibility of resistance. Power, on the other hand, works by what we might call *influence* instead of violence. It works not by restraint but by inducing something to happen. This is why Foucault says, "Power is exercised only over free subjects, and only insofar as they are free" (*ibid.*: 221). Power works by taking an open field of possible actions and constructing certain pathways of actions that are more likely to be taken. Normalization, for instance, does not work by violence upon the body but rather by observing and examining a body and leading it to become more efficient.

There is a kinship between this definition of power and the historical contingency to which Foucault is committed. If power works by influencing or by inducing a free body rather than by force, then its hold is more fragile than we might otherwise think. Although normalization lies deeply embedded in our conception of who we are, it does so only by means of its influence and by its inherence in so many of our practices. There are other ways we can be, ways that can be explored through the construction of new practices. Who we are now is historically contingent.

If this is Foucault's view of what power is, how does it work? What can we say about the ways power relations influence or induce our behaviour? In the first volume of his history of sexuality, Foucault offers what might be called his five theses on power: power is not a possession; power is not exterior to other relations; power comes from below; power relations are "intentional and nonsubjective"; power always comes with resistance (*HS*: 94–5). It is worth pausing over each of these theses.

To think of power as a possession is to think in accordance with the traditional view of power. It is to seek to understand and regulate the entity, usually the state, that has the most of it. But power can work without belonging to anybody. Actions can constrain other actions without anybody's possessing the power of that constraint. Tuke and Pinel, for instance, possess no power over the mad. Their interventions are merely expressions of discursive and practical regularities. But those interventions, actions upon actions, help to create and sustain a new type of bondage of the mad. In the terms we have been using, their interventions help make the mad who they were to become. Or again, those who work in the medical field or who teach or who engage in psychotherapy do not have the power of discipline over those they monitor or supervise. Rather, they are in a relation with those others that is itself one of discipline. Normalization is not something they impose, but instead something in which they participate.

To say that power is not exterior to other relations is to generalize the lesson of power–knowledge. Knowledge is not in a relation of exteriority to power. Neither is health, psychotherapy, penality, or, as we shall shortly see, sex. We must be careful here, though. As we saw with knowledge, to say that other relations are not immune to power is not the same thing as saying that they are all reducible to power, that they are "really about" power. Power is interwoven into these and other practices in complex ways. If one is to understand the operation of power within them, it requires a patient historical analysis of the way power arises within and across practices, not a sweeping generalization about everything being simply a matter of power.

This is, in part, because power comes from below. Power, in the sense Foucault approaches it, is not a possession of the state, a matter of the economy, or the expression of some overarching historical theme. It lies in the dispersion of everyday practices that are the aether of our lives. In my raising of my children, in the postal worker's interaction with customers, in the warden's observation of prisoners, in the holidaymaker's choice of hotels, there is power. It is not a power that one possesses over another (there may be that, too, but that is not what Foucault is getting at); rather, it is a power that lies in the practices itself, creating who we are through our participation in them. We would, of course, refuse to say that all of these practices are nothing but power at work. To say that would be at best silly, probably meaningless. There is more going on in what we do every day than merely power. And that would be Foucault's point. Power is everywhere, to be sure, but this does not mean that power is everything. The point that power comes from below, from what Foucault sometimes calls the "capillaries", reinforces that point.

Foucault's phrase that power relations are "intentional and nonsubjective" has often been misunderstood. It sounds as though there is a certain goal that power has in mind, even if that goal is not the motivation of particular individuals. Foucault's choice of words may reinforce this view. "[T]here is no power that is exercised without a series of aims and objectives. But this does not mean that it results from the choice or decision of an individual subject" (*HS*: 95). We need not, however, read any anthropomorphizing of power here. Power relations themselves do not want or aim at or seek to achieve anything. We might better understand the idea if we use the term *oriented*. Power relations are oriented in certain directions. They have regularities that conduce to some kinds of behaviour and not others.

Discipline involves a set of power relations that are oriented. Historically, a dispersion of practices – or at least elements of those practices – come together to induce individuals to become normalized and, inseparably, to think of themselves in terms of normalization. This orientation is not the aim or goal of anything. It is the product of various intersections and borrowings in a particular historical context and with a recognizable set of consequences. It is the task of a genealogy to trace those intersections and borrowings and to describe their consequences. The orientation of intersections, borrowings and consequences is what Foucault refers to with the term *intentional*.

The idea that "Where there is power, there is resistance" (*ibid*.) is an elusive one. It can be taken in at least two different ways. The first way would be to claim that, in principle, power requires resistance. There can be no power without resistance. I am uncomfortable with this claim.[14] If power is a set of actions upon actions that create objects in the way Foucault describes, it does not seem necessary to think of resistance as an inevitable part of power relations. Since force is not involved, could there not be relations of power that are without resistance? There is reason to think otherwise. However, we might understand this fifth thesis in a weaker sense. It is not that power relations require resistance and cannot exist without it, but rather that there always seems to be resistance where there are relations of power. In other words, power does not *imply* resistance, but often comes coupled with it. This seems a much more defensible claim. Justifying it is a matter of turning to the historical record. And indeed Foucault shows in *Discipline and Punish* that various power arrangements have been met with resistance, even if those resisting do not know exactly what it is they are opposing. For instance, near the end of the book Foucault describes the criticism of penal discipline in workers' newspapers of the nineteenth century, showing how they have an intuition of the stakes of discipline without a nuanced grasp of its operation.

These fives theses amount to a view of a type of power that does not merely suppress or repress but that actively creates. Without anyone's controlling it, power arises in everyday practices, orienting our behaviour and our knowledge in particular, historically contingent ways. We rarely understand these ways fully, but often try to resist them. And, by our participating in these practices, we ourselves become embedded in relations of power, even when we resist them. We become what those relations orient us to become, and we pave the way for others to become it as well. To put the point another way, power helps *create* who we are, or at least who we are now. Recall here Foucault's earlier statement that we often know what we do and why we are doing it; what we do not know is what our doing it does. What *our doing it does* is reinforce power relations that elude our cognitive grasp, not because we are distant from them but for the opposite reason that they are so much a part of who we are. It is the project of a genealogy to display those relations before us in their proximity, their complexity, and their historical contingency.

A history of sexuality

The first volume of Foucault's history of sexuality sketches another genealogical project, this one tied to sex rather than discipline. Although the next (and last two published) volumes of the history of sexuality take on a different approach from the one outlined in the first volume, the historical sketch Foucault offers there has been as influential as his book on the prisons, in part because it invites a radical reorientation of how we think about sex.

The *History of Sexuality, Volume I*, is published in 1976, a year after the book on the prisons. It announces and sketches a project on sexuality that appears less radical now than it does at that time, in part because we no longer live at a moment we would be tempted to call one of "sexual liberation". In the thirty years since the publication of this book, much of what seems novel then is now a matter of course. If anything, our sexual practices are a subject of attack from the right rather than, as it appears then, a provocation by the left.

At the beginning of the book on sexuality, Foucault describes our (then-) current view of sex under the term the *repressive hypothesis*. The repressive hypothesis is a story about our sexuality. It is a story of sexual awakening. Once we were sexually repressed. This sexual repression, which has long been with us, perhaps achieves its zenith in the Victorian period, but has been sustained throughout much of the twentieth century. With the various movements for liberation in the 1960s (and here recall the events of May '68), the recognition of the need for sexual liberation arises. Sexual repression, after all, is not only bad in itself; it also contributes to other ills, including the repression of women's sexuality, discrimination against homosexuality, a general cultural conformism, and the suppression of other desires. Now, in the period of the late 1960s and early 1970s, we have liberated our sexuality and with that liberation have opened the door to other liberations from the constraints of bourgeois society.

There is more than a little influence of psychoanalytic thought in the repressive hypothesis. The theme of sexual repression, the idea that such repression is linked to other social phenomena – in particular the sustaining of bourgeois society – and the focus on desire are all legacies of psychoanalysis.

In the United States and Britain, where psychoanalysis has always been less influential than during these years in France, the possibility of a psychoanalytic background to the repressive hypothesis may seem to be strained. However, it does find its way into Anglophone countries through such works as Herbert Marcuse's *Eros and Civilization*. In France, the rise of psychoanalytic thought under the influence of Jacques Lacan makes it, during this period, almost de rigueur for leftists to appropriate psychoanalytic elements into progressive theory. Perhaps the most lasting of these works is Deleuze and Guattari's *Anti-Oedipus*, a book that rejects psychoanalysis but which, on the other hand, appropriates and reworks a Lacanian concept of desire.

There are many questions one might put to the repressive hypothesis. Have we really liberated ourselves from sexual repression? If so, has this indeed led us to other forms of liberation? Hasn't sexual liberation simply been appropriated by capitalism to open up new products and new types of marketing? Foucault, however, follows a different path. He asks a question that casts doubt on the founding assumptions of these other questions. Has there ever been, he wonders, such a thing as sexual repression? If there hasn't, then not only could we not have liberated ourselves from it; we cannot wonder what effects this liberation might or might not have had.

It would seem odd to say that there has never been anything like sexual repression. Does the Victorian period not exhibit much greater discretion about sexual issues than we do? Hasn't the open discussion of sex long been a taboo subject? To say that there never was sexual repression, however, is not the same thing as saying that there was never any discretion in regard to sexual matters:

> It is quite possible that there was an expurgation – and a very rigorous one – of the authorized vocabulary. It may be true that a whole rhetoric of allusion and metaphor was codified . . . At the level of discourses and their domains, however, practically the opposite phenomenon occurred. There was a steady proliferation of discourses concerned with sex. (*HS*: 17–18)

Discourse on sex in periods previous to our own is discreet, to be sure, but it is also pervasive.

How does this concern with sex arise? In accordance with genealogical practice, Foucault finds its roots not in a single cause but in the convergence of disparate concerns. One of them has to do with the Catholic confessional. In the face of the Reformation, the confessional undergoes a change. Where previously one confesses forbidden acts, now one must confess not only the acts that one commits but also one's desires. It is not simply what one does that is the object of confessional; it is what one thinks and wants, especially with regard to sex:

> According to the new pastoral, sex must not be named imprudently, but its aspects, its correlations, and its effects must be pursued down to their slenderest ramifications: a shadow in a daydream, an image too slowly dispelled, a badly exorcised complicity between the body's mechanics and the mind's complacency: everything had to be told. (*Ibid.*: 19)

If we recall the project of normalization from *Discipline and Punish*, we can see here the change from a binary logic of the permitted and the forbidden to a wider logic of the normal and the abnormal.

In addition to changes in the confessional, there is an economic focus on sex. The beginnings of an industrial economy raise questions about how populations are to be sustained and utilized:

> One of the great innovations in the techniques of power in the eighteenth century was the emergence of "population" as an economic and political problem: population as wealth, population as manpower or labor capacity, population balanced between its own growth and the resources it commanded. (*Ibid.*: 25)

Where there is concern with population, there will also be concern with sex: how it happens, what it leads to, and how it should be regulated.

There are other sources as well, in biology, in medicine, in psychology, in pedagogy. In schools, for instance, while sex is not spoken of, the architecture of dormitories displays a greater concern with the partitions dividing boys and girls. What these various sources converge on is sex. Sex as the centrepiece, sex as the object, sex as the secret, and ultimately sex as the truth. In direct contrast to the repressive hypothesis, sex is not something hidden that has just come to light. "What is peculiar to modern societies, in fact, is not that they consigned sex to a shadow existence, but that they dedicated themselves to speaking of it *ad infinitum*, while exploiting it as *the* secret" (*ibid.*: 35). In this sense, the sexual liberation of the period in which Foucault writes is not a break from the past; it is simply a continuation of the concern with sex that has characterized the West for several hundred years. Moreover, psychoanalysis, which frames the repressive hypothesis, is far from being an abandonment of religion in favour of something more progressive or better grounded epistemologically. It is, instead, a form of the confessional carried on by other means.

Sex is our truth; in our sexual desire we discover the secret of who we are and the key to proper social regulation. Over the course of the past several centuries, sex has become one of the key pivots about which the answer to the question of who we are revolves. And because power is inseparable from knowledge, the investigation of sex is a political as well as an epistemic one. That investigation is not only a matter of discovery. It is also a matter of actions upon actions that create what is investigated. Both in the empirical and theoretical research into sex as well as the individual confession of one's desires – to the priest, to the psychoanalyst, to the counsellor or social worker – one is being studied and created. Practices that centre on sex are creating a sexual being, or better, different types of beings that are defining themselves by their relation to sex.

Foucault suggests four "figures" that arise from the concern with sex. They are elements of the creation, as he puts it, of *sexuality* (as a historical phenomenon) out of sex. These figures are the hysterical woman, the masturbating child, the perverse adult, and the Malthusian couple. The hysterical woman has her roots in earlier views of sex. The idea of hysteria comes from the movement of the womb around the woman's body. (The Greek term *hysterikos* means womb.) This theme is appropriated over the course of the nineteenth century to link women and their nervous conditions to sexuality. Sex is the truth of the hysterical woman, who is to be found in almost all women.

The masturbating child is the product of the discovery of the sexual character of childhood. The child, once thought to be pre-sexual, is now thought (and feared) to be saturated with sexuality from an early age. The question arises of what to do with this newly discovered sexual character of children. In one of the recently published series of lectures from Foucault's tenure at the Collège de France, *Abnormal*, Foucault documents measures used to channel childhood sexuality, measures that find their root in a profusion of texts from the middle of the eighteenth century on the dangers of childhood masturbation. In essence, at least for bourgeois families, there emerges a fear of outside caretakers as potential sexual abusers, provoking masturbation in children. This leads to a privileging of the nuclear family as the necessary condition for healthy childhood sexuality, and consequently to the responsibility of the parents for a child's sexual upbringing. "The child's sexuality is the trick by which the close-knit, affective, substantial, and cellular family was constituted and from whose shelter the child was extracted" (*ALCF*: 257).[15]

The perverse adult is exemplified, of course, by the homosexual. Homosexuals are defined – and to this day remain defined – by their sexuality. It is the key to who they are. This does not mean that homosexuality itself is a matter of sex: that is an obvious truth. It means that homosexuals themselves, as people, are defined by their sexuality. Who they are can be discovered through an investigation of their sexual desires. As Foucault sums it up:

> the sexual instinct was isolated as a separate biological and psychical instinct; a clinical analysis was made of all the forms of anomalies by which it could be afflicted; it was assigned a role of normalization or pathologization with respect to all behavior; and finally, a corrective technology was sought for these anomalies.
>
> (*HS*: 105)

The perverse adult is the person defined by a warping of sexual desire. That warping fulfils two roles. First, it warrants intervention by various psychological and social agencies. Secondly, since this warping is a possibility that can befall all sexual desire, it stands as a possibility for each of us. We must all be protected, not only against perverse adults themselves, but also against the perverse adult that lies in wait within each of us. One can see here the soil within which Freudian psychoanalysis will take root.

Finally, there is the Malthusian couple. This is the couple that is ideal relative to the social and economic needs of society. It is a product of population analysis and psychosexual research. We might say, in the terms introduced in *Discipline and Punish*, that the Malthusian couple is the *norm* (as in "normal") against which all existing families are compared. And, since nobody (or almost nobody) achieves perfect normality, the Malthusian couple becomes the justification for intervention into people's sexual lives. We all exist both in the shadow of and at a distance from the ideal of the Malthusian couple, which in turn provides both an ideal for us to achieve and the excuse for outside institutions to monitor and control our sexual lives, or, otherwise put, to take part in the constitution of and intervention into who we are.

In the final chapter of the first volume of his history of sexuality, Foucault suggests that the sexuality that emerges over the course of the eighteenth and nineteenth centuries is part of a larger configuration that he terms *bio-politics*. Bio-politics is a politics of living that concerns itself with how to promote and intervene in human life. It replaces the earlier concern with simply allowing one to live with an active intervention into the character and state of one's living. "One might say that the ancient right to *take* life or *let* live was replaced by a power to *foster* life or *disallow* it to the point of death" (*HS*: 138). We must be clear here that the *power* that replaces that ancient right does not belong solely or even primarily to the state. It arises as a more diffuse mechanism of power relations that come from dispersed sources and converge in a fluid and shifting unity. The fostering or disallowing of life is a decision that is rarely made in the name of or by means of a central government. It emerges in schools, hospitals, social agencies, clinics, doctors' offices, health manuals, and a myriad of other places whose decisions may resonate with one another but do not arise from a central core.

With the concept of bio-politics, Foucault returns to and integrates his earlier treatment of discipline. He suggests that discipline may be one of the twin poles of the constitution of bio-politics:

> starting in the seventeenth century, this power over life evolved in two basic forms . . . One of these poles . . . was ensured by the procedures of power that characterized the *disciplines*: an *anatamo-politics of the human body*. The second, somewhat later, focused on the species body, the body imbued with the mechanisms of life and serving as the basis of the biological processes . . . Their

90

supervision was effected through an entire series of interventions and *regulatory controls: a bio-politics of the population.* (HS: 139)

Discipline and population: the individual body and the collective group. These are the poles of bio-politics. What do the body and population have in common? Sexuality.

Sexuality, then, can be read back into some of the concerns developed in the earlier book on the prisons. This does not mean that the earlier book is mistaken, that the issue is really sex, not discipline. The suggestion rather is that the concern with sex brings a new dimension to the disciplinary interventions described in the earlier text. We can see the overlap between the two: the focus on normality and normalization, the concern with a person's interiority (the soul in one case, desire in the other), the connection with psychological and psychiatric practice. During this period of his writing, Foucault often says that his concern is with what he calls, in a play on words, *subjectification* or *subjectivation*: the creation of particular kinds of subjectivity through the subjection to various practices of power–knowledge. What the books on discipline and sex accomplish is to describe, from two different but convergent angles, the emergence of modern subjectivity. In that sense, these books reflect the genealogical method itself. Just as each describes dispersed sources of the unities of who we are, they are themselves dispersed sources in that history. Taken together, they account for two of the most important dispersions that form the historically contingent sources for who we are now.

Before turning to Foucault's last works and the concerns they raise, it remains for us to ask how the genealogical works we have discussed here fit with the five aspects of Foucault's writings cited in the first chapter, and how they compare on these counts with the archaeological writings. The first aspect is that of our collective constitution. One can see that aspect at work in the genealogical writings, perhaps even more clearly than in the archaeological ones. Although both sets of works operate at the level of social practices rather than the individuals' creation of themselves, the genealogical works show how this collective constitution arises on an everyday level. Because the genealogical works are less abstracted from our daily lives, they show how a *we* (or a group of different but overlapping *we*s) arises, not by imposition from institutions or forces above us, but from below, where we live.

Earlier, we saw that the archaeological works, although recognizing relations between the discursive and non-discursive elements of an archive, seem to privilege the former. This privilege disappears in the genealogical works, in part because the distinction between the discursive and non-discursive itself disappears. Since Foucault is concerned less with the archival shape of theoretical discourses, and more with how particular discourses of knowledge arise within concrete social practices, the issue shifts. It is no longer a matter of the relation of the discursive to the non-discursive. It is one of how practices create forms of knowledge. When one discusses a practice, one need not draw sharp distinctions between the discursive and the non-discursive elements, because at the level of a practice they are entwined. What we think we know and what we do are in constant interaction, and in fact bleed into each other. By focusing on practices rather than on bodies of knowledge, one can recognize this more clearly.

We can see this, for example, with the emergence of the four figures of sexuality or of the self-monitoring citizen of the disciplinary archipelago. In both cases, the way one knows and the way one is and behaves are entwined. Our knowledge creates who we are, and who we are in our relationships of power helps to create our knowledge. This, of course, is another of the five characteristics of Foucault's works, the close relationship of acting and knowing. Genealogy's focus on practices, as well as the introduction of power–knowledge, creates a type of analysis that renders the discursive and the non-discursive inseparable. At the same time, because these practices are social, they form the collective character of who we are.

This collective and politically charged character of who we are is at once historically contingent and something we cannot just shake off. The historical contingency is as strong here as it is in the archaeological works, but for a different reason. In the earlier writings, the fragility of our history is displayed in the breaks and discontinuities it contains. Different archives are governed by different rules and norms, and there are often shifts from one archive to another. This shifting of archives blunts the force of any claim that history follows necessary movement or has a single underlying theme. In the genealogical works it is not so much the discontinuities that matter – although they are there – but rather the shifting and changing character of the practices themselves as well as their complex interplay with one another.[16]

There is no necessary reason that sex should become so important to who we are now, any more than breathing or eating. The intersection of a changed Catholic confessional and the rise of population studies, for example, cannot be ascribed to an underlying movement of history that they both reflect. The Reformation does not have to take place in the way and at the time it does, and even if it had to, Catholicism does not need to respond to it by focusing the confessional on sexual desires rather than forbidden acts. At the same time, the rise of early capitalism does not require the emergence and importance of population studies. Capitalism could be studied and supported through other types of epistemological approaches. Further, the cross-fertilization of the modified confessional and population studies does not have to centre itself on a historically constituted sexuality. Even if both refer to sex, they do so in different ways. There is no historical inevitability to their coming together to form a unity.

We can see this historical contingency more clearly through the detailed approach of genealogy than through a more broad-brushstroke painting of history and historical change. Recall Foucault's depiction of genealogy: grey, meticulous and patiently documentary. From a great distance or height, our history may seem to have a necessary shape or pattern. However, when one begins to look at the complexity of our actual practices, when one approaches our lives at ground level, the contingency of those practices' emergence and interaction becomes more visible.

At the same time, and on the other hand, the unities that emerge through the contingent threads of our history, fragile as they are, are not simply to be shaken off. We have seen that in the archaeological histories the fact that action takes place in an archive means that actions are framed by their historical circumstances. Tuke and Pinel cannot just do and say anything they like; what they do and say is both constrained by and takes on its meaning through the circumstances in which it is done and said. The genealogical works are no different in this regard. However, by introducing the concept of power, Foucault's genealogies are more explicit about the constraining nature of our practices. Actions that affect other actions are inescapably actions that we cannot simply shake off. One need not embrace a conspiracy theory of history to recognize that who we are is subject to force or elements or relationships that, to a greater or lesser extent, are out of our control.

This does not imply, as some of Foucault's critics have maintained, that we are helpless before our historical constitution, that we are nothing more than the machinations of power relationships. We have already seen that the claim that power is everywhere does not imply that it is everything. One of the difficulties in understanding Foucault's work is that of thinking of contingency and constraint together. This is not a difficulty that belongs to some abstract or elusive facet of Foucault's work. It is just something we are not used to. Our intellectual legacy largely provides us with two options: either we are free or we are determined. Or, if we are more nuanced about it, we have our areas of freedom and our areas of determination. The former is an open space, untouched by the causal relationships of the world. The latter is completely subject to those causal relationships.

Foucault's histories do not subscribe to this view. There is no part of us that is immune to the vicissitudes of our history. And yet, those vicissitudes are not made of iron. They are fragile, contingent, changeable. Foucault, as we have seen, does not give us a solution to the philosophical problem of free will and determinism. Moreover, his approach implies a different orientation to the issue of constraint. There is, then, no reason to saddle him with a view he does not hold in the name of a theoretical approach that is not his.

There remains the characteristic of complexity. Genealogy leaves the ambiguity of archaeology's relation to complexity behind. Foucault's archaeological studies trace the rules and norms of particular archives. This leaves open the question of how general the archive is. Does it range over an entire cultural formation, or is it more limited? If it is the former, then historical formations are less complex than if there are different archives governing different areas of a society or a culture. Is ordered representation, or reason's treatment of madness as folly, a deep characteristic of the classical age? Do these aspects of the classical age describe that age in its entirety? Or are they aspects or parts or areas of the epistemological structure of the later seventeenth and eighteenth centuries? Might there be other knowledges, outside those of the theories of value, living beings and language, that are not oriented around ordered representation? Might the particular type of reason that engages with madness be only one way in which reason operates? These are questions that are ultimately unresolved in Foucault's archaeological works.

Not so with genealogy. Although there are times when Foucault may seem to suggest a reduction of cultural complexity to single themes (some, for instance, have read his concept of the carceral archipelago to indicate that the essence of modernity is carceral), a careful reading shows that each book treats an aspect of how we have come to be who we are now, not the entirety of it. Are we disciplinary beings? Yes. Are we sexual beings? Yes. Is there a relation between these two? Yes. Are they reducible to each other or to a third unity that encompasses them both? No. Foucault's genealogical works, even more insistently than his archaeologies, resist the temptation of much of traditional philosophy, of the philosophy that runs from Descartes through to Freud and Sartre, to discover the essential core of who we are and to see the rest of who we are as expressions of that core.

There are certainly more important aspects of who we are now, and sexuality and discipline are among them. Not every aspect of who we have come to be is an equally significant contributor to that being. We must not take the lesson of this, however, to be that there are one or two aspects of who we are now that are the essential ones. The complexity of Foucault's approach lies in carving a path between posing an essential ahistorical core of who we are and counting all aspects of our legacy as equally worthy of discussion.

There is another question that remains, one we have posed to the archaeological writings. The archaeologies are haunted by a question of reflexivity, a question having to do with their epistemological status. We can summarize the question this way: if all knowledge takes place in an archive, does this not also apply to Foucault's archaeologies, and if so, does that not somehow undermine their claims? However we answer this question with regard to archaeology, it is not a question genealogy must confront. The reason for this has to do with genealogy's relation to complexity. If there are many different and irreducible practices in which we are (or could be) engaged, we can count genealogy itself as one of them. Genealogy has its own norms and power relations, to be sure, but this does not necessarily undermine the historical claims it makes. Foucault underlines this point when, in an interview in 1983, he responds to a question about his treatment of reason by saying:

> I think that the blackmail which has very often been at work in every critique of reason or every critical inquiry into the history of rationality (either you accept rationality or you fall prey to the irrational) operates as though a rational critique of rationality were impossible, or as though rational history of all of the ramifications and all the bifurcations, a contingent history of reason, were impossible. (CT/IH: 27)[17]

Recall how genealogy operates in the critique of psychology that arises in the book on the prisons. Foucault does not criticize psychological knowledge for being false. In fact, part of its truth lies in the fact that it contributes to creating what it studies. The problem with psychological knowledge lies in its effects, not its truth: in the political character of what it creates rather than in the epistemic character of its claims. With genealogy, then, if we were to ask genealogical questions about *its* claims, if we were to do a genealogy of genealogy (or a genealogy of a particular genealogy) we would trace the emergence and descent of that genealogy, asking where it comes from and what the endorsement of it leads to. There is no bar to doing this, as long as one is willing to perform the spade work. That is, one cannot just say that genealogy has effects of power that are unacceptable or intolerable. One must show it: one must investigate the history itself. Recall Foucault's caveat with his own history of sexuality: he does not yet know whether, "beyond these few phosophorescences", he will discover that the repressive hypothesis is indeed correct. It will require historical research to determine. The same holds for genealogy.

Genealogy, then, does not face the problem of reflexivity that haunts archaeology because it does not reduce knowledge to a particular archive and because it does not claim that the objects of its critique are false. It is open to critique itself; but that critique must be shown, not just claimed. A critique of a Foucauldian genealogy, if it is to be compelling, must itself be *grey, meticulous and patiently documentary*.

CHAPTER FOUR

Who we are and who we might be

The Archaeology of Knowledge is published in 1969. Between 1961 and 1969 Foucault publishes six books. He does not publish another one until the first genealogy appears in 1975, followed by the first volume of the history of sexuality a year later. By then there are new themes, such as power, and a new methodology, that of genealogy. The first volume on sex promises several more to follow:

> [T]he domain we must analyze in the different studies that will follow the present volume is that deployment of sexuality: its formation on the basis of the Christian notion of the flesh, and its development through the four great strategies that were deployed in the nineteenth century: the sexualization of children, the hysterization of women, the specification of the perverted, and the regulation of populations. (*HS*: 113–14)

In 1984, the second and third volumes are published. They appear just before Foucault's death. And in them there are new themes, a new chronology, and a new approach, an approach that Foucault sometimes labels *ethics*.

Ethics

We already know that Foucault is resistant to patrolling the same intellectual territory. He has told us in *The Archaeology of Knowledge* that it is not for him to keep his papers in order, but for bureaucrats and the police. He says much the same thing in his preface to the second volume of the history of sexuality, *The Use of Pleasure*, when he tells us that what motivated him is a curiosity that allows him to "stray afield" of himself. We shall ask more about the character of this straying later. For now, it is enough that we not demand of him that he keep to the original schedule of announced works. In the meantime, between the publication of the first volume of the history of sexuality and the latter two volumes, the evidence of a change in orientation appears in his annual lecture series at the Collège de France.

Instead of beginning the investigation in the period of the Renaissance or post-Renaissance, a period that has always been Foucault's starting point, Foucault turns his attention to ancient Greece and Rome. The 1979–80 lectures series, "On the Government of the Living", discusses the theme of *governmentality* (a prominent theme of the next chapter of this book) as he finds it in early Christianity. But the real break appears the next year in a series of lectures entitled "Subjectivity and Truth". It is in those lectures, which are the basis for the third volume of the history of sexuality, that he develops the theme that will occupy the ethical period of his thought: the care of the self.

The care of the self involves several changes to the project on sexuality. First, its concern is not simply with sex. This should not be surprising, given the thesis of the first volume that sexuality as the placement of sexual desire at the centre of who one is has evolved over recent centuries. Sexuality is not an eternal phenomenon. By returning to ancient Greece and Rome, Foucault shows us a period in which sex is conceived differently from the way it is now. It is more integrated into other aspects of living. Instead of holding the secret to who we are, sex is a part of one's living. For the ancients, it is an aspect that is to be taken up into the larger project of taking care of oneself.

This first change is related to a second one. In Foucault's previous works, he traces aspects of the history of how we have come to be who we are now. He starts with historical periods before our own in order to show, in the archaeological works, the ruptures that have taken place and, in the genealogical works, the contingent emergence of our own situation from a very different one. We might say that the history he recounts allows him to do two things, one that we have focused on and another that we have not. We have focused on the contingency of historical emergence. We have not focused on the related idea that people can conceive the world very differently from the way we do now. That history did not have to take the path it has should, by now, be a familiar Foucauldian idea. In tracing that path, we have also seen that the stops along the way, whether they are archives or earlier arrangements of practices, involve very different approaches to things like madness and punishment than our own.

Why might this matter? Of course, one might say, people saw things differently in earlier periods. What is the lesson of that? The lesson emerges when we combine that idea with the recognition that the way people see things, and indeed the way people are, is historically contingent. If we do not have to see things the way we once did, if we do not have to be who we once were, then we do not have to be who we are now. Bringing into focus different ways of being allows us not only to *see* the contingency of our own historically given ways of being; it allows us to *feel* it. Being brought into the presence of another way of living, getting a sense of its themes, its parameters, its concerns, allows us to understand more viscerally that there are, indeed, other ways to live than our own. This does not mean we have to embrace those other ways. But they can help loosen the grip of naturalness that the present has upon us.

The loosening of this grip is in evidence in the latter two volumes on sexuality. If their goal is to permit our straying afield of ourselves, then seeing how we could have lived otherwise is a tool in this permission. We should distinguish this tool from another one that is sometimes mistaken for Foucault's intention. Foucault does not offer us the latter two volumes of the history of sexuality in order to provide models for our own living. It is sometimes thought that the sympathy with which he writes, particularly of Greek sexuality, implies that he wants us to return to it. I suspect that this view arises largely because of the intersection of Foucault's homosexuality with the Greeks' tolerance for it. In an exchange in an interview from 1983, Foucault makes it clear that the Greeks do not provide a model for him. "Q. Do you think that the Greeks offer an attractive and plausible alternative? M.F. No! I am not looking for an alternative; you can't find the solution of a problem in the solution at another moment by other people" (OGE: 343).

If Foucault's later studies focus on a different view of the role of sex from our own, and if they seek to loosen the grip our own views have on us by immersing us in another view, then this implies a third change, a shift in orientation in Foucault's thought. Up until now, we have said that the question that occupies Foucault is that of who we are now. In presenting us with ways of seeing and living very different from our own, however, he changes the question. The ancient Greeks and Romans are *not* who we are now. Moreover, while our history has evolved from their legacy (although not in a continuous thread), what Foucault emphasizes in his later studies, in contrast to the genealogical works, is not their *legacy to us* but their *difference from us*. It is not how the specific practices of the Greeks and Romans converge with other practices in order to form who we are that matters here. Rather, it is how distant they are from our practices that is at issue.

This relocation of focus has an impact on the question of who we are. At first glance, we might say that it shifts the concern from who we are now to who we once were. But that is not enough. As Foucault tells us, he is not interested simply in knowing who we were. His research is never simply an academic exercise. The stakes here concern freedom; they concern straying afield of ourselves. "The object was to learn to what extent the effort to think one's own history can free thought from what it silently thinks, and so enable it to think differently" (*UP*: 9). So the shift is not the simple one from who we are to who we were. It is better schematized in this way: it is from who we are now to who we might be. We must be careful here, though. Who we might be is not provided directly by the model of the ancients. Although there will be themes in the ancient approach to living that Foucault endorses, particularly concerning the idea of the care of the self as an aesthetics of existence, the ancients do not provide us with a concrete alternative. Rather, studying them loosens the grip our present has upon us. It allows us not only to conceive but imaginatively to inhabit a different way of living. It opens the door to our asking the question of who we might be.

Alongside these three changes there are a number of continuities with the earlier works. One of them is of particular moment. Foucault's attention remains focused on practices, on the structured forms of daily living. If he writes about philosophers like Plato and Seneca, it is with a different orientation from the one the history of philosophy has passed down to us. He is not interested in the ancients as theorists; he is interested in them as practitioners of what might be called *true living*. To live rightly, to live according to proper truths, is the task of ancient philosophers, rather than one of simply discovering the truth. In this, Foucault follows his contemporary, the philosopher of antiquity Pierre Hadot, to whom we will return. But he also remains faithful to his earlier genealogical orientation of looking on the ground, at the practices that make up a life, rather than ascending to a more purely theoretical plane.

If, looking backwards from our perspective, we see philosophy as a matter of discovering truths rather than orienting ourselves towards the proper care of the self, this is because we have lost the ancient approach to philosophy, and with it the understanding of what ancient philosophers were doing. In his lecture series of 1981–82, *The Hermeneutics of the Subject*, Foucault says,

> the more serious reason why this precept of the care of the self has been forgotten, the reason why the place occupied by this precept in ancient culture for nigh on one thousand years has been obliterated, is what I will call ... the "Cartesian moment." ... It came into play in two ways: by philosophically requalifying the *gnothi seauton* (know yourself) and by discrediting the *epimeleia heautou* (care of the self). (*HSLCF*: 14)

Although the care of the self dropped out of philosophical discourse, knowing oneself, which had been oriented towards the care of the self, became a matter of determining the conditions of a person's access to truth. Instead of maintaining itself as what Foucault sometimes calls a *spiritual* project, philosophical practice gradually transformed itself into an episte-mological one.

What is the care of the self? What is its character and what makes it a philosophical matter? Foucault's most sustained treatment of this concept is in the recently published lectures from which the above quote is drawn. In those lectures, Foucault traces the change in orientation of the care of the self from Plato through Hellenic thought, especially that of the Stoics and the Epicureans. What underlies Foucault's concern is the relation of what he calls the subject and truth.

This relation of subject and truth is a lens through which we can, if we like, read the entirety of Foucault's writings. The archaeological work is a matter of the subject's epistemic placement in an archive. By placing the subject of knowledge in an archive, Foucault rejects the phenomenolo-gical tradition that he was brought up in and that his earliest writings sustain. In phenomenology, the subject's relation to truth is more immedi-ate. It is a matter of being able to see perspicuously, almost in the sense of Descartes's clear and distinct perception, what needs to be grasped. The interference of history, politics, or language can all be overcome accord-ing to the phenomenological view. However, if knowledge is inescapably located within the rules and norms of an archive, if it is always historically bounded, then the possibility of a subject's immediate relation to truth is lost. The relation of subject to truth runs through the archive.

Genealogy maintains the same rejection of phenomenology, and adds a political dimension to the historical one. What one knows is not a matter of a pure seeing or grasping; rather, it concerns a series of political relation-ships in which truth – or at least claims to truth – is embedded.

Of course, Foucault's concern has never been with all areas of truth. He does not treat natural sciences such as physics and chemistry. The truth that concerns him has to do with what he sometimes calls the "human sciences". Psychology, linguistics, economics, medicine, psychoanalysis, biology: these are the areas of truth that form Foucault's target. We might say that it is not a matter of subjects' relation to truth, but their relation to *their own* truth that lies at the core of Foucault's interest. Or, to put it in the terms we are using here, the issue is subjects' relation to who they are, or to who they are now, and, as a part of this, to who they take themselves to be.

This is what makes Foucault's discovery of the ancient care of the self fascinating to him. The care of the self involves a different relation of the subject to its own truth. The care of the self, whether Platonic, Hellenistic, or early Christian, requires one to work on oneself in a way that trans-forms who one is. It is not simply truth but oneself that is at stake. And, in particular with Hellenistic thought, the care of the self involves a lifelong commitment to self-creation, to getting free of who one is so that one can become something else:

> Knowledge of the self, at this level at least, is not then on the way to becoming the decipherment of the mysteries of conscience and the exegesis of the self which develops in later Christianity. Useful knowledge, knowledge in which human life is at stake, is a relational mode of knowledge that asserts and prescribes at the same time and is capable of producing a change in the subject's mode of being. (*HSLCF*: 238)

If we compare this idea with Foucault's own project of philosophy as allowing one to stray afield of oneself, the importance of the care of the self becomes evident. In both cases, the relation of subject to truth is not epistemological. It is practical, practical not in the sense of Kant's moral law nor in the everyday sense of helping navigate one's world smoothly. In many ways, it is the opposite of the latter sense of the practical. The care of the self requires one to jettison one's normal relation to the practical world in favour of one that fails to conform to the expectations that are the web of that world.

The care of the self and Foucault's straying afield are practical because they are both matters of *practice*, in two senses of that word. First, they are matters of how one relates to and engages in the social practices of which one is a part. They are not merely projects of thought; they are projects of living. Secondly, to take care of oneself or to stray afield of oneself requires practice. It requires a vigilant attention to who one is being made to be by the society around one, and an often renewed commitment to become otherwise. The ancients often engaged in what Pierre Hadot calls *spiritual exercises*, in which one repeats a variety of philosophical formulas to oneself in order to keep reminding oneself of who one wants to be and of the forces that are arrayed against one's achieving it.[1] Marcus Aurelius, for instance, often reminds himself in his *Meditations* that he will soon be dead and forgotten, so that he might stop lusting after fame. Caring for oneself and straying afield of oneself are not simply products of a single epiphany. They require constant practice and renewed commitment.

If the relation of subject to truth is in some ways common to both Foucault and the ancients, so is the goal of philosophical practice. It is, in both cases, a certain freedom, a freedom that involves abandoning some of the norms that govern the society in which one finds oneself in favour of a vision of a better way of living.

We should not, however, interpret Foucault's project as identical to that of the Stoics, or of the ancients generally. There are important differences between Foucault's idea and that of the ancient philosophers, particularly regarding the character of the freedom one seeks to exercise. Among the most important is that for the ancients, there are proper ways to live, and the care of the self is required in order to achieve them. Foucault writes in a much later period, one in which the idea of essentially proper ways to live is foreign to many, and certainly to him. So the care of the self is differently oriented. It is not in the service of a right way of living, a way of living that would, for the ancients, be inscribed in the larger cosmic order. Rather, it is in service of bringing reflective thought to bear on what one might make of oneself. One cares for oneself in the sense of having it matter what one can make of oneself, who one can create oneself to be.

In an interview during this period of his work, Foucault comments that:

> What strikes me is the fact that in our society art has become something that is related only to objects, and not to individuals, or to life. That art is something specialized, which is done only by experts who are artists. But couldn't everyone's life become a work of art? Why should the lamp or the house be an art object, but not life? (OGE: 350)

This view could not be expressed by a Stoic or a Platonic philosopher. It orients the care of the self in a direction different from that of the ancients, but at the same time it reveals a philosophical approach that concerns itself not with conditions of truth but with forms of living.

In the lectures on the care of the self, Foucault contrasts three paths for caring for oneself that arise in the ancient world. There is the Platonic path, exemplified in the dialogue *Alcibiades*, where Socrates advises the young Alcibiades to know himself in the sense of discovering or recalling who he is. There is the Hellenistic path, in which caring for oneself is a confrontation with and modification of who one is. And finally there is the Christian path, which asks one ultimately not to modify but to renounce oneself. In the second volume of the history of sexuality, published two years later than the lectures on the care of the self, Foucault turns his attention to the ancient Greek form that the care of the self takes. Here the framework is wider than that of the Platonic path described in the lectures. And yet it follows the lectures in its emphasis on three areas: dietetics, economics and erotics (although it adds a fourth area on the relation to truth). In the lectures, Foucault tells us, with regard to letters of Marcus Aurelius, "The body; the family circle and household; love. Dietetics, economics, and erotics. These are the three major domains in which the practice of the self is actualized in this period, with, as we see, constant cross-referencing from one to the other" (*HS*: 161). Two years later, this division is read back from the Stoics into the Greeks as the framework for the proper construction of a life.

Foucault offers a rich description of ancient writings concerning these three areas. Before turning to them, he introduces a term that does not appear in the lectures, but that frames the enquiry: *problematization*. Although he does not define the term, one can get a sense of it from the passage in which he introduces it:

> It is often the case that the moral solicitude is strong precisely where there is neither obligation or prohibition. In other words, the interdiction is one thing, the moral problematization is another. It seemed to me, therefore, that the question that ought to guide my inquiry was the following: how, why, and in what forms was sexuality constituted as a moral domain? Why this ethical concern that was so persistent despite its varying forms and intensity? Why this "problematization"?   (*UP*: 10)

What is a problematization? Foucault contrasts problematizations with obligations, prohibitions and interdictions. The latter three terms will be familiar to us from their role in current moral thinking. We tend to consider the moral realm precisely as one of obligations and prohibitions. We might say that we think of the moral realm as divided into three areas: the prohibited, the permitted and the required. There are, to be sure, gradations within them. For instance, there are acts that are permitted but discouraged, or forbidden except under certain exceptional circumstances. But the broad framework is one of disallowances, allowances and requirements.

However, much of the normative intervention into people's lives and behaviours does not fall under this simple rubric. If moral theory is a matter of sharp divisions, the practice of living is more often a matter of problematizations.

We might say, at a first go, that problematizations occur regarding those areas of life that are considered problematic. For an area of life to be problematic is not for it to be a problem, as in a problem to be overcome. Rather, it is for that area of life to be fraught. Instead of prohibitions there are dangers. Instead of obligations there are opportunities. Instead of allowances there are multiple ways these dangers and opportunities can be navigated. Like our traditional conception of the moral realm, a problematic realm (and, in Foucault's view, much of the moral realm is in fact a problematic one) is normatively laden. But those norms have less to do with the question of *whether* and more with the question of *how*. And, correlatively, they are less concerned with individual behaviours and more with realms of life.

Foucault's earlier works have prepared us for this idea. As he tells us in the second volume:

> There was the problematization of madness and illness arising out of social and medical practices, and defining a certain pattern of "normalization"; a problematization of life, language, and labor in discursive practices that conformed to certain "epistemic" rules; and a problematization of crime and criminal behavior emerging from certain punitive practices conforming to a "disciplinary" model.   (*UP*: 12)

We must always be careful when Foucault reads his earlier works in light of his later projects. He often reinterprets what he has done in light of his current project. Here, however, the idea of problematization captures an aspect of the trajectory of his work. Much of who we are is constituted not by allowances and prohibitions, but by norms embedded in practices that determine how we go about constructing who we are and what we know. Foucault's work, whether archaeological, genealogical, or ethical, has always been a matter of the historical investigation of norms that determine that construction.

One might want to object here that the introduction of the idea of a problematization runs afoul of the concept of power Foucault develops in his genealogical works. In *Discipline and Punish*, for instance, Foucault sees the operation of power undergoing a historical change. Before the eighteenth century, power operates on the binary model of the permitted and the forbidden. It is only in the last two hundred years that a more nuanced type of power emerges, one that can normalize or discipline subjects. By seeing problematization in an ahistorical fashion, by seeing it as something that concerns the ancients as well as the moderns, is Foucault abandoning this view of power? Is he saying that power has always been positive and creative as well as negative and restrictive? Is he moving from a more historical view to a more essentialist one?

The situation may seem to be even worse for Foucault. Not only may the introduction of the concept of problematization have removed power from history; it may even have inverted modern and pre-modern forms of power. Our current moral conception is dominated by obligations, permissions and prohibitions. Ancient morality, as Foucault stresses, is not. So it might seem that in fact the type of power associated with normalization and the disciplines is more properly seen in ancient practices than in modern ones. It is the moderns who operate by means of a repressive power while ancient practices create subjects through various problematizations.

In replying to this objection, we must first distinguish our conception of morality from our practice of it. Regarding power, Foucault writes in the first volume of the history of sexuality that:

> One remains attached to a certain image of power–law, of power–sovereignty, which was traced out by the theoreticians of right and the monarchic institution. It is this image that we must break free of, that is, of the theoretical privilege of law and sovereignty, if we wish to analyze power within the concrete and historical frame-work of its operation. (*HS*: 90)

The operation of power has changed, but our conception of it remains bound to earlier models of its operation. The same is true for morality. Our practice of morality, as Foucault's problematizations show, is more complex than our rigid division of it into three areas. This is why Foucault, particularly in his works from 1975 on, focuses on practices rather than on theories, or better, why he focuses on theories only in their role of arising out of and relating to practices.

Yet another worry might encroach here. Foucault argues that our conception of ourselves on the one hand and who we are on the other cannot be divorced. But in his view of power (and my extension of this view to morality) he seems to do precisely the opposite. He says that our political and moral views do not reflect who we have come to be. Is there a problem here? No. For Foucault, our conception of who we are comes more from our practices than from political or philosophical theory. Who we are is a matter of our practices. Who intellectuals *think* we are is often a matter of theories that, although they are connected with certain practices in their own right, are often connected with practices that have less to do with who we are than with an intellectual legacy that has more tenuous relations to the practices that actually determine us. This does not mean that those theories are entirely divorced from who we are, any more than the rise of a positive, creative form of power has entirely displaced the negative power theorized by those under the sway of power-as-sovereignty. What it means is that those theories have yet to grasp what is happening on the ground, a grasp that Foucault turns to genealogy (and then to ethics) to achieve.

With this in mind, we can turn back to the initial worry that Foucault's introduction of the concept of problematization threatens to undo the historical character of his conception of power. In considering this objection, we should first ensure that we have distinguished problematization from power. They are not the same thing, although indeed they are related. Where problematization occurs, there is indeed the possibility of a power

105

relationship, of actions constraining other actions. What do we make of the idea, then, embraced by Foucault during his genealogical period, that the operation of power is more negative and repressive in pre-modern Europe and more positive and creative (which, bear in mind, does not mean better) in modern Europe?

I believe there is a shift here in Foucault's thought, but it is less stark than it may appear. Problematization does open the door to a power that creates subjectivity, but there are limits to its ability to do so that are bound by the technology and social state of the times. Recall that in order to monitor populations in the way that bio-power seeks to, there must be certain economic conditions in place, there must be concentrations of people, and there must be the ability to collect information across populations. Or again, in order to discipline a larger group of people, one must have the technology to monitor that group. What makes negative, repressive power more prominent in pre-modern societies is, perhaps among other things, the inability to engage in certain forms of control that many types of positive, creative power require.

This does not mean that there is no creative power in ancient practices, a point that Foucault's later studies do not deny. To be sure, Foucault does not consider power in his discussion of the care of the self. In an interview from 1984, Foucault has this exchange:

> Q. Thus there has been a sort of shift: these games of truth no longer involve a coercive practice, but a practice of self-formation of the subject.

> M.F. That's right. It is what one could call an ascetic practice, taking asceticism in a very general sense – in other words, not in the sense of a morality of renunciation but as an exercise of the self on the self by which one attempts to develop and transform oneself, and to attain to a certain mode of being.   (EC: 282)

Here the distinction Foucault allows the interviewer to makes seems, at least to me, too rigid. It is not that the "games of truth" involving the care of the self do not concern power. Rather, it is that power is not the focus of Foucault's analysis. There can be power in the way one is asked to care for oneself. Problematizations open up certain paths and discourage others: they involve actions upon actions that contribute to creating certain ways of being. However, the power that inheres in these practices and that does help create its subjects may not have the same coercive force as later forms of creative power that require more technological advancement and different economic conditions.

In the preface to the second volume of the history of sexuality, where Foucault discusses the change in his approach from the one originally outlined in the first volume, he seems to see problematization as more closely entwined with power:

> To speak of sexuality as a historically singular experience also presupposed the availability of tools capable of analyzing the peculiar characteristics and interrelations of the three axes that constitute it: (1) the formation of sciences [*saviors*] that refer to it, (2) the systems of power that regulate its practice, (3) the forms within which individuals are able, are obliged, to recognize themselves as subjects of this sexuality. (*UP*: 4)

The first two "axes" are, of course, archaeology and genealogy. The third axis is what requires a chronological re-orientation, because in order to accomplish it, Foucault believes he must "analyze the practices by which individuals were led to focus their attention on themselves, to decipher, recognize, and acknowledge themselves as subjects of desire" (*ibid.*: 5).

Thinking of ethics, and with it the issue of problematizations, as an axis that intersects with the axes of archaeology and genealogy brings it in closer contact with power. This, in turn, allows that power, even creative power, can be an aspect of ancient forms of problematization. This is where there is, I think, a shift in Foucault's thought. It is where power as a creative and not merely repressive force can appear in ancient practices of living. But the shift is one of emphasis, not an overturning of a historical view of power. Foucault does not say that the creative power he describes in the genealogical works is non-existent in the pre-modern period. Rather, it emerges as the dominant form of power, the one most in need of analysis. By introducing the concept of problematization, by ascribing it a place in all his works, and by seeing it as an axis that intersects with power, he opens the door to a recognition that different types of creative power can occur in different time periods. Yet by the same token, he can also say that the more urgent forms of that power are the more recent ones, for economic, political and technological reasons.

Foucault does not say any of this, because he does not address the problem. However, it is a perspective that allows us to see both the continuity and discontinuity of the later project with the earlier ones.

With this view of problematizations in hand, we can ask how the problematization that emerges among the ancients relative to sex occurs. As Foucault has emphasized, sex in the ancient world is not yet what he would call sexuality. It does not yet stand as the secret key to open the mysteries of who one is; it is not the centrepiece of one's identity. Rather, it is embedded in a larger ethical realm, the realm of the care of the self. What is this realm like? What makes something an ethical matter? If we are to understand the ancient care of the self, we need to know in general what ethical space looks like and then more specifically how that space is filled by ancient practices.

Foucault isolates four elements of the ethical: the ethical substance, the mode of subjection, the ethical work, and the telos. Together they form the framework of ethics, or more generally of any moral practice. On this view, moral theories of the type we have already discussed, those that focus on obligations and prohibitions, would find their place within the larger realm of ethical problematization.

The ethical substance is "this or that part of himself [that the individual must determine] as the prime material of his moral conduct" (*UP*: 26). Over the course of history, different ethical substances have been determined. For instance, many modern philosophers believe that behaviour is the ethical substance. For others, like Kant, the ethical substance is the will. It need not be either of these, however. It can be the soul, or desire, or the emotions or passions.

The mode of subjection (the French here is *mode d'assujettisement*, which can be translated as mode of subjection or mode of subjectification – becoming subject to or becoming a subject – and Foucault probably has both meanings in mind) is "the way in which the individual establishes his relation to the rule and recognizes himself as obliged to put it in practice" (*UP*: 27). For instance, if I enlist to fight in a war my country has declared, I can do so for many reasons. I can enlist because I believe it is my duty as a citizen of the country to protect it; I can enlist because I owe it to my family to protect them; alternatively, my enlistment can come from my sense that the country we are fighting poses a threat to a larger world order that must be maintained, or that to refuse to fight might endanger the lives of innocent people whom I have never met but to whom I am morally obliged. In all these possibilities lies the question of my relation to what is asked of me, and in that relation I establish myself as a particular kind of ethical subject.

The ethical work is the work "that one performs on oneself, not only in order to bring one's conduct into compliance with a given rule, but to attempt to transform oneself into the ethical subject of one's behavior" (*ibid.*). If, in the mode of subjection, one establishes how the ethical has a hold on one, in the ethical work one realizes that hold through what one does. Suppose I decide that my moral net ought to be cast more widely than I have previously thought; I am obliged not only to people I care about but also to those I have not met but who are suffering in their own right. How might I establish myself as the kind of person who exhibits this obligation? I might read novels about people in other cultures who are undergoing forms of deprivation that do not affect people I know. Alternatively, I might travel to some of these cultures. Yet again, I may decide that I do not need to experience their suffering, but instead to subtract part of my weekly paypacket and give it to an organization that deals with poverty in foreign countries. All of these methods are modes of ethical work.

The last element of the ethical framework is the telos. "[A]n action is not only moral in itself, in its singularity; it is also moral in its circumstantial integration and by virtue of the place it occupies in a pattern of conduct" (*ibid.*: 27–8). The telos, we might say, is the point of moral conduct. Is one to conduct oneself morally in order to become a certain kind of individual? And if so, what kind? A person of reason, as Kant would have it? A man of self-mastery, as will be the case for the ancient Greeks? A person of virtue? Or is the point of moral conduct instead to contribute to a certain kind of world, as the utilitarians would have it? In each case there is an ethical vision involved, a goal towards which the instances of conduct that establish or express certain relations to a particular ethical substance are directed. That goal is the ethical telos.

Together these elements form the framework of ethical action. As Foucault notes, in all of these there are matters of conduct and practices of self-formation. Modern moral views tend to emphasize the conduct over the self-formation, while the ancients tend in the other direction. For instance, modern moral philosophers more often think of the ethical work in terms of what one does to accomplish moral goals than in terms of who one becomes by the conduct one engages in. In that way, there can arise the emphasis on the permitted and the forbidden that seems to many to be the heart of modern ethics. If Foucault's characterization of the ethical is right, however, that emphasis takes place within a larger framework of practice that has other elements that are formative of ethical subjects but that may not be theorized as clearly. Otherwise put, ethical practice may outrun ethical theory, just as certain modern practices of power lie beyond the theories of power meant to account for power's operation.

Ethics in Ancient Greece

If this is the general shape of ethical space, or alternatively of the historical trajectory of ethical problematization, then we are prepared to ask what that shape looks like for the ancients. In particular, Foucault is concerned with that shape as it bears upon sex. Sex is not in itself a separate problematic area in ancient living, an area with its own particular ethical problematization. Rather, it is part of the larger arena of pleasures, of *aphrodisia*. Foucault leaves the term *aphrodisia* untranslated; he uses it as a term of art. Broadly, it has to do with pleasures associated with certain types of activity. Not only sex, but also food, wine, and relations with boys are activities associated with *aphrodisia*. What all these activities have in common is that they involve an intense pleasure, one that could tempt a person toward excessive indulgence. Excessive indulgence, in turn, upsets the natural order of living.

For the Greeks, *aphrodisiac* pleasures are not morally suspect in themselves, as they will be later for Christian practitioners, but they are inferior. The activities from which these pleasures arise are not among the noble activities. *Aphrodisiac* pleasures have a role in one's living, but it is a secondary role. The intensity of these pleasures, however, threatens to make them a primary focus of one's life. Although they are secondary in the proper order of living, they may become a primary focus of attention:

> It was just this acuteness of pleasure, together with the attraction it exerts on desire, that caused sexual activity to go beyond the limits that were set by nature when she made the pleasure of the *aphrodisia* an inferior, subordinate, and conditioned pleasure. Because of this intensity, people were induced to overturn the hierarchy, placing these appetites and their satisfaction uppermost, and giving them absolute power over the soul. (UP: 49)

How, then, is a person to approach the pleasures of *aphrodisia*, of which sex is an element rather than the whole? In Christian thought, the approach will be centred on renunciation. *Aphrodisia* will be associated with temptation and therefore with sin; the ethical relation to the pleasures of *aphrodisia* must then become one of abandonment, or, barring that, marginalization. One can begin to see here the birth of a conflicted attitude toward sex, one that remains with us today: if sex involves a tainted pleasure, but is yet an unavoidable activity, then indulgence in it is at once necessary and indecent. Necessary because of procreation, indecent because of the inescapably impure pleasure it entails. The Greek attitude toward such pleasures is more measured. Renunciation is not the proper relation to them; rather, it is knowing how and when to indulge.

Foucault isolates three elements in the know-how of one's proper relation to *aphrodisiac* pleasures: need, timeliness and status. There is no shame in sex; there is, however, a shame in overindulgence. One needs to engage moderately. One should be guided in one's sexual relations, as in one's culinary activity and one's consumption of wine, by need. Where the need is not urgent, one should refrain. That way, control remains with the subject of pleasures – the individual – and not with the pleasures themselves. Again, there are right and wrong times to engage in the activities that yield *aphrodisia*: times of day, times of the month, times of the year. Physicians in particular are concerned with understanding the proper rhythms of *aphrodisiac* indulgence. Finally, there is a concern with the status of those who indulge that is perhaps most foreign to us now. Particularly in men's relations with boys, issues of the class status of the partners, the positions taken during sexual activity (active or passive), and the age of the participants become matters of reflection in order to determine their proper levels and balance.

If moderation is the proper relation to *aphrodisia*, then the person who is capable of moderation is the person who can control his (in the Greek case, the ethics involved only concern men) desires. One must become a master of oneself. "One could behave ethically only by adopting a combative attitude toward the pleasures . . . These forces could not be used in the moderate way that was fitting for them unless one was capable of opposing, resisting, and subduing them" (*UP*: 66). This idea of mastery and particularly the image of battle against pleasures may sound Christian. It has a different inflection, though. In Christianity, one masters these pleasures because they are, ultimately, to be renounced. They are not to be controlled but to be, in so far as possible, abandoned. As will later become the Christian (and then Cartesian) approach, the pleasures of *aphrodisia* are pleasures of the body. Since the body is immersed in sin, one must seek to overcome its pleasures to the extent that it is in one's power to do so.

None of this characterizes the Greek approach to mastery. The pleasures of *aphrodisia* may be fraught, they may be dangerous, but their dangers are not matters of sin. They are not irremediably indecent. Instead, the dangers of *aphrodisia* have to do with upsetting the natural order of pleasures and activities. Self-mastery does not require renunciation. *Aphrodisia* remains, but it remains under the control of the subject of its pleasures. Foucault refers to images used to describe this mastery, for instance Plato's image of the team of horses with its driver or Aristotle's discussion of the child in relation to the adult. It is not necessary to kill the horses or the child, but instead to ensure that they remain under one's direction and control.

What does this self-mastery yield? It yields a sort of freedom. Freedom is the goal of the ethical relation to *aphrodisia*. This freedom is not, as we moderns may think, either a freedom from deterministic forces or from political oppression. It is a freedom in the self's relation to the self. "This individual freedom should not . . . be understood as the independence of a free will. Its polar opposite was not a natural determinism, nor was it the will of an all-powerful agency: it was enslavement – the enslavement of oneself by oneself" (*UP*: 79). As Foucault points out, this freedom is "virile" in character. It is active rather than passive, and involves power rather than the mere absence of coercion.

In this sense, the Greek approach to freedom and self-mastery brings together two qualities that often appear dissociated to us now: virility and moderation. We often think of virility as a matter of imposing one's will. The virile man bends others to his desire. Moderation, on the other hand, requires one to refrain rather than to impose. Combined in the same person, however, virility and moderation become a mastery of self, an imposing of one's will by means of moderating one's desires. This, in Foucault's view, is the Greek approach to ethics.

In this approach we can see the four elements of ethics Foucault cites. The ethical substance is *aphrodisia*. It is that part of the person that is the subject of ethical reflection and practice. The mode of subjection is the knowing-how associated with need, time and status. It forms what Foucault calls a type of *savior-faire*; instead of being a set of permissions and prohibitions, it forms a sense of how to navigate among dangerous but not necessarily impure desires. The ethical work is the battle itself, the training and effort required to bring the promised pleasures of *aphrodisia* under one's control. The telos is freedom.

Returning to themes from the 1982 lectures, Foucault claims that the self-mastery sought by the ancient Greeks is aligned with a particular form of truth. For Plato, for instance, in order to master oneself properly one has to know oneself, to recollect who one is. Again, we should not confuse the philosophical relation to truth here with the relation that has come down to us through what Foucault calls "the Cartesian moment". It is not a matter of epistemology, of understanding the conditions of the subject's relation to knowledge. It is a practical relation, a relation to truth as one of the conditions for a person to achieve freedom. The ancient relation to truth is subsumed under the larger project of the care of the self. It is not that the truth of things independent of oneself does not matter. Rather, it is that that truth matters in as much as it bears on one's relation to oneself. One of the current criticisms of contemporary philosophy is that it concerns itself with matters that are of interest only to the specialist; it is divorced from how we actually live. Not so ancient philosophy, in Foucault's view, since the project of ancient philosophy is nothing other than the articulation of proper ways to live.

In this relation to truth, Foucault discovers what he calls an aesthetics of existence. He contrasts this to the hermeneutics of desire of later Christian practice:

> Now, while this relation to truth, constitutive of the moderate subject, did not lead to a hermeneutics of desire, it did on the other hand open onto an aesthetics of existence. And what I mean by this is a way of life whose moral value did not depend either on one's

being in conformity with a code of behavior, or on an effort of purification, but on certain formal principles in the use of pleasures, in the way one distributed them, in the limits one observed, in the hierarchy one respected.   (*UP*: 89)

We can recall the hermeneutic of the self from the first volume of the history of sexuality. There one learns to confess who one is, in order to learn one's nature. Central to this is, of course, the confession of one's sexual desire. In contrast, the truth of ancient thought is bound, not to a hermeneutics, not to an interpretation of who one is through a reading of one's desire, but to the project of learning how to live.

One might ask here whether the hermeneutics of desire that Foucault discovers in Christianity is to be found in its earlier versions. This would seem to be a revision of his view from the first volume, where he sees it arising in response to the Reformation. He does not address this issue, but I do not believe a revision is necessary here. The confessional is, throughout its history, skewed towards even if not exactly a hermeneutics. Even when it is only a matter of saying what one does, those doings are still one's own. To confess them is to put oneself before another in the context of the larger project of renunciation or purification. Later, when what is required is the confession of desire, the hermeneutic character of the confessional becomes central. But the structure of the confessional is never far from a hermeneutics.

This confessional structure is distant from the ancient project that relates truth not to what one tells but to what one learns. As Foucault puts it in the 1982 lectures:

Now the subject's obligation to tell the truth about himself . . . did not exist at all in Greek, Hellenistic, or Roman Antiquity. The person who is led to tell the truth through the master's discourse does not have to say the truth about himself. He does not even have to say the truth. And since he does not have to say the truth, he does not have to speak.   (*HSLCF*: 364)

In the confessional, one tells the truth; in ancient practice, one learns it.

This learning takes place in four areas: dietetics, economics, erotics, and in relation to truth. Dietetics is not only about diet but concerns the general health regimen. A proper health regimen requires moderation and timeliness. Foucault suggests that there are two types of attention paid to dietetics, a "serial" vigilance and a "circumstantial" one. The serial vigilance concerns the order in which activities are performed: "activities were not simply good or bad in themselves; their value was determined in part by those that preceded them and those that followed" (*UP*: 106). Circumstantial vigilance requires an awareness of the circumstances in which the activity is to take place: "the climate of course, the seasons, the hours of the day, the degree of humidity and dryness, of heat or cold, the winds, the characteristic features of a region, the layout of a city" (*ibid.*). One must, in engaging in a proper health regimen, follow a reasonable order of activities. It is imperative not engage in excessive or deficient exercise, sex, or eating; to be aware of where and when the *aphrodisiac* pleasures are to take place; and at all times to maintain control over oneself in any engagement.

If sex has a distinctive character in ancient dietetics, it is because it, more than other activities, is associated with violence, expenditure and death. The sexual act is a violent one, involving a surge of spasmodic activity that threatens a person's self-mastery. It also involves expenditure. Sex involves the imparting of life-giving forces; they are transferred from oneself to another, and thus entail an expenditure of one's own life forces. Finally, there is in Greek thought an association of sex with death (as there is in the French language, orgasm being *le petit-mort*). Just as sex brings life, that bringing of life is in recompense for lives that are passing away. In regard to the dietetics of sex, Foucault concludes that:

> The sexual act did not occasion anxiety because it was associated with evil but because it disturbed and threatened the individual's relation with himself and his integrity as an ethical subject in the making; if it was not properly measured and distributed, it carried the threat of a breaking forth of involuntary forces, a lessening of energy, and death without honorable descendents.   (*UP*: 136–7)

Economics in ancient thought concerns the running of the household. For the ancients, of course, the man is the proper ruler of the household. This idea extends further among the Greeks to a lack of symmetry (with Plato an exception here) regarding household obligations. It is not just that there are different duties involved for the husband and wife. The nature of obligation is different. The woman is obliged to the husband, but the husband is obliged to himself. The project of the wife centres on fidelity, whereas for the husband it concerns self-mastery. Thus it is that if adultery is a wrong, it is not because a man has betrayed his wife; rather, it is because a wife has betrayed her husband and because another man has betrayed his civic duty toward that husband. In sum, then:

> The husband is self-obligated in this respect, since the fact of being married commits him to a particular interplay of duties and

114

demands in which his reputation, his relation to others, his prestige in the city, and his willingness to lead a fine and good existence are at stake. (*ibid*.: 182–3)

Erotics is the most vexed of the *aphrodisiac* activities. This has to do in particular with the fact that it concerns love between men, and between men and adolescent boys. For Christianity, the problematization of sex is centred on the woman, but, for reasons just mentioned, the problematization of sex among the ancient Greeks does not arise there. It arises in the sexual relations between males. On the one hand, these relations are characterized by equality, since each of the partners is an equal citizen of the city. On the other hand, since the ethical requirement placed on each is one of an active self-mastery, the issue of passivity becomes more urgent. The reason is that sex, for the ancient Greeks, is indissociable from penetration. Penetration requires an active subject and a passive subject. To become penetrated is to become dominated, to be mastered instead of master. This in itself is a dishonour, but the dishonour extends to questioning one's ability to govern oneself and even more generally to taking one's proper place in the governance of the city. "When one played the role of subordinate partner in the game of pleasure relations, one could not be truly dominant in the game of civic and political activity" (*ibid*.: 220).

This question becomes even more complex when the issue is one of sexual relations between men and adolescent boys. On the one hand, boys, like women, are objects of beauty, and can be appreciated and approached as such. On the other hand, boys are to become men, free citizens of the city-state. For a boy to allow himself to be dominated by another male is to imperil both his integrity and his reputation among fellow citizens. This seems to put the boy in a paradoxical situation where neither acceptance nor refusal can operate without leaving an unseemly remainder.

We can begin to see here why, although the Greeks engage in rather than prohibit sex between men, their ethical problematization of this sex does not provide a contemporary model for Foucault. Not only, as he indicates, is there no possibility of a return to earlier models of living. In addition, there is an irresolvable contradiction that lies at the heart of this problematization, "namely, the difficulty caused, in this society that accepted sexual relations between men, by the juxtaposition of an ethos of male superiority and a conception of all sexual intercourse in terms of the schema of penetration and male domination" (*ibid*.).

Foucault's treatment of the relation of sex and truth is more clipped, drawing from Plato and particularly from the *Symposium*. He suggests that the question of truth in regard to sexuality is one of true love. It arises in the relation between men and boys, since women are not considered equals and so are unable to rise to the occasion of true love. For Plato, however, the question of true love is transformed, in Socrates' hands, into the question of the nature of love. It becomes a reflection on Eros. This leads Socrates to endorse a love that is removed from physical relations between people and turns toward a love of higher things. This turn presages the later Christian privileging of renunciation, although it does so not as much through what it rejects as through what it seeks.

The third volume of the history of sexuality extends the themes of the second volume into the first two centuries of our era. We will not follow this extension in detail here. In the 1982 lectures, Foucault offers a more detailed discussion of the care of the self in general. The third volume on sexuality focuses on the care of the self as it bears on sex, particularly in regard to health, marriage, and the relation to boys. Foucault summarizes the changes from the Greek approach to these matters:

> A mistrust of the pleasures, an emphasis on the consequences of their abuse for the body and the soul, a valorization of marriage and marital obligations, a disaffection with regard to the spiritual meanings imputed to the love of boys: a whole attitude of severity was manifested in the thinking of philosophers and physicians in the course of the first two centuries. (CS: 39)

These changes may sound Christian, and indeed early Christianity draws from them. However, they appear in a Hellenistic context that inflects their meaning toward a form of self-cultivation rather than self-denial.

Foucault notes that these changes stem in good part from a different view of marriage and marital obligations on the one hand and a different political situation (Imperial Rome as opposed to the Greek city-state) on the other. The transformation of the view of marriage is one in which the wife becomes a more relevant factor, therefore beginning to shift the basis of love from that between males to that between a male and a female. Regarding politics, there are a number of modifications, including the complex bureaucratic institutions for governance that Rome develops. These replace the more personal democratic institutions of the Greek city-state, and require changes not only in the public sphere but also in the economic sphere and the interpersonal one.

Foucault's last two volumes on the history of sexuality are published just before his death. They have been welcomed by many scholars of ancient thought, if for no other reason than they confer on ancient studies the cachet associated with Foucault's name. Because Foucault is not, as he openly admits, a scholar of ancient thought, one might ask after the accuracy of his interpretations of Greek and Hellenistic texts and the contexts in which they are written. Perhaps the most trenchant criticism of his reading emerges from the French scholar Pierre Hadot, whom Foucault takes as a model for his own orientation toward the ancient texts.

One of Hadot's most important contributions to the study of ancient philosophy lies in his idea that ancient philosophy is centred on the question of how one should live.[2] Ancient philosophy is not, as anachronistic interpretations would have it, a project of interpreting the world. It is a matter of figuring out how one should conduct one's life. Therefore, philosophers are not limited to those who have particular doctrines they defend. A philosopher, in the ancient world, is anyone who conducts his life according to a proper doctrine of how one should live. To approach ancient thought this way opens it not only to a different interpretation but also to a different philosophical sensibility. One no longer asks whether the doctrine is correct in the sense of having explanatory power. Instead, one asks whether it provides a compelling picture of how a life should be conducted.

The affinities Foucault finds with Hadot's approach are obvious. Not only is Foucault's general method of focusing on knowledge as it arises with practices convergent with Hadot's work; his specific treatment of ancient philosophy, philosophy before the Cartesian moment, as a matter of the care of the self is in line with Hadot's. Indeed, Foucault credits Hadot's work as an influence on his own reading of the ancients.[3] In turn, Hadot has written an article, "Reflections on the Idea of the 'Cultivation of the Self'" that offers his assessment of Foucault's approach.[4]

Hadot, of course, is in sympathy with Foucault's emphasis on the care of the self and on his approach to ancient texts through practices rather than through abstract reflection. However, in Hadot's eyes Foucault misses a crucial element of ancient thought, one that renders Foucault's interpretation anachronistic in its own way. For the ancients, the care of the self is not directed solely toward one's self-development. There is a larger cosmic context within which one cares for oneself, and the goal of such care is to be in accord with that larger context. The universe has a structure and, for many ancient thinkers, a telos – a goal. To live properly is to live in accordance with that structure or to contribute in the right way to that telos. For instance, the Stoics think that the unfolding of the cosmos is a display of reason; the universe, although always in flux, accords with a rational principle. We might say that the universe expresses Reason, with all the connotations the capital letter brings with it. In being caught up in the everyday concerns of one's life, one neglects or is blind to that Reason and therefore does not live in the proper relation to it. The point of caring for oneself, for the ancients, is to be able to attune oneself to the larger context in which one lives.

To put the point another way, it is not freedom, as Foucault would have it, but objectively proper living that is the telos of ancient practices of the self. Hadot says:

> One seeks to be one's own master, to possess oneself, and find one's happiness in freedom and inner independence. I concur on all these points. I do think, however, that this movement of inter-iorization is inseparably linked to another movement, whereby one rises to a higher psychic level . . . which consists in becoming aware of oneself as a part of nature, and a portion of universal reason.[5]

Foucault, as a product of twentieth-century thinking, fails to recognize the larger cosmic framework assumed by the ancients. In the wake of Nietzsche and others who pronounce and work within the context of the death of God, Foucault forgets that for the ancients the existence of such a frame-work is inseparable from their thought.

If Hadot has the proper interpretation here, and Foucault admits that he is no scholar of ancient thought, what difference would this make for our relation to the last two volumes of the history of sexuality? It would intro-duce a greater distance between our lives and those of the ancients. To the degree that we do not see the universe governed by the type of Reason or natural hierarchy or cosmic order characteristic of the ancients, we are less likely to make ancient living a model for our own. Is this a problem for Foucault? In one way no and in another way yes. Foucault is clear, as we have seen, that he does not take the ancients as a model for contemporary living. He describes their lives in such a way as to loosen the grip ours have on us. His project is motivated, as he puts it, by "the only kind of curiosity, in any case, that is worth acting upon with a degree of obstinacy . . . that which enables one to get free of oneself". It is not because we should follow the ancients that he seeks to understand their lives, but because they allow him to see the contingency of our own self-understanding. In this sense, his failure to recognize the larger universal context they assume in their living is nothing more than an interpretative mistake that needs correction.

There is a sense, however, in which the error Hadot ascribes to Foucault does cause his project a difficulty, or at least introduces a cautionary note. It is clear that Foucault is attracted by the orientation of the care of the self. He finds it an attractive alternative to the current philosophical orientation, an orientation driven by concerns that are divorced from the question of how a life might go. When he complains that we think of objects, but not lives, as works of art, he is suggesting that the care of the self, self-cultivation, may be a way of introducing aesthetic considerations into the conduct of living. Indeed, he calls the ancient Greek attitude an aesthetics of existence. And perhaps the reason he neglects to consider the wider cosmic context in which the ancients think is that he seeks to bring the idea of the care of the self closer to us. If the ancients do not provide a model for living, at least we can borrow and rework for our purposes an important element of their philosophical approach.

If Hadot's reservations are right, then we must be circumspect in that borrowing and reworking. We cannot simply remove the orientation and apply it to our lives, because that orientation brings with it an assumption (or set of assumptions) that we can no longer embrace. This does not mean that we cannot use the orientation at all; but it does mean that we must be careful. We must see the orientation provided by the care of the self for what it is in the ancient world; and if we are to adopt elements of the philosophical orientation it provides, we must recognize the opportunities and dangers of the transformation we shall be putting it through. This vigilance is not foreign to Foucault's thought. It is he, after all, who calls our attention to details that more general discussions often miss. In this case, we must apply his criterion to his own work, with all the caution this implies.

It remains for us in this chapter to assess Foucault's work on ethics in the light of the five characteristics I have suggested lie at the core of his thought. All five characteristics are in evidence, although at times in different ways from the way they appear in some of the earlier works. First, it is clear, as is the case across the trajectory of Foucault's work, that the determination of who the ancients are is a collective one. Although the evidence for how that determination works is more scant than in recent history – at times Foucault's interpretations are based on the few extant texts that address a particular problem – he always assumes that these texts are reflective of a broader social and historical context. It is not what individuals recommend but how a people approaches life that interests him. That is why he focuses on problematizations. His task is to discover, in regard to sex, the normative issues the ancient Greeks and then the Romans face, and what paths are open to navigate them.

If Foucault retains a commitment to collective determination, however, there is a different inflection in his later work. We might, at the risk of oversimplifying, say that this collective determination is more inflected toward a collective *self*-determination. In the archaeological works, there is no discussion of how the determination of who we are happens. This is because of his focus on historical discontinuity. In the genealogical works, there is more of a causal story, but that story involves power. In the ethical writings the introduction of concepts like care of the self and self-cultivation seem to lend a sense of self-control to people's construction of who they are that is missing up until that point. In fact, many critics of Foucault's early writings have been sympathetic to the later ones. They take Foucault as finally conceding the importance of the role of subjectivity that is missing from both archaeology and genealogy.

My own view is that it is easy to overstate the differences between the earlier and later works on this point. To be sure, the idea of the care of the self and the orientation toward self-making appear more prominently in the writings on ancient thought. However, this is primarily because, in Foucault's view, the care of the self provides the framework for the ancients' view of their relation to their lives. If, as the genealogical writings suggest, we often see ourselves through the lens of psychology, the ancients often see themselves through the lens of self-care. The ancients are no more – and, just as important, no less – able to jettison their collective determination than we are.

This is not to deny that Foucault believes that there can be fruitful borrowing from the ancient framework for thinking about our lives. However, that borrowing will be in the service of living otherwise than we do now. And that project, the project of living otherwise, is never far from Foucault's writings. When he engages in genealogy, for instance, he does so with the goal of showing us that since who we are now is the product of a contingent history, living otherwise is always available to us. Perhaps, then, the difference between the ethics and the earlier works is that the ethical works, in addition to providing alternative views of how people have lived, offer positive elements to be appropriated. It is not that Foucault has rediscovered the subject. The constitution of who we are, the construction of the subject, is always, for him, both collective and contingent. Rather, it is that the orientation of his writings is less overtly critical than it is of our more recent history.

These considerations also address the second characteristic of Foucault's thought, that who we are is not just something we can shake off. This is as true of the ancients, with their care of the self, as it is of us. If, as we have seen, power operates differently in the ancient world, that is not because there is no power but because the forms it takes correspond to the social, economic, and technological orientation and capacities of the time. Foucault does not argue that the ancient Greeks or Romans are freer than we are now. Nor does he argue that they are less free. When Foucault discusses freedom his concern is not the more and the less. The question of free will and determinism is not a touchstone of his thought. That we cannot *easily* shake off the determinations of our history is a central commitment of his thought. But that those determinations are contingent and therefore can be shaken off is just as central a commitment. Whether, ultimately, this shaking off is a matter of free will or another form of determinism is a question that does not interest him.

The determination of ancient Greek and Roman lives is as complex in the ethical works as it is in the earlier studies. Who they are is not the result of a single overarching or underlying theme. It is the product of a network of interacting practices and concerns. Those practices and concerns converge on problematizations that are difficult to navigate and sometimes, as in the case of Greek male sex, paradoxical or contradictory. Moreover, the last two volumes of the history of sexuality are not discussions of Greek life per se, but rather of a single thread in that life, the thread of sex. Foucault holds that thread to be of great moment in the fabric of ancient life. But he nowhere argues that ancient life can be understood solely by reference to sex or that the problematizations of sex are the only problematizations in the ancient world. To the contrary: if we are to believe the lessons of the first volume, the attempt to make sex the pivot of understanding who one is is precisely the project of normalization that Foucault seeks to overturn.

In the archaeological works the question of complexity is a vexed one. To be sure, the archives Foucault describes are complex. The rules and norms he discovers in them are elusive and difficult to isolate from the practices and texts he studies. On the other hand, the question of generality haunts his archaeological writings. He seems uncertain about the extent to which the themes he unfolds are supposed to be characteristic of a larger social or cultural context. By contrast, the genealogical works are clearly limited in scope. Who we are is a product, not of a single set of themes, but of different intersections of diverse practices that follow a complex and contingent historical trajectory. Discipline is one theme, bio-power another. In the genealogical writings, Foucault holds to Berger's dictum that we can no longer tell a story as though it were the only one.

The last two volumes of the history of sexuality, although they treat a single theme, do not betray the lesson of genealogy. They remain faithful to the idea that who we are is a product of a complex history that cannot be reduced to a dominant theme or movement or process. There is no Archimedean point for understanding the ancients any more than there is for understanding ourselves.

The fourth characteristic of Foucault's thought, the intimacy of acting and knowing, is on full display in the ethical works. If one is not careful, one might be tempted to say that the ethical works show a more intimate bond between action and knowledge than the earlier works. This would be a mistake, although there is a right idea in it. Foucault's argument is not that the ancients *have* a deeper bond between their truths and their lives, but rather that they *see themselves* as having a deep bond. The philosophical truths with which the ancients are concerned contribute to the care of the self. Those who practise such a care are drawn to the truths that will assist them in that practice.

Compare this with the psychological truths characteristic of the disciplinary regime. On the one hand there is no formal project of self-care characteristic of the ancients, either in psychology or in philosophy. On the other hand, and more important, one sees who one is and how one should act in terms of the psychological truths that form the epistemic framework of discipline. One may not see oneself as constructing a life in the same way as the ancient Greeks; but one is concerned with being normal and conforming to the psychological concerns that preoccupy the carceral archipelago. The difference here is less than it might seem from a standpoint that sees a stark division between genealogy and ethics. It is less than it might seem if we draw too sharp a line between constitution and self-constitution. As Foucault reminds us with the concept of problematization, beyond the morality of duties and obligations there are always spheres of behaviour that are the object of scrutiny, ambivalence and uncertainty. It is not that the ancients face problematizations and we moderns do not. Rather, it is that different problematizations face each. One of the important problematizations for the ancients concerns sex in its role in the care of the self; for the moderns it concerns one's psychological state or one's sexual desire in relation to normality.

The last characteristic of Foucault's thought is that of the historical contingency of who we are. We have already seen the operation of this contingency in the discussion of our collective determination. In that discussion, the theme of freedom was broached. It is perhaps fitting to end a consideration of Foucault's treatment of the ancients with a discussion of the role of freedom in his thought.

There are many who see in Foucault, particularly in his genealogical works, a political fatalism. Everything is a matter of power, the product of unseen forces insidiously determining who we are. There is no reason to struggle, and no point in struggling anyway, since we shall only wind up in another nexus of power. Among those who see Foucault's earlier works this way, there is often a sigh of relief that greets the appearance of the ethical works. After all, here we are faced with a subject that can create itself, make something of itself, rather than being merely a node in an evolving system of power.

However, there is no great divide between the earlier works and the later ones. The concept of problematization should make that clear. Foucault nowhere argues that our lives are completely circumscribed by the archives he describes in the archaeological works or the powers he recounts in the genealogical ones. Conversely, he nowhere claims that the care of the self is free from the constraints of the practices and norms of the time. Quite the opposite. To ask whether Foucault sees us as having free will or as being completely determined by the contexts, rules, norms and powers he describes is to ask the wrong question. It is to impose the free will debate on a set of texts for which it is irrelevant. This is not to say that the debate itself is not important, or that its results do not have an impact on how we see Foucault's works. Rather, it is to say that Foucault's writings cannot be read through the lens of that debate without distorting them.

What, then, are we to make of the idea of freedom? How does it apply to Foucault's works, if at all? There are two separate questions we might ask here, only one of which we shall answer. One question concerns the normative status of the term *freedom*. How does Foucault justify his criticism of disciplinary power or his embrace of the care of the self or an aesthetics of living as an exercise in freedom? What reasons can he give us for valuing the latter and not the former? Is it simply a matter of personal preference, and if not, why not? If certain forms of power must be abandoned and others not, how do we mark the difference between the two? These are difficult questions, ones that Foucault's writings do not address, except perhaps to invoke the term *intolerable* with regard to particular practices or power arrangements. They are questions we cannot address here without taking the discussion too far afield, but are certainly worth the asking.[6]

The other question is, what does this freedom consist in? If it is not a matter of carving out a space of free will, then what are we to make of the freedom Foucault's works seek to offer us? One hint for understanding it relies on returning to Foucault's reference in the preface to the second volume on sexuality to curiosity. Curiosity, in Foucault's sense, means straying afield of oneself. Freedom, for Foucault, lies in this straying afield of who one is. But what is this straying?

Our history yields a particular complex of practices with their rules, norms, problematizations, knowledges and power arrangements. Each of us participates in some of those practices. By participating in them we subject ourselves to some of those rules, norms, problematizations, knowledges and power arrangements. That is how we become who we are. Our practices are laden with a politically, ethically and epistemically charged history that infuses us through the practices we engage in. What Foucault describes with different inflections in all his works are important moments and elements of that history. It is a history that is at once constitutive and contingent: it makes us who we are, but not by necessity. If we understand our history, understand who we have come to be, and understand that we do not have to be *that*, then we are faced with the possibility of being something else. That is our freedom.

We must be clear here. To say that we can be something else is not to say that we can be anything else. We cannot simply choose who we are to be. The recognition of how we have come to be who we are does not eliminate the history that has brought us here. It does not eliminate the context in which we choose, nor the constraints that context imposes. Moreover, the complexity of our historical legacy allows us to question some areas of our lives, but not all of them at the same time. We may question aspects of who we have come to be, but we cannot step outside ourselves, leap from our own historical skin to choose our lives from some vantage point beyond the vagaries of our history and context. To stray afield of oneself is not to recreate oneself out of whole cloth. Rather, it is to experiment with who one might be, to try other ways of being that may turn out to be more tolerable than who we are now. In Foucault's writings, and in his life, the theme of experimentation as an alternative to being who we are now is salient. To stray afield of ourselves is precisely to experiment with who we might be.

What characterizes experimentation is its probing and tentative character. When we experiment with who we might be we do so in the knowledge either that we might fail or, alternatively, that we might succeed. only to find that our success has created another form of intolerability. After all, the intersection of practices that has brought us to this point was not intended to deliver us here. Discipline and bio-power are not the products of design, but of a history that could very well have been otherwise. In the interview where Foucault denies that he sees the Greeks as providing a model for contemporary living, he tells us:

> My point is not that everything is bad, but that everything is dangerous, which is not exactly the same as bad. If everything is dangerous, then we always have something to do. So my position leads not to apathy but to a hyper- and pessimistic activism.
>
> (OGE: 343)

If everything is dangerous, if everything is capable of yielding the intolerable, then we must be vigilant not only about who we have come to be but also about who we seek to make ourselves to be. We must look as we create, taking account not only of what we intend but of what actually happens. We must bear in mind Foucault's dictum that people often know what they do and why they do it, but not what their doing it does. This is what it means to treat a life as an experiment.

To be free is to be able to experiment with who we are. It is to be able to make ourselves into something other than what we have come to be: to play with, overturn, undercut, rearrange, parody, go beyond the legacy that we are. And to do so is mostly, if not always or completely, a collective project. Freedom occurs as a *we*, not as an *I*. It should be clear to us why this is. If our determination is collective, if who we are is a product of a history we share with others, then any form of experimentation is likely to take place alongside others as well. It is difficult, although perhaps not impossible, to imagine that a single person can succeed in straying afield of themselves when the rest of the social field in which they are immersed remains unchanged. Even to engage in solitary activities – writing or painting, for instance – is to respond to current social norms and expectations, if perhaps through rejecting them. And it is to imagine others who are willing to engage with one's own efforts either through reading or viewing or writing or painting in turn.

To experiment requires that there are others who are willing to experiment, that there is a *we* willing to jettison the intolerable for something that is perhaps better. The freedom to become who we might be is, like the history that brought us here, at once collective and contingent. As there is neither necessity nor individuality to our historical inheritance, so there is neither to our freedom. We face our possibilities as a darkly lit path, together with those who are willing to travel it with us.

CHAPTER FIVE
Coda: Foucault's own straying afield

Do not ask me who I am and do not ask me to remain the same: leave it to our bureaucrats and our police to see that our papers are in order.

How is one to say something about Foucault's life in the wake of this request? Can one say anything at all without betraying him? Or are we to dwell within the irony that this thinker who told us so much about who we are now and opened doors to our asking who we might be is someone about whom we are barred from asking who he was?

We cannot do biography. This much is clear. We cannot say, Foucault is *this*; he is not *that*. Or better, if we want to say who Foucault is, we need look no further than his writings. There he seeks to tell us who we are, who we are now, and he among us. History, not psychology, is what is required to know who we are, and to know the contingency of that *who*, so we can make ourselves into something else: so that we can take care of ourselves, mould ourselves into a work of art.

We cannot place Foucault neatly in a set of psychological categories and think we have remained within the ambit of his own thought. And yet, in the wake of this last chapter, in the personal seeking his thought displays there, perhaps there is a way to say something about him that would reveal a bit about his own self-creation without placing him within an epistemic framework that his works constitute a constant struggle to abandon.

This much alone for standard biography: Foucault was born in 1926, and died in 1984. From here, let us ask instead who he made himself to be. We may ask this in many ways, but we shall let three suffice here. Foucault made himself a writer, a political activist, a sexual experimenter. There is more we could say, and some biographers have attempted it.[1] Our interest here is not in canvassing a life, but in seeing in Foucault's life an answer to the question of who one might be, how one might stray afield of oneself, given who one has been made to be.

126

First, a writer. This is the most obvious aspect of who Foucault makes himself to be, and for that reason the one whose implications we are most likely to miss. When Foucault tells us late in his life that he writes to stray afield of himself, this is in keeping with the quotation from fifteen years earlier that opens this chapter's coda. We know the aim of his writing: to tell us who we are now in its contingency, and this in order to open the question of who we might be. But what might this have to do with Foucault himself, the writer? Is he lost to his writings? Are they projects whose motivation lies solely with their intended effect on his audience?

Hardly. This is not how it is when one writes, or at least when one writes anything worthwhile. To write about who we are, who we have come to be, is not only to recount a history; it is to undergo it, to feel its movement, as well as its contingency, viscerally. When Foucault says he writes to become something other than what he is, this is not only as a *result* of the writing. It is not something that only comes afterwards, when the work is completed, when it is whole, when the words have been said. To think otherwise is to see a writer above his writing rather than within it. Foucault makes clear, however, that his writing is always an experiment, a way of making himself into something. It is a way of making himself into something other than he is.

In his writing, Foucault's present both emerges in its fullness and loses its grip upon him. That is where the power of the writing lies. It is not just a fantasy. It is not just that Foucault frees himself in his head by writing. He does not merely take a journey, if a true journey, on a personal intellectual itinerary. If our present has us in its grasp, if it can make us believe that who we are is who we must be, this is not solely by convincing us with arguments. It is not solely cognitive; it is affective as well. Maybe even more so. To see the present in its contingency, then, is not just to recognize it by argument, or by history. It is to feel it. And that is where the writing assumes its significance.

For Foucault, writing is not only a matter of telling us histories we should know. It is not only telling himself such histories. It is, for him, to undergo those histories affectively. It is to navigate the currents that have brought us here, and to see first-hand, not only with his mind but with the rest of his body, the openings that appear among those currents. Writing is a matter not only of telling himself what he needs to know in order to take care of himself. It is itself a way of taking care of himself, of making himself by means of straying afield of himself.

For some writers, this is enough. Foucault's colleague Deleuze responds to a critic who mocks him for writing about journeys he does not take, "If I stick where I am, if I don't travel around, like anyone else I make my inner journeys that I can only measure by my emotions, and express very obliquely in what I write."[2] This is not Foucault's way. To write is indeed to make oneself into something else. There are other ways as well, and Foucault chooses some of them.

For instance, politics. There is a long history of the involvement of French intellectuals in public political discourse. This will strike many in the United States in particular as strange. Public debate in the United States seems bereft of intellectuals. On the one hand, most of them have abandoned the field, especially philosophers, who have created a discourse that often seems to immunize itself against public understanding. On the other hand, those who place themselves – or are placed – at the centre of public debate seem themselves immune to intellectual rigour. Not so in France, where at least since Sartre the role of the public intellectual in modern history is taken for granted. In Foucault's case, it is not surprising that the events of May '68 push Foucault, as he attempts to grasp the operation of power, into the role of taking public stances and engaging in debate about current issues.

Among those issues, there are four that may be worth noting. First, he becomes involved in 1971 in the formation of the movement *Groupe d'Information sur les Prisons* (GIP). This group works alongside prisoners in order to call attention to prison conditions, to unjust punishment, and to the political nature of the penal system. Undoubtedly it informs Foucault's own thinking. His next book, published four years later, is *Discipline and Punish*. However, although Foucault is a leader in this movement, he does not act as its spokesperson. This would be a violation of his thought. One does not tell prisoners what they should think; one allows them to speak for themselves. One works alongside prisoners, not in their name. The publications of the GIP use information gleaned from first-hand contact with prisoners and also create space for prisoners themselves to write about their own experiences and offer their own analysis of the prison system.

In 1979, Foucault briefly becomes involved in the plight of the Vietnamese boat people. Recall that in the late 1970s many Vietnamese fled the communist dictatorship of Vietnam by boat, often taking dangerous journeys in flimsy ships, and often refused entry by countries such as the United States and France, which contributed so much to that country's destruction. In 1981, Foucault participates in a press conference, where he reads a document that not only signals his solidarity with the boat people, but eloquently states the bonds that might exist among all those who are subject to power. He says:

> There exists an international citizenry that has its rights, that has its duties, and that is committed to rise up against every abuse of power, no matter who the author, no matter who the victims. After

all, we are all ruled, and as such, we are in solidarity . . . The will of individuals must be inscribed in a reality that the governments wanted to monopolize. This monopoly must be wrested from them bit by bit, each and every day. [3]

Foucault is in sympathy with those who stand against authority. In one case, this leads him astray. During the Iranian revolution of 1979, Foucault visits Iran several times as a journalist and becomes taken with the movement against the Shah. He speculates that an Islamic movement against the government might offer new models for living and for self-governing, models that reject both liberal democracy and the totalitarianism of many postcolonial regimes. This optimism is mistaken, and Foucault soon distances himself from it. Among many whose view of Islamic movements is more measured, Foucault's sympathy for the Islamic resistance is thought to be naive, and he is excoriated in the French press for it. For a while, he withdraws from public comment on current affairs.

Not permanently, though. With the rise of Solidarity in Poland, Foucault again lends his name and his time to a resistance movement against rulers. In this, he goes against the established left. In 1981, the Socialist François Mitterrand becomes France's President, ushering in hopes for a renewal of the left in France. The government, however, never fulfils these hopes. Early on, it offers a signal of its movement toward the centre by refusing to stand with the Solidarity movement against the Polish communist regime. Foucault refuses to support the government's stand, and, alongside other prominent intellectuals, openly supports Solidarity.

There is a common theme among these four political involvements. They are all in support of movements against established authority. In two cases, Vietnam and Poland, Foucault opposes the rule of communists; in the case of Iran, he opposes those who support the Shah in the name of anti-communism. With the GIP he works alongside prisoners against those who rule them, and, more important, who silence them. There is a reason for this, one that is in keeping with Foucault's genealogical orientation.

In an interview in 1977, Foucault distinguishes what he calls "universal" and "specific" intellectuals. Universal intellectuals speak in the name of humanity:

For a long period, the "left" intellectual spoke and was acknowledged the right of speaking in the capacity of master of truth and justice. He was heard, or purported to make himself heard, as the spokesman of the universal. To be an intellectual meant something like being the consciousness/conscience of us all.   (TP: 126)

The specific intellectual, by contrast, does not represent humanity. He does not represent anybody. Instead, he works alongside those who struggle, providing intellectual tools in specific areas that can be appropriated by those who are capable of resisting the intolerable in their own name. If the universal intellectual courts the danger of speaking in the name of others, the specific intellectual courts the symmetrical danger of failing to see the larger picture within which he operates. The task, Foucault argues, is to remain a specific intellectual without losing sight of the general politics of truth within which those struggles take place.

One can see *Discipline and Punish* and the first volume of the history of sexuality in this light. They follow specific threads of our history, of the constitution of who we are now. At the same time, they have larger and more general implications. They capture important ways in which the politics of truth – power–knowledge – has infiltrated our society. Foucault's political involvements reflect the same approach and attitude. On the one hand, he works alongside and in solidarity with specific struggles. He does so not in the name of humanity but in the name of those struggles themselves. On the other hand, there is a larger issue at stake, one that informs all his involvements. "We are all ruled, and as such, we are all in solidarity." Against those who would tell us who we are and where we should stand – whether they be from the established right or the established left – Foucault stakes out a position that resists the truths that we are told are the only truths on offer.

In the interview where he speaks of universal and specific intellectuals, Foucault says:

> The essential political problem for the intellectual is not to criticise the ideological contents supposedly linked to science, or to ensure that his own scientific practice is accompanied by a correct ideology [Foucault is referring here to Louis Althusser and contemporary Marxist intellectuals], but that of ascertaining the possibility of constituting a new politics of truth.   (TP: 133)

We can see this possibility at work in Foucault's public political stances. It is not in the name of or against an established ideology that he speaks. He aims instead towards the possibility of seeing who we are and where we are differently from how we have been taught. This is what makes him so maddening politically for those who take comfort in received political categories.

Finally, sexual experimentation. Much has been made of the last years of Foucault's life in this regard. He speaks of his own homosexuality, and, more notoriously in the eyes of some, he engages in the practice of sado-masochism. James Miller has written a breathless biography of Foucault that details his sexual experimentation and his encounters in the bathhouses of 1980s San Francisco. He ascribes it to Foucault's search for limit-experiences and fascination with death.[4] Foucault's death of AIDS seems to some to confirm this reading of his sexual life. I suspect the truth is both more pedestrian and more in keeping with Foucault's intellectual orientation. Near the end of the first volume of his history of sexuality, Foucault tells us that "The rallying point for the counterattack against the deployment of sexuality ought not to be sex-desire but bodies and pleasures" (*HS*: 157). Why not see his sexual experimentation in that light? Foucault himself offers this interpretation of his sado-masochist activities. "The practice of S/M is the creation of pleasure . . . and that's why S/M is really a subculture. It's a process of invention. S/M is the *use* of a strategic relationship as a course of pleasure (physical pleasure)".[5]

To create ourselves is, in Foucault's view, an experiment. It involves straying afield of oneself in order to see where that may lead. Foucault's sexual experimentation should be seen as exactly that. If it is titillating to some, this is not because Foucault has chosen to titillate, but because his experimentation has crossed the boundaries of their own experience.

In writing, politics and sex, Foucault seeks. He experiments. His life, like his works, is restless. There are those who stray afield by immersing themselves in a single activity, seeing what it offers, where it leads them, but always further down a single road. Foucault's self-creation is different. He is in constant renewal. He does not allow himself to become comfortable on a particular piece of terrain before he moves on. *Do not ask me to remain the same.* There are many ways to experiment, many ways to create or to take care of oneself, many ways towards a new politics of truth. In his own life, Foucault explores a number of them, but leaves behind enough markers for us to go further along our own chosen paths.

CHAPTER SIX

Are we still who Foucault says we are?

As I write this, it is twenty-one years since Foucault's death. His last published book that does not deal with ancient practices is twenty-nine years old. Since his death, we have seen the rise of the internet, DVDs, cell phones, gated communities, Tivo, sport utility vehicles, email and instant messaging. The United States has started three wars: two in Iraq and one in Afghanistan. Terrorism, not communism, is the chosen enemy of what would charitably be called Western democracies. Neoliberalism has come to replace welfare liberalism in many quarters as the reigning economic philosophy of the state. Europe has made steps toward integration; the Soviet Union has disintegrated. China seeks to position itself as the next great national power as the United States squanders its resources, its military and its good will. In short, much has changed.

To admit that much has changed requires us to ask of Foucault a question that is an ineluctably Foucauldian one. Are we still who Foucault has said that we are? Do we remain the normalized beings of discipline, the "empirico-transcendental" doublet – the man – of *The Order of Things*, the products of bio-power, the moral legacy of a Reason that seeks to keep its madness at bay? Are the accounts Foucault offers us still accounts of the character of our being? Or have we moved on? Are we in another *episteme*, another archive, another genealogical moment from the one Foucault has brought us to?

Foucault writes that his work is a contribution to a "history of the present" (*DP*: 31). Is that present the same one we now inhabit? Or are we in another present, one that requires another thinker and another history? To be sure, Foucault sees himself, in Nietzsche's term, as an *untimely* thinker. But to be untimely is to think against the grain of one's time, to offer a thought outside or beyond the time in which one lives. To be untimely is not the same as being anachronistic. Are Foucault's works still untimely, or are they merely behind the times?

Are we now different?

There are many who believe we have moved on, that Foucault's works describe the emergence of the period before the one we are living in. Foucault never uses the term *postmodern*, which for some stands as an indicator of a new historical condition. Jean-François Lyotard would be among those who embrace the term and the novelty it implies. For others who either do not use the term, such as Jean Baudrillard, or who reject it as empty or misleading, like Gilles Deleuze, there is still reason to think that our history has taken another turn, that we need new concepts and new analyses if we are to understand who and where we are now, as well as what we might become.

Some may respond by saying that twenty or thirty years is not a long time. Historical change is more often gradual than not, particularly when what is at stake is not revolutionary upheaval but more often the quotidian practices that make us who we are. But we need look no further than Foucault's own works to see that this is not true. In *The Birth of the Clinic*, a work we have not discussed here, Foucault traces the change in medical views of disease, and thus of the relation of life and death, from a model of disease as essence to one of disease as lesion. This change takes place from the end of the eighteenth century to the beginning of the nineteenth in a period of little more than two dozen years (*BC*: chs 9 & 10).

We cannot avoid a confrontation with the question of Foucault's relation to the present. There is no philosophical fiat by which we can spare him scrutiny, any more than there is a philosophical manoeuvre that would allow him to be dismissed without being read (although there are some who would wish the latter). Even if we cannot, and we will not, close the debate on this question, we must surely open it. After all, the stakes concern who we are now. Are we now still who Foucault says we are?

We can refer to the three thinkers cited a moment ago in order to engage this question. Deleuze has written a small but influential piece arguing that we have gone beyond the historical juncture Foucault designates as the disciplinary society. Baudrillard argues that Foucault's concept of power no longer applies to a world that is more virtual than real. Lyotard does not situate his famous work, *The Postmodern Condition*, in relation to Foucault's writings, but we can draw from it and related works the conclusion that we have entered a new historical period, one characterized by a new type of capitalism. Between the three works we can situate the three most important characteristics that many have invoked, at times with the term *postmodern*, to argue that we have entered a new historical situation: fluid networks of control, the rise of the electronic media, the emergence of transnational capitalism and rampant consumerism. These characteristics are, we shall see, related. Each thinker, though, places the accent on a different aspect of that relation.

Deleuze's "Postscript on Control Societies" is only a few pages long. It is, however, one of the most often discussed of Deleuze's writings. No doubt this is in part because it is one of the most accessible. But it is also one of his most engaged attempts to offer an account of the world we inhabit. It does not, as do many of his other works, refer to the present either in passing or indirectly. It directly asks the question of where we are. How are we situated historically, logically and programmatically? Written in 1990, it is prescient in its reference to the unfolding character of our time.

Deleuze begins the text by situating himself in relation to Foucault: "Foucault associated *disciplinary societies* with the eighteenth and nineteenth centuries; they reach their apogee at the beginning of the twentieth century . . . But Foucault also knew how short-lived this model was."[1] The latter remark is not merely a gesture of generosity. Near the end of *Discipline and Punish*, as Foucault is describing the tenacious ability of the prison to survive its ongoing failures, he notes the suffusion of processes of normalization across society, and remarks that, "In the midst of all these mechanisms of normalization, which are becoming ever more rigorous in their application, the specificity of the prison and its role as link are losing something of their purpose" (*DP*: 306). As a prediction of the future of the prison, in the United States at least, this is premature. However, the thrust of the remark is aimed not so much at the prison itself as at the idea that normalization may not, in the future, require disciplinary enclosure.

This is the idea that animates Deleuze's "Postscript". "We're in the midst of a general breakdown of all sites of confinement – prisons, hospitals, factories, schools, the family."[2] The confined areas in which discipline is instilled are no longer operative. We are no longer subject to the particular training that discipline involves because the closed and enclosing sites in which that training has happened have lost their integrity. This is not to say, and Deleuze does not claim, that these sites have become entirely irrelevant. Rather, it is that they are no longer central to the historical dynamic that is unfolding. The disciplinary society is giving way to what Deleuze calls *control societies*.

The reason for this has to do with what Deleuze calls the logic of control societies. He cites several differences between the logic of discipline and that of control. First, the temporal movement of discipline is circular, and in control it is endlessly forward. "In disciplinary societies you were always starting all over again (as you went from school to barracks, from barracks to factory), while in control societies you never finish anything."[3] Disciplinary societies move individuals from enclosure to enclosure. At each enclosure, one is moulded according to the ways Foucault describes in *Discipline and Punish*. In control societies, by contrast, this serial moulding does not exist. One is instead always moving to the next thing and the one after that, whether it be, as in Deleuze's example, continuing education with continuous assessment, or the next fashion, the next philosophy of management, the next relationship. Discrete spaces do not matter in this continuous movement; they can happen in any space or, with electronic communication, in no particular space at all.

Similarly, disciplinary societies work within particular parameters and control societies work with modulating fluxes:

> Money, perhaps, best expresses the difference between the two kinds of societies, since discipline was always related to molded currencies containing gold as a numerical standard, whereas control is based on floating exchange rates, modulations depending on a code setting sample percentages for various currencies.[4]

Just as discipline occurs within a circular time associated with discrete spaces and control works with an endless time that is not pegged to any particular space, discipline applies norms and values both to individuals (discipline) and groups (bio-power), and control floats among and between individuals and groups substituting codes for norms.

To understand the difference between codes and norms, we might use the analogy of quantum physics and Newtonian physics. For Newtonian physics, the universe consists in discrete elements in particular lawful relations. The laws are like the norms of a disciplinary society. Quantum mechanics, on the other hand, works with probabilities rather than laws. It is not that there are no regularities and that everything is chaos. Rather, there are probabilistic regularities that are associated with the movement of the whole rather than of any particular element within that whole. Codes are like those probabilistic regularities.

As an example, one might think here of the movement of fashion. No longer are the styles produced by designers the standard by which others create clothing. Now clothing and shoe companies send employees into urban areas to discover what the dominant youths, usually males, in those areas are interested in. In addition, there is a range of niche products that seek to appeal to increasingly narrow market demographics. The fashion industry does not impose a set of sartorial norms; it modulates a code that arises from an array of shifting interests.

Finally, the logic of capitalism has changed. It is no longer concerned with production; that can be farmed out to less developed countries. Rather, it focuses on what Deleuze calls *metaproduction*: the oversight, coordination and marketing of production. "Markets are won by taking control rather than by establishing discipline, by fixing rates rather than by reducing costs, by transforming products rather than by specializing production."[5] Discipline is associated with factory production, and factories in turn with the establishment and maintenance of norms. Control societies do not need a particular space because nothing is made and no norms are imposed. One might say that the Internet or perhaps the laptop computer is to control societies what factories are to disciplinary ones.

Movement without end or enclosure, modulating codes, and meta-production: these are the aspects of control societies, the societies that have replaced disciplinary ones. Far from being chaotic, these societies are indeed regulated, not by imposing regimes of order in specific spaces but by intervening in the fluid and probabilistic unfolding of the activities that constitute them. Deleuze does not argue that there is nothing left of discipline, but he sees a new historical, political and economic arrangement unfolding that is one step beyond the arrangement Foucault describes.

One might ask of Deleuze whether control really is very different from normalization, or whether it is instead a modification. Certainly, as Foucault admits, there seems to be less urgency for enclosed spaces. According to Foucault, the reason for this is that normalization has so deeply infiltrated our society that one does not have to construct discrete spaces in order to instill it. Is this very different from what Deleuze calls control?

Although the idea of diffuse oversight is characteristic of both non-enclosed normalization and control, there are still important differences. Deleuze is describing a dynamic distinct from that of Foucault's discipline. Normalization involves the training of individuals according to particular standards; it requires personal intervention and oversight. This is one reason why earlier societies could not have a project of normalization; normalization requires a certain level of social interaction and technological communication, processes associated with the rise of capitalism. What Deleuze sees, however, no longer requires an individualized inculcation of particular norms. Rather, it is a more amorphous matter involving codes and probabilities. To be sure, there are certain norms, in the broad sense of the term. There are sartorial fashions, ways of acting and talking, things people find valuable, and so on. However, norms are products not of individualizing projects of normalization. They are codes that arise across societies that individuals pick up more or less as they go along. Later we shall return to the question of whether in fact control has replaced normalization (as well as the discipline that produces it). For the moment, it is enough to recognize that they are distinct processes.

Recently, Deleuze's friend Antonio Negri, along with Michael Hardt, has written a book, *Empire*, that extends Deleuze's discussion on control societies.[6] They argue that the world is moving away from the structure of nation-states characteristic of the previous few centuries (at least in much of the world), and towards a more fluid structure comprising nation-states, transnational corporations and non-governmental organizations. Although the United States might be dominant among nation-states, it cannot dominate the world in the way, say, that Britain did during the heyday of imperialism. What Hardt and Negri call empire is distinct from imperialism precisely in that the latter is structured by discrete nation-states pursuing their interests through subjugation and exploitation, whereas empire is structured by fluid and intersecting political and economic networks with no particular centre and only relatively demarcated geographic boundaries. Empire, they argue, has three imperatives: the inclusion of all, an affirmation of differences, and a management and hierarchization of those differences. In this sense, what is often called postmodernism and the rising force of fundamentalism are coordinate ideologies: one embraces the new situation uncritically, the other rejects it by seeking to move backwards. Like Deleuze, Hardt and Negri do not claim that there are no winners and losers in this new situation, or that control does not exist. Rather, they claim that winners are not to be seen as a particular class of people who can manipulate the system from above – everyone is included – and that they are not to be associated solely with a particular class or nation. They are those who monitor, exert a measure of control over, and benefit from the operation of empire.

Deleuze, Hardt and Negri focus on the *structure* of the new historical situation they believe we inhabit. Baudrillard, by contrast, focuses on the *content*, and in particular on the technological content, of our current historical juncture. Baudrillard's early writings invert the Marxist concern with production, arguing that a radical analysis of society ought instead to focus on consumption. In his view, our identities as producers have been surpassed by our identities as consumers; if we are to understand ourselves, it is the latter that should receive the analytical weight. More recently, his work has been associated with hyperreality, the replacement of concrete lived reality by a virtual electronic reality that is now the true aether of our lives. Hyperreality, if not by name, is already on display in a work Baudrillard publishes in 1977, a year after Foucault's first volume on the history of sexuality. Entitled "Forget Foucault", it is an argument that the operation of power Foucault describes is already outmoded. Foucault's genealogical works depict a world that no longer exists:

> Something tells us . . . that if it is possible at last to talk with such definitive understanding about power, sexuality, the body, and discipline, even down to their most delicate metamorphoses, it is because at some point *all this is here and now over with*.[7]

"Forget Foucault" levels a number of charges against Foucault's work, including the already refuted idea that Foucault reduces everything to power and therefore subverts his own position. Baudrillard's most interesting thought, however, is that Foucault's stress on the role of power is part of a productivist model of society of the kind that Baudrillard criticizes in Marx. We need to replace the concept of power with that of *seduction* if we are to understand what is going on in our society.

In what sense is the idea of power productive? We have already seen it. One of Foucault's most striking challenges to the traditional conception of power is that, in his view, much of the power to which we are subject works not by repression but by creation. Rather than preventing us from being who we are or from realizing our true nature, power operates by making us who we are. We are produced by power. In this sense, Foucault's work is, in Baudrillard's eyes, continuous with Marx's. They operate on different terrains, but they both embrace a view of reality that emphasizes the production of that reality.

Baudrillard argues that this conception of power:

> is still turned toward a reality principle and a very strong truth principle; it is still oriented toward a possible coherence of politics and discourse (power no longer pertains to the despotic order of what is forbidden and of the law, but it still belongs to the objective order of the real).[8]

Here is where we can see the emergence of the idea of hyperreality. At first glance, it might seem incongruous to accuse Foucault of too strong an attachment to a reality principle and particularly to a "very strong truth principle". Is it not Foucault, after all, who introduces the concept of power–knowledge, a concept that seems to weaken rather than strengthen our attachment to what we consider our truths? For Baudrillard, however, Foucault has not yet jettisoned the most important attachment: the attachment to a reality to be analysed.

Consider Foucault's dictum on the soul in *Discipline and Punish*:

> It would be wrong to say that the soul is an illusion, or an ideological effect. On the contrary, it exists, it has a reality, it is produced permanently around, on, within the body by the functioning of a power that is exercised on those punished.   (*DP*: 29)

This is the reality principle Baudrillard refers to. Power produces a reality that genealogy, in turn, can describe or account for. It can tell truths about it because there is something out there, something produced, for truths – genealogical truths – to be true of.

In Baudrillard's eyes, a reality (produced or not) that can be theoretically accounted for is precisely what we no longer have. We live in a world governed not by a reality but by a virtuality that has no reality. In the terms used by Baudrillard in "Forget Foucault", we are not *produced*, we are *seduced*.

To begin to grasp this idea, we can turn to a later text of Baudrillard's, *Simulations*. There he offers a chronological summary of "three orders of appearance" that have governed our relation to reality since the Renaissance:

- *Counterfeit* is the dominant scheme of the "classical" period, from the Renaissance to the industrial revolution;
- *Production* is the dominant scheme of the industrial era;
- *Simulation* is the reigning scheme of the current phase that is controlled by the code.[9]

What is the difference between simulation and production? If production works by creating reality, simulation works by feigning one. There is no real world in which our lives take place; or better, the real world is no longer of any account. The world in which our lives take place is a simulated world, one given to us by images that either no longer reflect the real world or no longer need to. We are plugged into images via our media, especially television and the internet, that simulate a reality. That simulated reality is now our own. There is no longer a reality principle, because the concrete reality described by those, like Foucault, still in thrall to thinking in terms of production, has been replaced by a simulated reality that is neither produced nor pre-existing. There is nothing, or need be nothing, beyond the image. In an arresting encapsulation of his view, Baudrillard tells us that:

> Disneyland is presented as imaginary in order to make us believe that the rest is real, when in fact all of Los Angeles and the America surrounding it are no longer real, but of the order of the hyperreal and of simulation.[10]

Seduction is a matter of simulation and the hyperreal rather than of production and the real. *"To seduce is to die as reality and reconstitute oneself as illusion."*[11] Seduction works, not by creation, but by lure:

> *Seduction* is that which is everywhere and always opposed to *production*; seduction withdraws something from the visible order and so runs counter to production, whose project is to set

139

everything up in a clear view, whether it be an object, a number, or a concept.[12]

Consider the activity of seduction in the everyday sense of the term. To seduce someone is not to dominate them, to subject them to one's will. Seduction does not make an appearance on the scene as something visible. It works more by what is suggested but not there rather than by what is there. To seduce someone is not to impose something; it is to set things up so that they do the imposing, they make the move, they fill the void left by the seduction itself.

In Baudrillard's view, if there is such a thing as power in our current situation of hyperreality, it operates not by production but by seduction:

> "against Foucault's functional vision in terms of relays and transmissions, we must say that power is something that is exchanged. Not in an economical sense, but in the sense that power is executed according to a reversible cycle of seduction, challenge, and ruse ... power seduces by that reversibility which haunts it, and upon which a minimal symbolic cycle is set up.[13]

The reversibility of seduction is Baudrillard's answer to the question of how to resist power. Seduction is a game. It is a game that can be played by either side. In fact, the complexity of this game is such that it can become unclear who is seducing and who is being seduced:

> The law of seduction takes the form of an uninterrupted ritual exchange where seducer and seduced constantly raise the stakes in a game that never ends. And cannot end since the dividing line that defines the victory of the one and the defeat of the other, is illegible.[14]

Baudrillard substitutes the game of seduction for the couple power/resistance in Foucault. Rather than a power that impresses itself against the resistance it meets in reality, there are the reversible lures of seduction that work without reference to a reality that would coalesce them.

In a world of simulation, it is seduction rather than power that is the motor of political and social movement and exchange. Seduction has no reference to reality, and nothing within it ever becomes solid or stable. Seduction "never belongs to the order of nature, but that of artifice – never to the order of energy, but that of signs and rituals".[15] Foucault's genealogy of power remains stuck in the previous historical epoch, the epoch that ended with the rise of simulation and hyperreality. We are governed not by relations of power but by the seduction of images in a game without end that we, too, participate in.

Jean-François Lyotard's *The Postmodern Condition* is perhaps the most famous of all discussions of postmodernism. *The Postmodern Condition* is commissioned in the late 1970s by the Quebecois government as a report on the current state of knowledge. The themes of the book, however, have been taken to have much broader application than just the epistemic one. In the book, Lyotard defines postmodernism as "incredulity toward meta-narratives".[16] This definition, which he admits at the outset oversimplifies matters, points towards an attitude that characterizes postmodern movements in literature, art, academics and politics. We might put the core idea this way. Humanity has for much of its history seen itself in the context of a larger narrative in which each of our lives is an element. This larger narrative brings together the smaller narratives that constitute our knowledge of ourselves and our world. In that way, it is a metanarrative, a narrative under whose umbrella other epistemic and moral narratives find their place.

For much of human history – at least recorded human history – our metanarratives have been religious in nature. During recent centuries, however, other metanarratives have come to compete with and often to replace religion. Lyotard points to two metanarratives that have situated our knowledge over the past several centuries. One is the Enlightenment narrative that sees the rise of science as a liberation from the superstitions of the past. The other is the Hegelian metanarrative of the spirit coming to self-understanding. In both cases, there is a story about the operation of our knowledge that places it in a broader narrative context.

One of the roles, and perhaps the major role, of this context is to justify our knowledge. This justification is a broad one. It is not a justification in the sense that a science experiment justifies a hypothesis. Metanarratives justify knowledge by offering it a sense of meaningfulness or significance. It is the role that knowledge plays, whether it be in the service of coming closer to God or of the liberation of humanity from superstition or of the process of the spirit's coming to know itself, that justifies knowledge as a whole.

The incredulity toward metanarratives that characterizes the postmodern condition is a wariness towards this larger justifying picture. In the postmodern condition, which is *our* condition, there is a loss of belief or faith that knowledge can be justified as meaningful or significant. This leads to a crisis of knowledge, since the point of epistemic projects now becomes uncertain.

In *The Postmodern Condition* Lyotard provides an alternative view of knowledge that he believes will fill the hole left by the decline of metanarrative. I would like to focus on another aspect of his thought. My concern here is not what Lyotard says *might* serve as a better justifier for knowledge but what he says actually *does* serve as the justifier. The latter has to do with capitalism, and the criterion of justification is what Lyotard calls *performativity*. Performativity has to do not with moral justification nor with spiritual uplift nor with liberation; it has to do with results. In the absence of a credible metanarrative, what justifies knowledge are the results it can give in terms of efficient application to or manipulation of our world.

What, however, justifies performativity? That is a question that once would have been answered by appeal to a metanarrative. Performativity would be justified by some story in which we saw ourselves playing a role, a story that would tell us who we are and at the same time what role performative knowledge plays in making us who we are. But there is no narrative like that any longer, at least none that grips most of us. Performativity must be its own criterion, its own justifier: which is to say that it is unjustified.

Even if we can live with performativity being unjustified, however, there is still another question that remains unanswered. Which types of performativity ought to be fostered? This again is a question to which a metanarrative might offer an answer. Lacking that, however, how have we come to approach it? After all, efficient functioning depends on what one is trying to be efficient about. What are the criteria or the goals that allow us to decide how to direct the performativity of our knowledge? In *The Postmodern Condition*, Lyotard does not offer us an answer to this question, but he begins to suggest one near the end of his later book *The Differend*. He constructs his answer in terms of the relation of capitalism to time, but I would like to simplify it a bit in order to focus on a key phrase: "Capitalism does not constitute a universal history, it is trying to constitute a world market (while deferring it, since it also needs the gaps between national communities)."[17]

A universal history is metanarrative. Capitalism does not supply a metanarrative. It supplies a world market. What govern a world market are not values of the kind one might find in a metanarrative, values that confer meaning or significance. What governs a world market is exchange. In the void left by the loss of metanarratives, capitalism has stepped in and offered exchange as the guiding standard for performativity. How does it work? Those who have studied elementary economics will be familiar with the operation. Those forms of efficiency to be fostered are those that people are willing to exchange for. Performativity is to be directed toward what the market holds as valuable, and what the market holds as valuable are those things for which people are willing to exchange something in order to receive or own. Stripped to its essentials, performativity is to be directed towards what people will buy.

One might want to argue here that the distinction drawn between a universal history and a world market is misleading. In particular, the idea that the former embodies values and the other does not is wrong. Does the structure of exchange not embody its own values, perhaps not the values of traditional metanarratives, but values nonetheless? If metanarratives promote values of service to God or liberation from superstition, does the rise of performativity and particularly of exchange not promote the values of individual choice? Can we not say that where once common national or human values reigned, values that brought us together in a common struggle or destiny, now we are beholden to individualist values that are more in keeping with the dispersed multicultural world in which we live? The issue is not one of choice between values and no values, but between the types of values embraced. And if this is true, is it not also true that contemporary capitalism does have its own metanarrative, one involving the rise of individual choice and freedom from cultural or social or national or ideological hegemony?

The objection is a forceful one. However, I do not believe that it is, in the end, compelling. It is not that there is no privileging of individual choice in our world. There certainly is. And it is not that that privileging is not held as a value. The problem is that, from the perspective of the individual, and particularly the individual consumer, it is held as a personal value, not a common one. With the dominance of exchange, each of us believes in *our own* individual choice. Each of us believes that we should receive what we desire. We do not hold this as a value for others, a value that brings us together, a value that would form the basis of a metanarrative. Rather, we might say, we hold it as a personal right rather than a universal value.

Moreover, from the perspective especially of the corporations that engage in performativity and that drive the world market, values are not an issue. Profit is. If the current world is more in thrall to a world market than to national entities or traditional metanarratives, then one of the results of this has been the decline of the concept of common values generally and the rise of a profit motive that does not answer the question of what that profit is for. Its story ends with profit, not with any values that underlie it, just as individual choice rests on personal desire rather than on the general value of such choice for humanity.

In Lyotard's introduction of the world market as the arbiter of performativity, we can see the intersection between his thought and that of Hardt and Negri. Whereas Hardt and Negri are concerned with the structure of forces in the emerging transnational world order, Lyotard focuses on the market and the way performativity and exchange work in that market. Both works, however, see what we might call a horizontal integration of markets and transnational entities displacing (while, as the quote from Lyotard notes, not entirely *re*placing) the old vertical order of national entities that confront or interact with one another as exterior to

143

one another. The rise of transnational entities, particularly of transnational corporations, has been documented exhaustively in recent years.

Masao Miyoshi, for instance, details in a 1993 article the transition from colonialism to transnationalism particularly with regard to the decline of nation-states and the rise of transnational corporations.[18] He argues that transnational corporations are beginning to replace multinational ones as their allegiance to particular nation-states diminishes and their global mobility increases. Miyoshi notes that among the effects of the rise of transnational corporations are a loss of concern for the welfare of indigenous populations, a homogenization of wealthier classes across national borders, a greater displacement of workers who follow the migration of jobs, environmental degradation arising from a lack of concern about local conditions, and a co-optation of academic institutions to which transnational corporations provide funding and from which they receive expertise. If we think of the structure of control that Deleuze depicts, the transnational structure delineated by Hardt and Negri, and the rise of performativity based on exchange that Lyotard discusses, these effects of transnationalism will not seem foreign to us.

From another angle, we can also see the intersection between Lyotard's thought and Baudrillard's early inversion of Marxism. Recall that before Baudrillard's turn toward hyperreality, he argues that Marx's focus on production should be turned around. It is consumerism, not production, that forms the core of contemporary capitalism. Alongside the rise of transnationalism, the emergence of consumerism is another effect of the substitution of performativity and exchange for the values embedded in metanarratives. This might seem unlikely. After all, one might ask, is not performativity a matter of production rather than consumption? Does it not have to do with efficiency in what is made regardless of the ultimate point of making it? On the other hand, what guides performativity is exchange. It is consumption that determines what is to be produced. If Lyotard is right here, then people think of who they are more centrally in terms of what they consume than in terms of what they make. It is the houses they live in, the cars they drive, the clothes they wear, the restaurants they eat in, that determine who they are to themselves, rather than the jobs they do. Performativity, yes; but performativity in the service of consumption.

Lyotard's thought, then, like that of both Deleuze and Baudrillard, argues that we have entered a new historical period. There is a break, what Foucault might call a historical discontinuity, between earlier historical epochs and the one we are inhabiting now. We are no longer who we were thirty or even twenty years ago. Whether the stress on who we are now should be placed on the structure of the world we live in, its increasingly virtual and mediated character, or the loss of metanarratives in favour of performativity and exchange, we must recognize that histories that deposit us in the mid-1970s can no longer account for who we are. A new chapter, or a set of new chapters, must be written. The genealogies must be extended. We are no longer who Foucault says we are.

There is much to consider here. In order to address these ideas adequately, I would like to proceed in three stages. First, it would be worth addressing each proposal individually from a Foucauldian perspective. Each, I think, has shortcomings in as much as it proposes that we have moved beyond Foucault's thought. (We must bear in mind, however, that Lyotard does not address Foucault's thought directly, so we are reading that idea into his perspective.) Secondly, the three proposals share a commonality in their approach that make them in an important way distinct from Foucault's own approach. I would like to show that, from Foucault's perspective, this commonality is a weakness in as much as these approaches are attempts to account for who we are now. Finally, however, I believe that it is undeniable that the changes these thinkers discuss are important ones. I would like to recognize that by appeal to the lectures that Foucault gives at the Collège de France in 1979. These lectures, which have just been published and as of this writing remain untranslated, can be read as a contribution to the historical changes Deleuze, Baudrillard and Lyotard discuss. This contribution offers a different stress from that of each of the other three. However, it is pointing in a direction that would not be entirely foreign to the intersection of their thought.

Deleuze argues that we now live in a society of control. Our lives are characterized by a lack of particular enclosures, a new temporal rhythm, codes instead of normalization, and metaproduction. We have already seen that Foucault is ready to concede the decline of particular enclosures as a site of discipline. Should he be ready to concede that discipline itself has been surpassed? The question hinges on the relevance of normalization. Deleuze argues that we live in the modulating flux of codes rather than the individualizing discipline of normalization. Has the former replaced the latter, or is normalization still an important force today?

I do not see a decline in the power of normalization. In fact, the situation may well be the opposite. Normalization, rather than giving way to codes, seems both to exist alongside them and, at times, to be a necessary support for them. If we think of normalization arising from discipline in particular spaces, we can perhaps see a bit of a decline. But it is easy even to overstate this. Think, for instance, of the operation of schools, one of the central sites of discipline. Diagnoses of Attention Deficit Hyperactivity Disorder (ADHD) in its various psychological subtypes have, at least in the United States, not declined. They have increased.[19] They are as rampant as the medications that are supposed to control them. School personnel, as every parent knows, work diligently to ensure that each child too energetic to sit quietly at a wooden desk for six hours at a stretch is diagnosed, medicated, and brought back into the fold of quiescent conformism to school routines. This is discipline in its classic form.

However, if we move away from traditional discipline we can still see normalization at work. During the recent presidential election in the United States the issue of "moral values" was thought of as a central one. I live in the state of South Carolina, a heartland of such values. Chief among these are what has come to be called "family values". Family values have nothing to do with supporting families. They do not concern such issues as financial or social assistance for working mothers, nutrition and health care for children, educational opportunities, or relief for impoverished families. They have to do with promoting what some consider the ideal structure of a family. That structure consists of a man, usually as the primary wage earner, a woman, and children (the Malthusian couple). Particularly anathema are single mothers (hysterical women) and gay couples (perverted adults). Not to mention the perennial problem of the masturbating child.

If we think of Foucault's analyses of sexuality in the first volume of his history, we should not be surprised that homosexuality and abortion are central among the issues that exercise Christian pastors. These sexual matters are taken to be central determinants of who we are. To be a homosexual in the United States is to be defined by one's sexual orientation. It is to have one's identity reduced to a single set of desires. Even in the South, where many people refuse to consider Catholicism a form of Christianity, the continuity of belief with the changes in the Catholic confessional in the seventeenth century is unmistakable. Moreover, one can see as well the operation of power as Foucault analyses it. In as much as gays take up their sexual identity as central, forming gay communities with their own integrity and practices, they become what the operation of sexuality makes them: people defined by the character of their desire.

In the disciplinary operation of schools and in the theological approach to sexuality, we can see the process of normalization at work. Codes have not replaced normalization; they operate alongside of it. Further, normalization helps support the rise of certain codes. Return to the example of fashion we used earlier to understand how codes operate. A shoe designer goes to the inner city with different shoe models and asks the dominant males in various urban groups to evaluate them. This may seem like a movement away from normalization. It is certainly a movement away from discipline in its classic form. However, in order for this method of shoe design to work, it requires a different type of normalization. It requires a convergence between shoe design, marketing techniques and dominant urban males. This convergence creates a set of norms that, although not disciplinary, are certainly as forceful in their way as the normalization that arises from discipline.

One might want to object here that this last example is not one of normalization, but simply of conformity. Is normalization as Foucault depicts it not a more precise practice or set of practices, involving the intervention into behaviour through hierarchical observation, normalizing judgement, and examination? We might see these operations at play in current theological practices in regard to sexuality, but is it not a stretch to see them in support of the types of codes Deleuze discusses? I do not believe that it is. Through the development of technology, people see themselves mirrored or not mirrored through the images they are presented with. Those images, in league with people around them, present a normalizing force that, in a different way from traditional discipline, retains all three elements. Hierarchical observation becomes comparison of oneself with the images one sees and with one's peers and superiors. Normalizing judgement and examination come from those same sources. And even if the processes of judgement and examination are more informal, nevertheless they apply to as minute elements of behaviour as those intervened upon in the training of Prussian soldiers. Normalization has not been replaced by codes, but exists with them, at times in collaboration and at times independent of the movement of codes. The rise of codes has certainly changed the character of some normalizing procedures, in particular with regard to the enclosed spaces associated with traditional discipline; but it has not replaced normalization.

Turning to Baudrillard, we must ask whether indeed we live in hyperreality. Baudrillard has a penchant, one that the reader will no doubt have noticed, and that many readers of Baudrillard have commented on, for stating his position in its most extreme form. As a rhetorical ploy, this is effective, and it allows him to create striking formulations such as the one on the role of Disneyland. Foucault's approach, however, is more measured. So we must ask whether the hyperreality Baudrillard posits indeed captures the world we live in. This is not a question of whether our experiences have become increasingly mediated by electronic technology. It would be foolish to deny that they are, or that they have taken a leap in this direction since the publication of Foucault's first volume on the history of sexuality. Rather, the question is, do we live in hyperreality?

The answer here, it seems to me, is no. The reason for this is that, contra Baudrillard, the referent of images still has an important role to play in our interaction with the world. What images are or purport to be images of still matters. And as long as this remains the case, our experience cannot accurately be described as one of hyperreality.

Although it is true that the power of the media to shape people's perceptions is far greater than it once was, it is also true that people hope the media offers an accurate portrayal of the world they live in. Critiques of the media are often formulated in terms of misleading or false portrayals of world events. For instance, one of the central justifications for President Bush's initiation of war against Iraq concerns the claim that Iraq had weapons of mass destruction, a claim we now know to be false. It is the comparison of what the President claimed and the media dutifully reported with what turned out actually to be the case that is the heart of the matter here. This seems to undercut Baudrillard's view that we inhabit a world of hyperreality.

However, perhaps we should take a subtler look. What Baudrillard might argue here is that the example as I have presented it ignores an important aspect of what happened. It is not, he might say, the non-existence of weapons of mass destruction that matters. Rather, the central point is that this non-existence was brought before the media and is still kept alive in the media. Reporters refer to it, talk show pundits analyse it, anchorpeople use it as a touchstone of their reporting on the administration's policy in Iraq. Should the Bush administration have been successful in covering up the non-existence of the purported weapons, the fact of their non-existence would not matter. It would not figure in the configuration of our experience. It would be as though there had indeed been weapons of mass destruction in Iraq, and the United States had found them. Their absence would be irrelevant. In this way, it is the images that determine our world, not the reality to which these images refer.

Put this way, Baudrillard's point is powerful, but at the expense of becoming ahistorical. If people are led to believe something false, by whatever means, and cannot have access to the truth, then that truth will remain foreign to their experience. They will be unable to reflect or act upon what is really the case. This point does not apply simply to contemporary society, but to all societies. It is a broad philosophical point rather than a historical marker of our time. Moreover, the point itself does not support the idea that the reality referred to by images is no longer of moment. Instead, it makes the more modest claim that often people do not have access to that reality.

None of this is meant to deny that in a world where electronic media play such an important role images are often taken for reality, nor that one of the most prevalent ways that reality is distorted or hidden is through the media. Rather, the idea is that although Baudrillard's claim that Foucault's view of power remains trapped within a reality principle may be true, that would be a point in Foucault's favour rather than Baudrillard's. We may live in a world where images play a far more important role in determining our experience than they once did. We do not, however, live in a hyperreality.

The stakes for Foucault in this discussion are enormous. For instance, if we did live in hyperreality, among the things that would become irrelevant are our bodies. It is what we see, rather than any intervention of the world on our bodies, that determines who we are. That is why seduction would be a preferred strategy of resistance; it does not refer to bodies but instead to a suggestiveness that has no corporeal form. In Foucault's view, power often operates at the level of the body. Both discipline and sexuality centrally involve a relation of various practices to our bodies. Perhaps what is necessary here is not, as Baudrillard would have it, a claim that practices of power oriented towards our bodies have passed away, but instead an analysis of the role images play in determining the orientation and character of our bodies. What have our bodies become in the wake of the rise of electronic media and its images? And what does that say about who we have become? These, it seems, are the relevant questions. There are many ways to address them, and among those ways a Foucaultian genealogy might not be entirely beside the point.

Turning to Lyotard, we must ask after his concept of postmodernity and particularly after the role that capitalism plays in replacing metanarratives with exchange. It is probably worth noting in passing that this replacement, although distinct from Deleuze's claim that normalization is being replaced by codes, has affinities with it. In particular, there is a relation between the idea of unfettered exchange and that of codes.[20] Before turning to capitalism, however, it is worth lingering a moment over an important similarity between Lyotard's view and Foucault's.

Lyotard believes that the postmodern world exhibits a wariness toward metanarratives. No single, overarching story about who or where we are or are headed compels people's assent. Foucault, in turn, jettisons overarching views of who we are, particularly in his genealogies. He sees who we are as a result of the intersection of a number of threads of practice, threads whose weave forms, not a single pattern, but many. Moreover, for Foucault the operation of power in the modern age has become increasingly dispersed. It is no longer primarily the repressive exercise of several centuries ago. It is increasingly a creative force that emerges through various and often unrelated practices. In this sense, both Lyotard and Foucault are looking at our world with a similar eye. Although Lyotard grounds his view in the twentieth century, and Foucault takes a longer view, there are resonances between their approaches.

In this resonance, however, there is a discordance that distinguishes their views. Lyotard values the loss of the grand narrative, if not the capitalism that has commandeered that loss. For him, incredulity toward metanarratives opens out onto novel ways of living. It allows for a recognition of competing narratives and for respect for different *genres* of discourse – different ways of conducting speech and engaging in language – from the epistemic to the moral to the aesthetic. In *The Differend*, for instance, one of his criticisms of contemporary capitalism is that it blunts the power of genres, reducing them all to the single discourse of exchange. Although the loss of the grand narrative has created a space in which different smaller narratives could flourish, capitalism has filled that space by translating all narratives into matters of exchange, and thus closed the possibility that postmodernism opens.

Foucault, by contrast, does not turn to the dispersion of practices in order to find something to value. We might put the point by saying that his orientation, in contrast to Lyotard's, is analytic rather than normative. It is not because there is something of value in the loss of an overarching theme or narrative that Foucault focuses his attention on minor, everyday practices. It is because that is where we are being created. If we want to understand who we are now, and in particular how we have been made to be who we are now, then we need to look on the ground rather than from some overarching perspective. The various and dispersed practices that constitute the current aether of our lives are not necessarily better than anything offered by a grand narrative. As we have seen, in many cases they are intolerable. For Foucault, then, in contrast to Lyotard, there is no privileging of smaller practices in contrast to larger ones informing his embrace of the details of our history. There is, instead, the project of asking about the character of our present.

This discordance leads to his divergence from Lyotard. Lyotard worries that contemporary capitalist ways of thinking and acting have subsumed and reduced others to their own parameters. Foucault would be uncomfortable with this view. He need not deny the importance of the discourse of exchange or of the related phenomena of globalization and transnational capitalism, any more than he need deny the place of codes or images in constituting who we are now. In fact, as we shall see, Foucault has a contribution to make to the discussion of contemporary views of capitalism. Rather, it would be Lyotard's insistence on the primacy of exchange that runs afoul of Foucault's analytic scruples. If what I said above in response to Deleuze about the persistence of projects of normalization is right, then there are indeed forms of discourse that are both outside the genre of exchange and politically oppressive or intolerable.

Neither all discourse nor all politically charged discourse is in the process of being reduced to the capitalist discourse of exchange that Lyotard describes. Although much discourse intersects with capitalism, each has its own parameters, its own integrity, and requires its own treatment if it is to be understood. This is the salience of Foucault's appeal to smaller discourses as an analytic rather than normative endeavour. The picture of capitalism on the one side and smaller, better genres on the other must give way to a picture of various intersecting genres with capitalism dominating in some, playing a minor role in others, and being nearly absent in others still.

The problem with Lyotard's approach, and it is a problem common to all three announcements of a new era, is that it seeks to account for who we have become in terms of a single register. Deleuze, Baudrillard and Lyotard look for the one thing that has made us who we are now as distinct from who we were twenty or thirty years ago. Codes as distinct from discipline, hyperreality and seduction as distinct from reality and power, the capitalist genre of exchange: each of these is posited to account for who we have become. In the first two cases, where the contrast with Foucault is stated, the authors posit a false symmetry between their thought and Foucault's. They operate by way of saying, "No, it isn't that; it's this." But that is not how Foucault operates. Discipline is only one among the forces that have made us who we are. And Foucault does not, contra Baudrillard's reading, see everything as a matter of power. Multiplicity is inherent in Foucault's approach, and has been since the beginning. In that sense, a historical criticism of Foucault's approach would more likely be of moment than a broad philosophically oriented criticism that seeks to subsume particulars under an overarching structure. At least a historical criticism, if it were not in the service of a broad philosophical agenda, need not posit the approach of a particular one of his works as a microcosm of his larger view.

The problem common to these three approaches is that they take a bird's-eye view. They glide far above the realities that make us who we are. This is what allows them to reduce the complexity of our historically formed present to a single explanation or a single factor. It is not that they see nothing of who we are. To the contrary, they offer acute insights into our current condition. The problem is that they try to take in too much at a glance. If we are to follow the lesson of Foucault's methodology, we need to return to the ground and investigate the space in which we live. Genealogy is grey and patiently documentary; it is not bright and reductively explanatory.

In this sense, the projects of Deleuze, Baudrillard and Lyotard are aligned with those of Descartes, Freud and Marx. They are looking for the key explanatory factor rather than investigating the world in its proper dispersion. This is not to say that their thought is in all ways continuous with those of Foucault's predecessors. Far from it. For instance, each of the three recent thinkers focuses on the character of our present rather than on a timeless essence. However, they share with those earlier thinkers a commitment to a single explainer, and in that commitment they have not yet reached Foucault, must less gone beyond him.

One might want to face Foucault straight on here, however, and argue that his problem is precisely that his thought is one of dispersion. One might say that our world has indeed changed radically, so radically that there now *is* a single explanation for who we are, a single account that can be given of our present. It might be the account that Deleuze offers, or that of Baudrillard or Lyotard. Or it may be some combination of the three. It may be that we live in a world of transnational capitalism that is guided by codes, mediated through a hyperreality, and in the process of reducing all discourse to that of capitalist exchange. Perhaps each of these thinkers has caught an aspect of the larger web in which we are now caught. In any case, and this would be the crucial point, it is a single web, and no longer the myriad of intersecting but distinct practices Foucault describes. Globalization and technological development have deposited us on new shores, shores that are characterized by a single coastline and a common inland. That is where we live now.

I have suggested by way of criticizing each of the thinkers that there are reasons to believe otherwise. For instance, normalization seems to be a more dispersed set of projects than a single explanation would have us believe. However, in the face of this possibility, these remain merely suggestions. In order to resolve this disagreement, we would have to go much further, further indeed than can be gone in this book.

What would be required in order to answer the question of whether who we are now is subject to a single account? There would need to be a study of the kinds of texts Foucault relies on, only focused on the past thirty years or so, in order to see what they yield. For instance, if we were to ask about the relation of sexuality to globalization and the electronic media, we would have to investigate sex manuals, sexual advice and pornography on the Internet, practices of sexual counselling, sex education in schools, church discourse on sex, clinical and theoretical approaches to sexual deviances, the role of the confessional, and the appeal to sex by politicians, among other sources, in order to understand the changes that have occurred since the first volume of Foucault's history of sexuality. We would have to ask of these texts and practices what kinds of norms and/or codes and/or values they promote, how they relate to previous texts and practices, with what other texts and practices they intersect, what their role is in contemporary capitalism, how the electronic media affect our interaction with them, and what the consequences of all this have been. In short, we would have to do a genealogy or, rather, a number of genealogies.

If there is a single account of who we are now, if our world has gone beyond the one Foucault describes, then we shall have to discover this by means of a Foucauldian methodology. To proclaim the existence of a new era without engaging in the patient labour of archival work is not to have gone beyond Foucault but instead not yet to have achieved him. What that work will yield, "beyond these phosphorescences", as Foucault has said, is a story yet to be told. But let us not fool ourselves into thinking that we already know the outcome.

I am not arguing here that our world has not changed, that it has remained static since 1976. That would be foolish. And again, I do not want to claim that Deleuze, Baudrillard and Lyotard are seeing nothing. They are palpating important changes in who we have become. But we do not yet know the full character of those changes, their nature or their place. There is too much work in front of us before we can say definitively or at least justifiably what exactly it is that these thinkers have seen.

Governmentality

Ironically, it is Foucault who has offered us a beginning in the way of spade work on this new project. In two lecture courses at the Collège de France offered in 1977–78 (*Sécurité, territoire, population*) and 1978–79 (*Naissance de la biopolitique*), Foucault traces the history of what he calls *governmentality* from its beginnings in the sixteenth century up until the middle of the twentieth century. Foucault sees these lectures as a contribution to his project on bio-politics that we discussed above. He focuses on the practice of government, particularly as it passes from the more pastoral mode of the Christian medieval period to the early modern and then contemporary period.

What is particularly striking for current purposes is the second set of lectures, in which Foucault discusses the rise of neoliberalism. It is, to my knowledge, Foucault's only extended discussion of twentieth-century history. In these lectures, he traces the rise of early-twentieth-century neoliberalism in among post-Second World War German thinkers and its appropriation more recently in US thought. Those of us who live in the English-speaking world will recognize immediately the themes that characterize this discussion.

Governmentality, as Foucault defines it, has little to do with political philosophy. It does not concern the nature of justice, the concept of a right, or the question of whether the proper political ends justify the use of otherwise inappropriate means. Governmentality is a matter of the *practice* of government. How ought government to be done? What are its proper roles? Whose benefit ought it to seek and how? These are the driving questions of governmentality. Foucault defines governmentality as involving three things: first, an "ensemble formed by the institutions, procedures, analyses and reflections" concerning a "complex form of power which has as its target population, as its principal form of knowledge political economy, and as its essential technical means apparatuses of security"; secondly, a tendency toward the pre-eminence of this type of power; and thirdly, the process of the transformation toward this pre-eminence (Gov.: 102–3). It requires the substitution of the idea of power for that of institutions, of strategies for that of governmental functions, and of the creation of a field of objects for the assumption of pre-existent objects (*STP*: 120–21).

We can see here that the project of studying governmentality is continuous with Foucault's genealogical method. Focusing on practices rather than abstract theory, oriented toward issues of power, and positing the creation of objects through power rather than accepting their pre-existence, Foucault's lectures on governmentality are of a piece with his preceding work.

Over the course of the seventeenth and eighteenth centuries, a practice of governmentality arises that is concerned with the power of the state on the one hand and the rights of the individual citizen on the other. The state, particularly its administration through what Foucault calls the *police*, seeks to draw the most out of the resources of its citizens as well as concern itself with their proper well-being. Here we must understand the concept of police in a broader sense than the everyday one. Policing is not simply a matter of providing internal security through an armed force. It involves all those measures that are directed toward state and citizen well-being, from census-taking to health policy to security to education. The police ensure a vital state through and alongside their knowledge of and intervention into the population, a concept that arises at the same time as that of the state. We might think of the sexual measures developed as a result of population studies as policing in this sense.

Over and against the propriety of state policing stands the concept of individual rights. The realm of rights constitutes the area in which the state and its police cannot intervene. The space of rights is, one might say, a free zone, immune from the powers that might otherwise overwhelm the individual. Much discussion of governmentality during this period is centred on the shape of that free zone, its extent and its limits, which are correspondingly the extent and limits of governmental intervention.

Early into the emergence of this type of governmentality, however, there exists alongside it an economic view that will eventually come to compete with it. This view might be summed up in Adam Smith's image of the invisible hand. For these thinkers, it is impossible for the government to have the proper knowledge of the population, particularly with regard to the mechanisms of the economy, required to intervene in the right way to optimize state flourishing. Rather than police intervention, what is required is a certain state modesty, a willingness to allow certain things rather than promoting them, in order to achieve its proper goals. Recall here Adam Smith's idea that if everyone is allowed to act freely in their own interest, at least in the realm of production and trade, everyone will wind up better off.

It should be stressed, and we shall return to this point, that this competing view, which is indeed that of liberalism, does not substitute individual freedom for state intervention. It does not enlarge the realm of individual action and shrink that of the state. Rather, it shifts the types of interventions the state can make from those of traditional policing to those of ensuring that the proper mechanisms of the market are in place and allowed to operate.

What are the characteristics of this early liberalism? Foucault cites three: "veridiction of the market, limitation by the calculus of governmental utility and . . . the position of Europe as a region of economic development unlimited by relationship to a world market" (NB: 62). The idea here is that, in contrast to earlier economic views, liberalism posits, first, that the market is no longer a space of justice but one of truth. It is no longer a matter of ensuring that exchange relations are just (recall the early Christian critique of money-lending as usury), but of understanding how they work in order to maximize their beneficence. Secondly, that understanding requires a limitation on governmental intervention into the market. Thirdly, knowledge of the operation of the market shows that economics is not a zero-sum game. Winners do not arise at the expense of necessary losers. This is the lesson of Smith's invisible hand: everyone can win through proper market cooperation.

Liberalism, Foucault points out, reverses the traditional relationship between the state and the market. Now, rather than utilizing the market in order to profit the state, the state is seen as needing to support the mechanisms of the market. This does not mean that the state necessarily assumes a secondary importance – although this may happen – rather that the continued health of the state requires that it no longer engage in the earlier project of policing.

It is in post-Second World War Germany that liberalism in its contemporary and highly influential form begins. Ordoliberalism, which had begun to be developed in the pre-war period by thinkers such as Wilhelm Röpke, comes to dominate discussions of rebuilding the German state. Ordoliberalism answers to a question that arises for Germany in the aftermath of the war. It is a question that is the opposite of the one most states face. The problem for the already existent states is that of asking how to limit state power in order to create a space of free exchange. "The Germans had the exact inverse problem to resolve. Given that a state does not exist, how to make it exist starting from this non-state space which is one of economic liberty?" (NB: 88). The ordoliberals answer that one must create a state that supports the market, rather than the reverse.

This answer has resonances for those engaged in the reconstruction of postwar Germany because, by submitting the state to the market, it forms at the same time a critique of state power. Ordoliberals argue that states, by their nature, seek power, and that offering states the power to intervene in the lives of people will lead them down a road that ends in totalitarianism. Thus the idea of a more limited state appeals to those who have been the object of German fascism. But their critique is more pointed. Putting power, particularly economic power, in the hands of *any* state is a step down the road toward totalitarianism. There is a continuity between the New Deal and Nazism that lies in the concentration of power in the state. What is required is "a state under the surveillance of the market rather than a market under the surveillance of the state" (*ibid.*: 120).

This idea is picked up in the United States by the theorists who form the early vanguard of neoliberalism. Foucault emphasizes that neoliberal doctrine is not a doctrine of non-intervention by the state. It requires non-intervention into the direct workings of the market. However, there are a number of interventions that can be made into the framework that supports the market. The ordoliberals pose the question, "it being given that the processes of economico-political regulation are not and cannot be those of the market, how can one modify material, cultural, technical, and juridical bases that are given in Europe?" (*ibid.*: 146). The neoliberals answer this question by positing individuals as *homo oeconomicus*, and designing social policy from that assumption.

Who is *homo oeconomicus*? He is the person oriented toward market production and exchange. He seeks to maximize his welfare by means of making the best use of his resources and his environment. He is, in short, a capitalist in all aspects of his life. He sees the projects of his life in terms of enterprises that requires certain inputs and have the possibility of yielding particular benefits. Foucault offers examples of this way of thinking by American neoliberals in child-raising, work and other areas. It would perhaps be worth drawing out his analysis of Gary Becker's neoliberal treatment of criminality, since it provides a contrast to disciplinary models Foucault discusses in *Discipline and Punish*.

For Becker, a criminal is someone who is calculating the benefits and costs of committing crimes. In fact, he defines a crime as "any action that makes an individual run the risk of being condemned to a penalty [*peine*]" (*ibid.*: 256). The question facing those who design such penalties, then, is one of how to create penalties that can deter crimes. Penalties are thought of as negative externalities; they are what are likely to accompany crimes but as unwanted side-effects (at least in the criminal's view). The penal system, then, must design negative externalities that will have the maxmimum deterrence value.

Of course, deterrence itself has costs to the system. These are opportunity costs: resources that are diverted from other possible social purposes to those of deterring crime. So the state must consider the best balance between gaining deterrence by placing negative externalities on the one hand and losing opportunities by a diversion of resources on the other. Those costs are then integrated into a supply/demand curve relative to crime: "The enforcement of the law is the ensemble of instruments of action on che criminal market that oppose to the supply of crime a negative demand" (*ibid.*: 260).

We are far removed here from the realm of discipline. Where discipline seeks to focus on each individual in order to modify their behaviour, neoliberalism attends to the general supply of crime. Where discipline works through training and normalization, neoliberalism works through a calculation of rewards and costs. Where discipline assumes a pliable body that can be intervened upon, neoliberalism assumes a *homo oeconomicus*. Where discipline seeks to eliminate crime, neoliberalism seeks "an equilibrium between the supply curve of crime and negative demand" (*ibid.*: 261). In short, in contrast to discipline and normalization, neoliberalism seeks:

> a society in which there would be optimization of systems of difference . . . in which there would be action taken not upon the players but on the rules of play, and finally in which there would be an intervention which would not be a type of subjectivization [*assujettissement*] internal to individuals, but instead an intervention of an environmental kind. (*ibid.*: 265)

What are we to make of Foucault's analysis of neoliberalism? First, it should be noted that Foucault emphasizes that the neoliberal approach remains, in 1979, marginal to mainstream discourse. It is not that neoliberalism has replaced discipline and normalization; rather it has arisen as a form of governmentality that competes with it. Foucault is measuring the rise of a view of the world, of human beings, of governing, and of economy that, at the time he offers his lectures, is beginning to have an impact. As we know, the twin emergence of globalization and electronic media has helped neoliberal doctrine move more towards the mainstream of political and economic governmentality. In this sense, Foucault has fore-seen changes that have become more salient since the writing of *Discipline and Punish*.

These changes converge with those studied by Deleuze, Baudrillard and Lyotard, although with two important differences. First, they are seen as a strand, albeit an important one, in thinking about who and where we are now. The neoliberal approach is not taken to be the whole cloth. Although Deleuze can admit that codes have not entirely replaced normalization, Foucault, by situating his analyses closer to the ground, can *show* it. And by keeping to the genealogical method, Foucault can ask more precise questions about the place of neoliberalism in creating who we are and how we think of ourselves than those thinkers who stand above or outside the details of our history. It is true that, since 1979, the place of neoliberalism has become far less marginal than it was in Foucault's time. But again, this means that we need to continue his analyses, not abandon them.

The second difference, and here the contrast with Baudrillard is particu-larly acute, is that in the neoliberal view that Foucault describes, *homo oeconomicus* is not so much a consumer as an enterprising capitalist. "*Homo oeconomicus* . . . is not the man of exchange, he is not the consum-ing man, he is the man of enterprise and of production" (*ibid.*: 152). We must be careful here. Foucault is not saying that who we have become is entirely *homo oeconomicus*. Not only is neoliberal theory not in the ascendance in 1979, but also the approach embraced by neoliberals must be placed alongside other threads in order to reveal the character, and even the bio-political character, of our world. It is entirely possible that, in one sense, we are becoming consumers as much as producers, and in another we are becoming capitalist entrepreneurs. For instance, President Bush's recent vision of an "ownership society", for all its hypocrisy, is an idea that needs to be investigated from both the consumerist and the entrepren-eurial perspectives. My claim is not that Baudrillard is wrong here, but that Foucault's contribution is not reducible to his. It approaches the emergence of who we are from a different angle.

We are left, then, with the question of who we are now. In this chapter, we have surveyed those who would leave Foucault behind, and I have argued that there is still much to be gleaned from using Foucault's works and particularly his method. We have seen that Foucault's contributions continue to have a grip on us. Whoever we are, we have not entirely shed who we were, nor has it been established that we have become something unified that can be placed under a single descriptive or analytical category. We have not, however, settled the question of who we are now. If Foucault is right, then we cannot appeal to his works uncritically in order to under-stand ourselves. We are historical beings, contingent and changeable. If we are to understand who we are, who we are *now*, it remains to us to ask the question closely and vigilantly. To discover who we are, to become who we might be: these are projects we are never done with. In that sense, Foucault's work lies not only with our past and with our present, but with our future as well.

Notes

Chapter 1: Introduction: who are we?

1. Gilles Deleuze, *Empiricism and Subjectivity: An Essay on Hume's Theory of Human Nature*, C. V. Boundas (trans.) (New York: Columbia University Press, [1953] 1991), 106.
2. Gilles Deleuze & Félix Guattari, *What is Philosophy?*, H. Tomlinson & G. Burchell (trans.) (New York: Columbia University Press, [1991] 1994), 82.
3. René Descartes, *Meditations on First Philosophy*. L. J. Lafleur (trans.) (Indianapolis, IN: Bobbs-Merrill, [1641] 1951), 3.
4. *Ibid.*, 74–5.
5. For more on this, see Descartes's *Passions of the Soul*, S. Voss (Indianapolis, IN: Hackett, 1990).
6. Descartes, *Meditations on First Philosophy*, 75.
7. *Ibid.*, 80.
8. Sigmund Freud, *Introductory Lectures on Psychoanalysis*, J. Strachey (trans.) (New York: W.W. Norton, [1916] 1963), 285.
9. Jean-Paul Sartre, "Existentialism", B. Frechtman (trans.), in *Existentialism and Human Emotions* (New York: Philosophical Library, 1957), 15.
10. *Ibid.*, 33.
11. Jean-Paul Sartre, *Being and Nothingness: A Phenomenological Essay on Ontology*, H. Barnes (trans.) (New York: Philosophical Library, [1943] 1956), 101.
12. Karl Marx, "Economic and Philosophic Manuscripts", in *Early Writings*, R. Livingston & G. Benton (trans.), 279–400 (New York: Random House, 1975), 327.
13. Karl Marx, "The Communist Manifesto", in *Karl Marx: Selected Writings*, L. H. Simon (ed.), 157–86 (Indianapolis, IN: Hackett, 1994), 158.
14. "The Eighteenth Brumaire of Louis Bonaparte", in *Karl Marx: Selected Writings*, 188.
15. Personal communication cited in Hubert Dreyfus & Paul Rabinow, *Michel Foucault: Beyond Structuralism and Hermeneutics* (Chicago, IL: University of Chicago Press, 1982), 187.

Chapter 2: Archaeological histories of who we are

1. All references will be to the English abridgement except in a couple of instances where the translation lacks the appropriate passage.
2. Descartes, *Meditations on First Philosophy*, 18. There is an article by Jacques Derrida, and an acrimonious reply by Foucault, on the proper interpretation of this passage.

Derrida holds, against Foucault's view, that Descartes neither dismisses nor privileges madness. See his article "Cogito and the History of Madness", in *Writing and Difference*, A. Bass (trans.), 31–63 (Chicago, IL: University of Chicago Press, [1967] 1978), 45–58. Foucault's reply, entitled, "My Body, This Paper, This Fire", which was an appendix to the second edition of *Histoire de la folie* in 1972, appears in English in the collection *Aesthetics, Method, and Epistemology: The Essential Works of Foucault, Vol. 2*, J. D. Faubion (ed.), 393–417 (New York: The New Press, 1999).

3. Derrida, "Cogito and the History of Madness", 33.
4. *Ibid.*, 35.
5. The term *statement* here is a technical one for Foucault, referring to the relation of what we would normally call statements to the practices in which they arise, but that does not alter the sense of the passage for our purposes.
6. For example, Robert Castel in his book *The Regulation of Madness: The Origins of Incarceration in France*, W. D. Halls (trans.) (Berkeley, CA: University of California Press, [1976] 1988) acknowledges a deep debt to Foucault's book.
7. H. C. Midelfort, "Madness and Civilization in Early Modern Europe: A Reappraisal of Michel Foucault", in *After the Reformation: Essays in Honor of J. H. Hexter*, B. Malament (ed.), 247–65 (Philadelphia, PA: University of Pennsylvania Press, 1980).
8. *Ibid.*, 254.
9. *Ibid.*, 255.
10. *Ibid.*, 257.
11. K. Doerner, *Madmen and the Bourgeoisie: A Social History of Insanity and Psychiatry*, J. Neugroschel & J. Steinberg (trans.) (Oxford: Basil Blackwell, [1969] 1981), 299.
12. For a view of Foucault's archaeologies as more "regional" rather than universal, see Gary Gutting's *Michel Foucault's Archaeology of Scientific Reason* (Cambridge: Cambridge University Press, 1989).
13. Plato, *The Republic*, G. M. A. Grubbe (trans.), C. D. C. Reeve (rev.) (Indianapolis, IN: Hackett, [380 BCE] 1992), 43 (367d).
14. Foucault discusses these four oscillations in Chapter 9 of *The Order of Things*, see esp. OT: 312–35.
15. I have tried to show how the question cannot be resolved in archaeology, but can in genealogy, in *Between Genealogy and Epistemology: Psychology, Politics, and Knowledge in the Thought of Michel Foucault* (University Park, PA: Pennsylvania State University Press, 1993).

Chapter 3: Genealogical histories of who we are

1. Of course, one cannot recommend a history of the events without also being committed on these questions. For my part, I would recommend Kristin Ross's recent *May '68 and its Afterlives* (Chicago, IL: University of Chicago Press, 2002), which details not only a number of the events themselves, but also the attempt to bury their revolutionary character in more recent years.
2. F. Nietzsche, *On the Genealogy of Morals*, D. Smith (trans.) (Oxford: Oxford University Press, [1887] 1996), 57–8.
3. As an example of Foucault's invocation of this term, see, for example, his discussion with Gilles Deleuze, "Intellectuals and Power", in *Language, Counter-Memory, Practice*, D. Bouchard (ed.), D. Bouchard & S. Simon (trans.), 205–17 (Ithaca, NY: Cornell University Press, 1977). Near the end of the discussion, Foucault says that, "if the fight is directed against power, then all those on whom power is exercised to their detriment, all who find it intolerable, can begin the struggle on their own terrain and on the basis of their proper activity (or passivity)" (IP: 218).

THE PHILOSOPHY OF FOUCAULT

4. F. Nietzsche, *The Will to Power*, W. Kaufman (ed.), W. Kaufman & R. J. Hollingdale (trans.) (New York: Random House, 1967), 364.

5. J. Berger, *G* (New York: Pantheon, [1972] 1980), 133.

6. Near the end of this book, we shall return briefly to this idea, although in a very different context, in discussing the neoliberal approach to punishment.

7. P. Spierenberg, *The Spectacle of Suffering: Executions and the Evolution of Repression: From a Preindustrial Metropolis to the European Experience* (Cambridge: Cambridge University Press, 1984).

8. *Ibid.*, ix.

9. *Ibid.*, 108.

10. In a footnote to *Discipline and Punish* (*DP*: 309), Foucault says that he is limiting his study to French prisons. Although he focuses on the French penal system, he does make a number of forays outside it.

11. Spierenberg, *The Spectacle of Suffering*, 206.

12. *Ibid.*, 108.

13. The historical situatedness of this new form of power is missed by Deleuze in his study of Foucault's thought, *Foucault*, S. Hand (trans.) (Minneapolis, MN: University of Minnesota Press, [1986] 1988). Deleuze seems to think that, in Foucault's view, all power operates this way and it always has.

14. I articulate this discomfort at greater length in May, *Between Genealogy and Epistemology*, 105–9.

15. As Foucault points out, while childhood sexuality is the concern of bourgeois parents, the social pressures brought to bear on working-class adults has more to do with the promotion of marriage and the discouraging of more informal sexual relations.

16. One might wish to ask, at this point, what exactly a practice is. Foucault himself does not say. However, I have tried to give an account of the nature of practices, one that is Foucauldian in inspiration, in May, *Our Practices, Our Selves* (University Park, PA: Pennsylvania State University Press, 2001). There I define a practice as, "a regularity (or regularities) of behavior, usually goal-directed, that is socially normatively governed" (p. 8).

17. I treat this issue in more depth in May, *Between Genealogy and Epistemology*.

Chapter 4: Who we are and who we might be

1. See especially Hadot's "Spiritual Exercises", in *Philosophy as a Way of Life: Spiritual Exercises from Socrates to Foucault*, M. Chase (trans.), A. Davidson (ed.), 81–125 (Oxford: Blackwell, 1995).

2. For an overview of his thought, see Hadot's clear and elegantly written *What is Ancient Philosophy?*, M. Chase. (trans.) (Cambridge, MA: Harvard University Press, 2002).

3. See, for instance, *UP*: 8, and the chapter on the "cultivation of the self" in *CS*, where he explicitly refers to Hadot's work.

4. See Hadot, "Reflections on the Idea of the 'Cultivation of the Self'", in *Philosophy as a Way of Life*, 206–13.

5. *Ibid.*, 211.

6. Habermas engages much criticism along this line, although perhaps the most trenchant critique is offered by Nancy Fraser in her article, "Foucault on Modern Power: Empirical Insights and Normative Confusions", *Praxis International* 1 (1981), 272–87. I try to construct a scaffolding for defending Foucault's (as well as Deleuze's and Jean-François Lyotard's) normative positions in T. May, *The Moral Theory of Poststructuralism* (University Park, PA: Pennsylvania State University Press, 1995).

Chapter 5: Coda: Foucault's own straying afield

1. One of the first biographies of Foucault, Didier Eribon's *Michel Foucault*, B. Wing (trans.) (Cambridge, MA: Harvard University Press, [1989] 1991), remains the most sensitive. Many of the details I recount here are drawn from this book.
2. G. Deleuze, "Letter to a Harsh Critic", in *Negotiations: 1972–1990*, M. Joughin (trans.) (New York: Columbia University Press, [1990] 1995), 11.
3. Cited in Eribon, *Michel Foucault*, 279.
4. J. Miller, *The Passion of Michel Foucault* (New York: Simon & Schuster, 1993).
5. Interview in the *Advocate*, quoted in Eribon, *Michel Foucault*, 315.

Chapter 6: Are we still who Foucault says we are?

1. G. Deleuze, "Postscript on Control Societies", in *Negotiations*, 177.
2. *Ibid.*, 178.
3. *Ibid.*, 179.
4. *Ibid.*, 180.
5. *Ibid.*, 181.
6. M. Hardt & A. Negri, *Empire* (Cambridge, MA: Harvard University Press, 2000).
7. J. Baudrillard, "Forget Foucault", N. Dufresne (trans.), in *Forget Foucault*, 7–64 (New York: Semiotext(e), [1977] 1987), 11.
8. *Ibid.*, 12.
9. J. Baudrillard, *Simulations*, P. Foss, P. Patton & P. Beitchman (trans.) (New York: Semiotext(e), 1983), 83.
10. *Ibid.*, 25.
11. J. Baudrillard, *Seduction* (New York: St Martin's Press, [1979] 1990), 69.
12. Baudrillard, "Forget Foucault", 21.
13. *Ibid.*, 43–4.
14. Baudrillard, *Seduction*, 22.
15. *Ibid.*, 2.
16. J.-F. Lyotard, *The Postmodern Condition: A Report on Knowledge*, G. Bennington & B. Massumi (trans.) (Minneapolis, MN: University of Minnesota Press, [1979] 1984), xxiv.
17. J.-F. Lyotard, *The Differend: Phrases in Dispute*, G. Van Den Abbeele (trans.) (Minneapolis, MN: University of Minnesota Press, [1983] 1988), 179.
18. M. Miyoshi, "A Borderless World? From Colonialism to Transnationalism and the Decline of the Nation-State", *Critical Inquiry* 19 (summer 1993), 726–51.
19. For a discussion of the rise of ADHD diagnosis and treatment see, for instance, D. W. Dunne, "Statistics Confirm the Rise of Childhood ADHD and Medication Use", *Education World*, www.education-world.com/a_issues/issues148a.shtml (accessed Dec. 2005).
20. This should not be surprising. Lyotard's book *Libidinal Economy*, Iain Hamilton Grant (trans.) (Bloomington, IN: Indiana University Press, 1993) is written in response to Deleuze and Guattari's *Anti-Oedipus: Capitalism and Schizophrenia*, Robert Hurley, Mark Seem & Helen R. Lane (trans.) (New York: Viking, 1977), seeking to take up and radicalize the idea of capitalism as destroying the guiding norms of previous social existence.

Further reading

What are probably generally agreed upon as the main works in Foucault's corpus are *Histoire de la folie*, *The Order of Things*, *The Archaeology of Knowledge*, *Discipline and Punish*, and the first and second volumes of *The History of Sexuality*. Some feel this slights *The Birth of the Clinic*, Foucault's archaeology of the rise of medical science. Others find the third volume of *The History of Sexuality* to be as important as the second volume. In addition to these works, Foucault authored a book on the writer Raymond Roussel in 1963 (*Death and the Labyrinth: The World of Raymond Roussel*, C. Ruas (trans.) (Berkeley, CA: University of California Press, 1986)) and a shorter one on the painter René Magritte in 1973 (*This is Not a Pipe*, J. Harkness (trans.) (Berkeley, CA: University of California Press, 1983)). He also collaborated on a number of works, including *Herculine Barbin* (New York: Pantheon, 1980) and *I, Pierre Riviere, Having Slaughtered My Mother, My Sister, and My Brother*... (Lincoln, NE: University of Nebraska Press, 1982).

For those who would like to start with some shorter works, *Language, Counter-Memory, Practice: Selected Essays and Interviews* (Donald F. Bouchard (ed.), Donald F. Bouchard and Sherry Simon (trans.) (Ithaca, NY: Cornell University Press, 1977)) focuses on the archaeological period, and *Power/Knowledge: Selected Interviews and Other Writings 1972–77* (Colin Gordon (ed.), Colin Gordon *et al.* (trans.) (New York: Pantheon, 1980)) focuses on the genealogical period. They are both good places to start.

There are mountains of secondary works on Foucault. Dreyfus and Rabinow's *Michel Foucault* is considered a classic, although some would dispute their interpretation of Foucault. My favourite general works are two short books: John Rajchman's *Michel Foucault: The Freedom of Philosophy* (New York: Columbia University Press, 1985) and Gary Gutting's *Foucault: A Very Short Introduction* (Oxford: Oxford University Press, 2005).

Bibliography

References to Foucault's works

Abnormal: Lectures at the Collège de France, 1974–1975, G. Burchell (trans.). New York: Picador, 2003. Originally published in 1999 as *Les Anormaux: Cours au Collège de France, 1974–1975*.

The Archaeology of Knowledge and The Discourse on Language, A. M. Sheridan Smith (trans.). New York: Harper & Row, 1972. *The Archaeology of Knowledge* was originally published in 1969 as *L'Archéologie du Savoir* and *The Discourse on Language* was originally published in 1971 as *L'ordre du Discours*.

The Birth of the Clinic, A. M. Sheridan Smith (trans.). New York: Random House, 1973. Originally published in 1963 as *Naissance de la Clinique*.

The Care of the Self, R. Hurley (trans.). New York: Pantheon, 1986. Originally published in 1984 as *Le souci de soi*.

"Critical Theory/Intellectual History" (an interview with Gerard Raulet), J. Harding (trans.). In *Politics, Philosophy, Culture*, M. Foucault, L. D. Kritzman (ed.), 17–46. New York: Routledge, 1988.

Discipline and Punish: The Birth of the Prison, A. Sheridan (trans.). New York: Random House, 1977. Originally published in 1975 as *Surveiller et Punir: Naissance de la prison*.

"The Ethics of the Concern of the Self as a Practice of Freedom". In *Ethics: Subjectivity and Truth*, P. Rabinow (ed.), 281–301. New York: The New Press, 1997.

"Governmentality". In *The Foucault Effect: Studies in Governmentality*, G. Burchell, C. Gordon & P. Miller (eds), 87–104. Chicago, IL: University of Chicago Press, 1991.

The Hermeneutics of the Subject: Lectures at the Collège de France 1981–1982, F. Gros (ed.), G. Burchell (trans.). New York: Palgrave Macmillan, 2005. Originally published in 2001 as *Herméneutique du sujet: Cours au Collège de France, 1981–1982*.

Histoire de la Folie á l'âge classique, 2nd edn. Paris: Éditions Gallimard, 1972.

The History of Sexuality, Volume I: An Introduction, R. Hurley (trans.). New York: Random House, 1978. Originally published in 1978 as *La Volonté de savoir*.

"Intellectuals and Power". In *Language, Counter-Memory, Practice*, D. Bouchard (ed.), D. Bouchard & S. Simon (trans.), 205–17. Ithaca, NY: Cornell University Press, 1977.

Madness and Civilization: A History of Insanity in the Age of Reason, R. Howard (trans.). New York: Random House, 1965. This is an abridged translation of *Histoire de la folie*.

"My Body, This Paper, This Fire". In *The Essential Works of Foucault, Vol. 2*, J. D. Faubion (ed.), 393–417. New York: The New Press, 1999.

Naissance de la biopolitique: Cours au Collège de France 1978–1979. Paris: Gallimard, 2004.

"Nietzsche, Genealogy, History". In *Language, Counter-Memory, Practice*, D. Bouchard (ed.), D. Bouchard & S. Simon (trans.), 139–64. Ithaca, NY: Cornell University Press, 1977.

"On the Genealogy of Ethics: An Overview of a Work in Progress". In *The Foucault Reader*, P. Rabinow (ed.), 251–80. New York: Pantheon, 1984.

The Order of Things: An Archaeology of the Human Sciences. New York: Random House, 1971. Originally published in 1966 as *Les Mots et les Choses*.

"Practicing Criticism", A. Sheridan (trans.). In *Michel Foucault: Politics, Philosophy, Culture*, L. Kritzman (ed.), 152–6. London: Routledge, 1988.

"Questions of Method", C. Gordon (trans.). In *The Foucault Effect: Studies in Governmentality*, G. Burchell, C. Gordon & P. Miller (eds), 73–86. Chicago, IL: University of Chicago Press, 1991.

Sécurité, territoire, population: Cours au Collège de France 1977–1978. Paris: Gallimard, 2004.

"The Subject and Power". In *Michel Foucault: Beyond Structuralism and Hermeneutics*, H. Dreyfus & P. Rabinow, 208–26. Chicago, IL: University of Chicago Press, 1982.

"Truth and Power". In *Power/Knowledge: Selected Interviews and Other Writings 1972–1977*, C. Gordon (ed.), 109–33. New York: Pantheon, 1980.

The Use of Pleasure: Volume 2 of The History of Sexuality, R. Hurley (trans.). New York: Pantheon, 1985. Originally published in 1984 as *L'usage des plaisirs*.

"What is Enlightenment?" In *Ethics: Subjectivity and Truth*, Paul Rabinow (ed.), 309–19. New York: The New Press, 1997.

Other references

Baudrillard, J. 1983. *Simulations*, P. Foss, P. Patton & P. Beitchman (trans.). New York: Semiotext(e).

Baudrillard, J. [1977] 1987. "Forget Foucault", Nicole Dufresne (trans.). In *Forget Foucault*, 7–64. New York: Semiotext(e).

Baudrillard, J. [1979] 1990. *Seduction*. New York: St Martin's Press.

Berger, J. [1972] 1980. *G*. New York: Pantheon.

Castel, R. [1976] 1988. *The Regulation of Madness: The Origins of Incarceration in France*, W. D. Halls (trans.). Berkeley, CA: University of California Press.

Deleuze, G. [1986] 1988. *Foucault*, S. Hand (trans.). Minneapolis, MN: University of Minnesota Press.

Deleuze, G. [1953] 1991. *Empiricism and Subjectivity: An Essay on Hume's Theory of Human Nature*, C. V. Boundas (trans.). New York: Columbia University Press.

Deleuze, G. [1990] 1995. "Letter to a Harsh Critic". In *Negotiations: 1972–1990*, M. Joughin (trans.), 3–12. New York: Columbia University Press.

Deleuze, G. 1995. "Postscript on Control Societies". In *Negotiations: 1972–1990*, M. Joughin (trans.), 177–82. New York: Columbia University Press.

Deleuze, G. & F. Guattari [1972] 1977. *Anti-Oedipus: Capitalism and Schizophrenia*, Robert Hurley, Mark Seem & Helen R. Lane (trans.). New York: Viking.

Deleuze, G. & F. Guattari [1991] 1994. *What is Philosophy?*, H. Tomlinson & G. Burchell (trans.). New York: Columbia University Press.

Derrida, J. [1967] 1978. "Cogito and the History of Madness". In *Writing and Difference*, A. Bass (trans.), 31–63. Chicago, IL: University of Chicago Press.

Descartes, R. [1641] 1951. *Meditations on First Philosophy*, L. J. Lafleur (trans.). Indianapolis, IN: Bobbs-Merrill.

Descartes, R. [1649] 1990. *Passions of the Soul*, S. Voss (trans.). Indianapolis, IN: Hackett.

Doerner, K. [1961] 1981. *Madmen and the Bourgeoisie: A Social History of Insanity and Psychiatry*, J. Neugroschel & J. Steinberg (trans.). Oxford: Blackwell.

Dreyfus, H. & P. Rabinow 1982. *Michel Foucault: Beyond Structuralism and Hermeneutics.* Chicago, IL: University of Chicago Press.

Dunne, D. W. 2000. "Statistics Confirm Rise in Childhood ADHD and Medication Use". *Education World,* www.education-world.com/a_issues/issues148a.shtml (accessed Dec. 2005).

Eribon, D. [1989] 1991. *Michel Foucault,* B. Wing (trans.). Cambridge, MA: Harvard University Press.

Fraser, N. 1981. "Foucault on Modern Power: Empirical Insights and Normative Confusions". *Praxis International* 1, 272–87.

Freud, S. [1916] 1963. *Introductory Lectures on Psychoanalysis,* J. Strachey (trans.). New York: Norton.

Gutting, G. 1989. *Michel Foucault's Archaeology of Scientific Reason.* Cambridge: Cambridge University Press.

Hadot, P. 1995. *Philosophy as a Way of Life: Spiritual Exercises from Socrates to Foucault,* M. Chase (trans.), A. Davidson (ed.). Oxford: Blackwell.

Hadot, P. 1995. "Spiritual Exercises". In *Philosophy as a Way of Life: Spiritual Exercises from Socrates to Foucault,* M. Chase (trans.), A. Davidson (ed.), 81–125. Oxford: Blackwell.

Hadot, P. "Reflections on the Idea of the 'Cultivation of the Self' ". In *Philosophy as a Way of Life: Spiritual Exercises from Socrates to Foucault,* M. Chase (trans.), A. Davidson (ed.), 206–13. Oxford: Blackwell.

Hadot, P. 2002. *What is Ancient Philosophy?,* M. Chase (trans.). Cambridge, MA: Harvard University Press.

Hardt, M. & A. Negri 2000. *Empire.* Cambridge, MA: Harvard University Press.

Lyotard, J.-F. [1974] 1993. *Libidinal Economy,* Iain Hamilton Grant (trans.). Bloomington, IN: Indiana University Press.

Lyotard, J.-F. [1979] 1984. *The Postmodern Condition: A Report on Knowledge,* G. Bennington & B. Massumi (trans.). Minneapolis, MN: University of Minnesota Press.

Lyotard, J.-F. [1983] 1988. *The Differend: Phrases in Dispute,* G. Van Den Abbeele (trans.). Minneapolis, MN: University of Minnesota Press.

Marx, K. 1975. "Economic and Philosophic Manuscripts". In *Early Writings,* R. Livingston & G. Benton (trans.), 279–400. New York: Random House.

Marx, K. 1994a. "The Communist Manifesto". In *Karl Marx: Selected Writings.* L. H. Simon (ed.), 157–86. Indianapolis, IN: Hackett.

Marx, K. 1994b. "The Eighteenth Brumaire of Louis Bonaparte". In *Karl Marx: Selected Writings.* L. H. Simon (ed.), 187–208. Indianapolis, IN: Hackett.

May, T. 1993. *Between Genealogy and Epistemology: Psychology, Politics, and Knowledge in the Thought of Michel Foucault.* University Park, PA: Pennsylvania State University Press.

May, T. 1995. *The Moral Theory of Poststructuralism.* University Park, PA: Pennsylvania State University Press.

May, T. 2001. *Our Practices, Our Selves.* University Park, PA: Pennsylvania State University Press.

Midelfort, H. C. 1988. "Madness and Civilization in Early Modern Europe". In *After the Reformation: Essays in Honor of J. H. Hexter,* B. Malament (ed.), 247–65. Philadelphia, PA: University of Pennsylvania Press.

Miller, J. 1993. *The Passion of Michel Foucault.* New York: Simon & Schuster.

Miyoshi, M. 1993. "A Borderless World? From Colonialism to Transnationalism and the Decline of the Nation-State". *Critical Inquiry* 19 (Summer), 726–51.

Nietzsche, F. [1887] 1996. *On the Genealogy of Morals,* D. Smith (trans.). Oxford: Oxford University Press.

Nietzsche, F. [1901] 1967. *The Will to Power,* W. Kaufman & R. J. Hollingdale (trans.), W. Kaufman (ed.). New York: Random House.

Plato [380 BCE] 1992. *The Republic*, G. M. A. Grubbe (trans.), C. D. C. Reeve (rev.). Indianapolis, IN: Hackett.

Ross, K. 2002. *May '68 and its Afterlives*. Chicago, IL: University of Chicago Press.

Sartre, J.-P. [1943] 1956. *Being and Nothingness: A Phenomenological Essay on Ontology*, H. Barnes (trans.). New York: Philosophical Library.

Sartre, J.-P. 1957. "Existentialism", B. Frechtman (trans.). In *Existentialism and Human Emotions*. New York: Philosophical Library.

Spierenberg, P. 1984. *The Spectacle of Suffering: Executions and the Evolution of Repression: From a Preindustrial Metropolis to the European Experience*. Cambridge: Cambridge University Press.

Index